Technology and the Logic of American Racism

Critical Research in Material Culture

Series editor: Sally R. Munt

Other titles in the series:
Technospaces, edited by Sally R. Munt

Technology and the Logic of American Racism

A Cultural History of the Body as Evidence

SARAH E. CHINN

CONTINUUM
London and New York

Continuum
Wellington House, 125 Strand, London WC2R 0BB
370 Lexington Avenue, New York, NY 10017-6503

First published 2000

British Library Cataloguing-in-Publication Data
A catalogue record for this book is available from the British Library.

ISBN 0-8264-4729-5 (hardback)
    0-8264-4750-3 (paperback)

Library of Congress Cataloging-in-Publication Data

Chinn, Sarah E.
    Technology and the logic of American racism : a cultural history of the body as
evidence / Sarah E. Chinn.
        p. cm.
    Includes bibliographical references (p.) and index.
    ISBN 0-8264-4729-5 — ISBN 0-8264-4750-3 (pbk.)
    1. United States—Race relations. 2. Race awareness—United States—History.
3. Racism—United States—History. 4. Body, Human—Social aspects—United
States—History. 5. Body, Human—Symbolic aspects—United States—History.
6. Afro-Americans—Legal status, laws, etc.—History. 7. Technology—Social
aspects—United States—History. 8. Race awareness in literature. 9. Afro-Americans
in literature. I. Title.

E185.61 .C56 2000
305.8'00973—dc21

                                                                00-027622

Typeset by BookEns Ltd, Royston, Herts
Printed and bound in Great Britain by Biddles Ltd, Guildford & King's Lynn

Contents

To Kris
who is more precious than rubies

Series foreword

One of the founding figures of Cultural Studies, the historian E. P. Thompson, once claimed that:

> No piece of timber has ever been known to make itself into a table: no joiner has ever been known to make a table out of air, or sawdust. The joiner appropriates that timber, and, in working it up into a table, he is governed both by his skill (theoretical practice, itself arising from a *history*, or "experience", of making tables, as well as a history of the evolution of the appropriate tools) and by the qualities (size, grain, seasoning, etc.) of the timber itself.
>
> (*The Poverty of Theory* (1978), pp. 17–18)

This series is concerned with the realness of matter, of the substance of culture as a material force that carves, cleaves and sculpts social identities, that forms human experience. Materialist philosophy, since the fifth century BC, has discussed civilization, society and morality in terms of the physical body in motion, offering various sets of explanations for the meaning produced by human activity, in space and time. There are limits to these efforts, and there are effects, for our analysis of the realm of ideas is always embedded in real, material human lives. In this series we offer original research which is intended to critically augment what, in the humanities, has been called "the cultural turn". We intend to re-emphasize how culture makes us real, how it confers citizenship, selfhood and belonging, and how it simultaneously inflicts alienation, fragmentation and exile.

Culture is a dynamic process — ambivalent, contradictory, unpredictable; it flows to forge human needs, and is in turn innovated by the vicissitudes of those needs. Culture is intersubjectively produced in the junctures between such oppositional fields as the private/public, the economic/social, the institutional/individual, the material/symbolic, the mind/body. In recent years we have learned how to deconstruct such totemic binaries without losing sight of their specific significance, to trace the relationships between them with critical intelligence. Crucially, because the terrain of culture is constantly changing, emergent and newly distinct structures of feeling demand that we revise our techniques of scholarly engagement. What will be the new strategies, tactics or dispositions to be lived out in the proclaimed Information Age? Does technological convergence really herald the compression of space/ time? What will happen to identity *after* the Postmodern? Will cyberlife ensure further fractured forms of consciousness and social atomism? We live in a political moment when the map of the public sphere is being redrawn in terms of rights, yet when we are said to be scurrying towards the post-national, towards the golden goal of globalization. Will hegemony endure, will capitalism reinvent itself using the hoary divisions of race, gender, sexuality and class? What new cultures of dissidence will arise from the bricolage of the twenty-first century? In what senses, and to what effect, is culture "material" at all?

Critical Research in Material Culture intends to avoid ephemeral solipsism. Instead, it hopes to illuminate how discourses of representation create embodied experiences, to argue how the matter of life is substantiated in the performance of culture, to disseminate a critique of that culture which engages with its ethical implications, and to ask for an intellectual accountability that recalls that knowledge and power are not dissociated. Our cultural inscriptions can vandalize the tree of knowledge, our pen/knives are out.

Sally R. Munt
Series Editor

Acknowledgments

Academic life has the reputation, well earned, of being solitary: research and writing are usually done alone, and teaching, while practiced in the presence of others, can sometimes be an oddly isolating experience. But solitariness is not the whole story. Our work grows out of collaboration, explicit or not: with colleagues, students, friends, family, lovers, the work of scholars we admire.

My research was aided by a host of librarians and archivists. Thanks go to the staff of the Columbia Rare Books and Manuscripts collection; Tab Lewis, Civilian Records Archivist at the National Archives and Records Administration; and the New-York Historical Society. My most heartfelt thanks, though, go to the librarians at McGraw-Page Library at Randolph-Macon College, especially Nancy Newins, Head of Library User Services, and Cynthia Hartung, the Interlibrary Loan Co-ordinator. Their generosity and good humor in dealing with my seemingly endless requests for obscure texts from around the globe showed me that there are no small libraries, only small librarians.

Patricia O'Hara and the anonymous reader at *Nineteenth Century Studies* provided great insight into my discussion of *Pudd'nhead Wilson*. Alan Rice was the first person to read the entire manuscript from beginning to end, and his comments helped me understand what it means to write a book, rather than a collection of chapters. The advocacy of Jane Greenwood helped get this project off the ground, and Janet Joyce at Continuum was indefatigable and patiently encouraging in seeing it through. Genie Cesarski was an enthusiastic indexer, more than I could manage myself at the tail-end of this process.

My colleagues at Randolph-Macon College were encouraging and supportive of me as a brash new faculty member. Especial thanks go to Ritchie Watson and Donna S. Turney for taking me under their wings, and to Amy Goodwin, Mark Parker, Tom Peyser, Ted Sheckels, and Maria Scott for being ideal colleagues: humorous, welcoming, and tartly cynical. Tom Peyser's astute responses to Chapter 2 were (as he is) clear-eyed and right on target. The input of the Feminist Writing Group gave me the kick I needed to sharpen up Chapter 4, particularly the comments of Nathalie Lebon and Amy Hubbard.

Much of the research for this book was financed by the Walter Williams Craigie Fund, for which I am enormously grateful. I was also supported by faculty development grants from Randolph-Macon.

More important than money, though, is time. The final push for this project came over the summer of 1999, as I was moving back to New York, and buying and renovating a house with my brother and my partner. We agreed that I would work on the book during the day, and the house at evenings and weekends. I cannot thank enough my brother Benjamin for watching uncomplainingly as I sat on the deck reading Bruno Latour while he ripped up kitchen tiles in the sweltering heat. That kind of generosity is precious.

Sarah Kelen, Sally Munt, and Mareike Herrmann have been, and are, steadfast friends; they have offered me both intellectual and emotional support, challenge, and refuge. Conversation with Bob McRuer is always such a pleasure that I forget how much I'm learning. Thanks, too, to Lisa Botshon, Eric Schocket, Tanya Monier, Hayley Gorenberg, and various other friends who were patient sounding-boards for the ideas that finally found their way into this book, and to Ann Douglas, Priscilla Wald, Paul Lauter and David Kastan, models as scholars and as allies. The encouragement of my parents, Carol and Geoffrey Chinn, has been unstinting from the start.

I dedicate this book to Kris Franklin. There is no part of it that does not bear her imprint: her passion for justice, her tenderness, her fierceness, her eye for crucial detail. I have learned from her the meaning of words I thought I knew: courage, joy, love.

Note: Chapter 2, "A Show of Hands: Establishing Identity in Mark Twain's *The Tragedy of Pudd'nhead Wilson*," appeared in a shorter form in *Nineteenth Century Studies* (Volume 9, 1999, © The Nineteenth Century Studies Association).

Preface

One of my favorite jokes: two Martians meet at a party. They chat for a while and as they're about to mingle some more, they realize they haven't told each other their names. "I'm 3458703," says the first. "My name's 908322," says the second. "That's funny," says the first Martian. "You don't look Jewish."

My reasons for liking this joke: I have heard it told only by Jews to Jews. It replicates the "we are everywhere (even on Mars)" rhetoric in which I was immersed while growing up, a childhood punctuated with the parental observation "he's/she's Jewish, you know" about public figures who had changed their names and emerged as film stars or television personalities. Rendered invisible in the dominant culture, and yet always available for anti-Semitic attacks, we looked for our own reflections in figures that denied their kinship with us.[1]

I have always fantasized that both Martians are Jewish, and that the first Martian's punchline is a tacit recognition of that. The joke acknowledges that we keep an eye open for each other, a particularly important strategy in explicitly Christian cultures like the 1970s Britain in which I grew up. At the same time, it recognizes the risks of not assimilating and changing your name, as did so many Jews of my grandparents' and parents' generation (and in fact, as did all the branches of my mother's family, transformed into Leighs and Smiths). If the first Martian is not Jewish, then her (his? its? do Martians have gender?) punchline is a quasi-aggressive act: you may hide under your *retroussé* antennae and green skin, but your name unmasks you.

This joke may also refer subliminally to the reduction of Jews during the Shoah to numbers, and the dehumanizing effects of anti-Jewish legislation, ghettoization, and life and death in the camps. An iconic image of the Jew in the 1970s, when I first heard this joke, was the tattooed number on the wrist, a bodily sign of the end result of European anti-Semitism. That the Martians' names are numbers (rather than Star Trek-y bisyllables, for example) can be read as an ironic reversal of the heroic efforts Jews undertook to carve a sense of self out of the imposition of numbers: in the joke, numbers signify the legibility of personal and group identity rather than the extinction of it.

The most important reason I like this joke is that it feels real to me. I have heard the punchline in my own life more times than I care to remember, and mostly from non-Jews (so much for my fantasy of Martian solidarity). The worst part about the "punchline" (which retroactively transforms my Jewishness into the joke) is that the expected response often seems to be "thank you," as though "you don't look Jewish" were a compliment rather than, as I experience it, an insult.

Sander Gilman has written at length and in depth about the etiology and effects of images of "the Jew" in Western Europe.[2] The ugliness of "the Jew" represented the very marrow of difference through bodily signs (flat feet, big hooked nose, circumcised penis) and psychic degeneration (cowardice, avarice, depravity, linguistic difference).[3] But the Jew can also hide — change speech patterns, change names, even not "look Jewish" — so as to infiltrate and weaken the dominant culture. I hear this fear of invisibility and infiltration in the statement "you don't look Jewish," as well as the effortless recapitulation of the anti-Semitic stereotypes of Jewish noses, Jewish hair, Jewish pushiness, and so on.

I recognize, too, that the distance between my identity and the bodily signs that are supposed to act as conduits for and markers of that identity causes surprise and discomfort. The implication is that Jews *should* look Jewish, in the way that Jews are imagined to look. The signs of Jewishness having been long established, Jews should inhabit them, and thereby be treated *as* Jews.[4] It is this internalized but everywhere occluded knowledge that modernity expects bodies to speak the visible identities they have been assigned that led me to write this book. To "look Jewish" is to bear upon the body the *evidence* of Jewishness, incontrovertibly, legibly, identifiably. And yet that evidence is always weighted against the subordinated body: our bodies are thought to testify against us ("You don't look Jewish." "Thank you.").

Ironically, looking Jewish does not figure in this work — an earlier plan to discuss Al Jolson's blackface performance in *The Jazz Singer* next to the racial passing in Nella Larsen's *Passing* gave way to a different set of concerns. But what this book does take up is the question of how bodily signs, both on the outside like skin and fingerprints, and on the inside like blood and DNA, are constructed as evidentiary material in a case of identity, where "case" takes on the multiple meanings of law, medicine, and experimental science, as well as detective fiction and newspaper reporting.

Most of *Technology and the Logic of American Racism* orbits around the meanings of whiteness and blackness in the United States from the 1890s to the 1990s. Those meanings circulate around or intersect with other discourses of the self: what it signifies to be an American citizen, for example, or the ways in which mass communication mediates modes of looking/at, or the popularity of the memoir in U.S. writing in the final decade of the twentieth century. Moreover, the processes by which identity is defined and disseminated are not unidirectional. As many of the stories in this book amply demonstrate, once evidence is laid out it is vulnerable to multiple (re)interpretations both along and against the grain. To be spoken of and for is *not* necessarily to be silenced.

Part of my project in this book has been to demonstrate the ways in which subordination and resistance have been continual although necessarily unequal partners in the forging of national identities in the United States. Sometimes resistance is individual, unformed, almost imperceptible except through close and committed attention by a reader. It is a faint humming sound that one must listen hard for. Other times it is organized, public, vocal, taking the form of political protest, pamphlets, cartoons, or editorials, but still beneath the radar of the majority discourse (an excellent example of this is, of course, the thriving black press of the 1940s, a topic I deal with in Chapter 4). One of the most brutal powers of dominant discourses is to erase opposition, render it invisible, and thereby reduce it to irrelevance, ridicule, or impotence. I hope this book will in part be a conduit for the oppositional strategies that have always existed in subordinated communities, both those of the past that were often not heard by the majority, and those of the present that would do well to learn from the past.

A word on methods. This book is organized chronologically, beginning at the end of the nineteenth century and ending at the close of the twentieth. However, it does not pretend even to approximate a survey of the ways in which bodies were deployed as evidence during that tumultuous hundred years. It is arranged around moments that I found deeply suggestive, where a confluence (and sometimes a cacophony) of voices converged around a part of the body, brought it into relief and theorized a whole set of meanings around it. Sometimes those meanings maintained their grip upon the public imagination – the best example of this is the hold that fingerprints have sustained for over a century, to such an extent that they have taken on metaphorical meaning in other fields. DNA is called a "genetic fingerprint," and fingerprints are still regarded as the yardstick against which irreproducible and quantifiable identity can be known. Other bodily signs have shifted meaning over time, such as skin color and blood, which have both, at different times, been imagined as the ground in which identity is rooted, and an empty signifier for race.

Second, this project is invested in a vision of culture as a series of what

Stuart Hall has called "articulations": that is, concurrent but contingent cultural phenomena, spoken into being together by culture. An articulation is "the form of the connection that *can* make a unity of two different elements, under certain conditions. It is a linkage which is not necessary, determined, absolute and essential for all time" (Hall, 1986: 53). Articulation happens for ideological rather than necessary reasons, and the theory of articulation "asks how an ideology discovers its subject rather than how the subject thinks the necessary and inevitable thoughts that belong to it" (*ibid.*). Different elements, such as skin color and a sense of identity, have no necessary "belongingness" one to the other, but in the contemporary United States they form a single articulation (which is also articulated with a series of other meanings and consequences). A theory of articulation recognizes cultural change, and the possibility for resistance: it helps us to recognize modes of understanding the world not as unchanging and static "traditions" but as (re)combinations of elements that make each other intelligible.

For my own work, an important articulated element that helps us make sense of the world is literature (and by association film). While I'm not sure that writers (and film-makers, and artists in general) can necessarily stand outside their world, I do believe that they pull into sharper focus the nagging questions that a culture would rather not hear asked and certainly does not want to answer. "The world is out there," Richard Rorty comments, "but descriptions of the world are not" (1989: 5). Descriptions of the world are "in here," inside the cultural matrix, and fiction is an often insightful, sometimes banal, occasionally revelatory conduit for those descriptions. As Mikhail Bakhtin has observed, fiction is particularly well equipped (and in fact exists in order) to represent the multiple bubblings up of culture as it is manifested in

> the internal stratification of any single national language into social dialects, characteristic group behavior, professional jargons, generic languages, languages of generations and age groups, tendentious languages, languages of the authorities, of various circles and of passing fashions, languages that serve the specific sociolopolitical purposes of the day, even of the hour ... present in every language at any given moment of its historical existence.
>
> (Bakhtin, 1981: 262–3)

In some of the chapters, a literary text is at the centre of my investigation of evidentiary tropes of the body. In others, fiction acts more as an accessory to my analysis in all senses of the word: it matches and/or contrasts the larger discussion, aids and abets my scrutiny of a given cultural-historical moment, and provides a passageway into the past that might otherwise be blocked from view.

Finally, this book isn't about science or law, but what people do with them. While I have endeavored to explain the science behind various kinds of knowledge (be they fingerprint technology, eugenics, blood typing, or DNA) or the legal intricacies of miscegenation law or jury decisions, I am not attempting an analysis of scientific or legal questions. Instead, I want to know how concepts of evidence formed an explanatory network of systems that claimed to help one recognize different kinds of people, particularly in terms of race, through looking at their bodies.

Technology and the Logic of American Racism starts with an exploration into theorizing the body as evidence. I work through a series of sites where ideas about evidence and how bodies could be used as vectors for evidence of their own identity were produced during the nineteenth century, specifically the law, medicine and the natural sciences, and the academic discipline of history. Much of this work depends upon theorizing the role of the visible as a category both for the development of professional expertise, and to undergird the implementation of racial segregation.

Chapter 2 takes off at the end of the nineteenth century, with Mark Twain's *The Tragedy of Pudd'nhead Wilson*. I survey an element of the novel that has been neglected in Twain criticism, the palm-reading episode near the beginning of the text, and trace its suppression by the evidentiary technology of fingerprinting. In this chaotic novel, Twain shows us how his scientific contemporaries constructed a sense of order by shifting racial discourse away from the corporeal and towards the quantifiable, away from sciences of touching, like phrenology and cheirosophy, and towards sciences of charting and graphing.

Chapter 3 moves us into the 1920s, to the intersection of fictional and judicial texts: Nella Larsen's *Passing* and the newspaper reports of the civil fraud trial known as the Rhinelander case. In this case, the son of a socially prominent New York family, Leonard Kip Rhinelander, sued his new bride for fraud, and by association annulment, claiming that she had lied to him about her background, which was partly Caribbean of African descent. Both Larsen's novel and the reports of the court case focus on racial identity as a thing to be fixed and held in place through the evidence of skin color; Clare Kendry and Alice Jones Rhinelander attempted, with differing degrees of success, to keep moving above, below, or beyond the gaze that could pin and identify them as specimens of a racial identity that would otherwise be ambiguous. The chapter ends with an analysis of Wallace Thurman's mordant novel *The Blacker the Berry*, whose protagonist Emma Lou Morgan wants nothing more than to escape what she (not unjustifiably) feels is the fixing sign of her dark skin. In this text, Thurman exposes how blackness comes to represent *the* pejorative evidence of "Negro-ness" within black communities even as repressive Jim

Crow laws and the regime of lynching made no legal distinction between African Americans of different colors.

In Chapter 4 I deal with the overriding metaphor for race, but the most elusive and least visible evidentiary proof of it: blood. The late l930s and early 1940s saw enormous advances in blood storage and transfusion technology, most importantly in the capability to extract and desiccate plasma for on-site reconstitution. The very *visibility* of blood weakened the blood-as-race trope that had previously dominated racist discourse. I follow the changes in meaning of blood from evidence of race to evidence of citizenship through the vehicle of blood donation drives during the course of World War II, and the concomitant segregation of blood by "race." At the same time, I reconstruct black responses to and appropriation of the new language of blood-as-citizenship. I end with a comparative reading of Japanese American citizenship during the same period, and the delegitimation of Nisei citizenship that led to Japanese internment during the mid-1940s.

Technology and the Logic of American Racism concludes by jumping to the present day, and the language that has grown up around the evidence, both medical and legal, of DNA. A reading of Shirlee Taylor Haizlip's *The Sweeter the Juice*, which explicitly invokes genetics as a way to understand racial genealogy, leads me to a meditation on the wrangling over the identity of the posterity of Sally Hemings, Thomas Jefferson's slave, supposed mistress, and, according to her descendants, mother of his children, a struggle in which DNA evidence has played a major role. In this case, questions of blood, skin, and self combine: we see the phenomenon of Americans who have never been anything but white, and who continue to think of themselves uncomplicatedly as white, publicly acknowledging black "blood" as a constitutive part of themselves.

Too often over the past century, bodies have been interpellated as a bundle of evidentiary signs in order to shore up the hierarchies of race. It has been crucial to the operations of white supremacy that the juridical lines between the categories of "white" and "black" appear impermeable.[5] But those lines have been challenged, crossed, and recrossed again and again. As a committed anti-racist, I can hope (perhaps extravagantly) that this book will make some contribution to the struggle to void the matrices of white hegemony altogether. More modestly, I hold on to the aspiration that by revealing the past and present workings of racism, and the strategies that people of color have used to thwart its operations, this project might give us space to imagine modes of identity that are lodged in more flexible imaginings of bodies and selves.

Notes

1. Of course, this is not the whole story. My family was both leftist and Zionist in political orientation, and we looked to Israel on the one hand and the Upper West Side of New York on the other for images of "out" Jews (even though both kinds of tough-talking Jewishness seemed ineffably exotic to me as a child).

2. See, for example, Sander Gilman, *The Jew's Body* (New York: Routledge, 1991); *Jewish Self-Hatred: Anti-Semitism and the Secret Language of the Jews* (Baltimore: The Johns Hopkins University Press, 1986); *Difference and Pathology: Stereotypes of Sexuality, Race, and Madness* (Ithaca, NY: Cornell University Press, 1985).

3. James S. Shapiro's *Shakespeare and the Jews* (New York: Columbia University Press, 1996) shows that the European obsession with Jewish difference stretches back to before the Middle Ages, encompassing the standard beliefs (horns and tails, drinking the blood of Christian children) as well as the less well-known (the menstruating Jewish man, Jews infiltrating Scotland after the expulsion from England in 1290).

4. A subset of art about the Shoah works with this circular logic, placing at its center Jews who don't "look Jewish," and thus manage to escape death but not psychological and emotional injury. See, for example, Agnieska Holland's film *Europa, Europa* (1990), and Letty Cottin Pogrebin's short story "Isaac", in *Deborah, Golda, and Me* (New York: Crown, 1991).

5. But not the lines of fantasy, as the immense support for blackface minstrelsy from the mid-1850s through to the World War II era shows. For a history of minstrelsy in the nineteenth century, see Eric Lot, *Love and Theft: Blackface Minstrelsy and the American Working Class* (New York: Oxford University Press, 1995). The popularity of Al Jolson in the 1920s is a classic example of the white American fascination with blackface, and in my research on World War II I found newsreels representing the ways in which servicemen relaxed, one of which was to put on minstrel shows.

1

Theorizing the body as evidence

That theory will be most generally believed which besides offering us objects able to account satisfactorily for our sensible experience, also offers those which are most interesting, those which appeal most urgently to our aesthetic, emotional, and active needs.

(William James, *Principles of Psychology*)

Perhaps we need a moratorium on saying "the body." For it's also possible to abstract "the" body. When I write "the body," I see nothing in particular. To write "my body" plunges me into lived experience, particularity. ... To say "the body" lifts me away from what has given me a primary perspective. To say "my body" reduces the temptation to grandiose assertions.

(Adrienne Rich, "Notes toward a Politics of Location")

Body counts

From 1997 to 1999, a contest sizzled over how to conduct the U.S. Census[1] for the year 2000. One argument focused on how people would be counted at all. President Bill Clinton favored "statistical sampling," which detractors ridiculed as taking the census like an opinion poll (one of the ongoing criticisms of Clinton being that he listened more to polls than to a sense of what was right). Republican Party members wanted to count the old-fashioned way, head by head, a method that the Clinton camp maintained had led to serious miscalculations in the 1990 Census, overcounting the white middle classes and undercounting people of color, the poor, and the homeless.[2]

The debate over the 2000 Census was not just about how to count, however. It had already erupted over *whom* to count, or rather, how to classify different kinds of people. In 1997, the Census Bureau suggested adding another category to the pre-existing racial and ethnic classifications — white, black. Asian/Pacific Islander, American Indian/Native Alaskan, Hispanic, and other — "multiracial" ("Experts Clash"). Federal officials argued that interracial marriages had profoundly changed the make-up of the United States, citing golf star Tiger Woods, with a mixed African American and Native American father and Thai mother, as the poster child for the new multiracialism, which counted for about two million U.S. citizens in 1990 ("Experts Clash").[3]

Responses to this new possibility were mixed. The Census Bureau found that few people would choose to call themselves "multiracial," particularly if one parent was white. Instead, they would align themselves with the racial identity of the other parent. This was particularly true if the other parent was of African descent; only between 0.7 and 2.7 percent would shift their classification from "black" to "multiracial" ("Poll Finds Few").

The desire for a new "multiracial" category dovetailed with calls for other previously uncounted ethnicities: Arabs, Creoles, Native Hawaiians, among others. But the census does more than just count. In the first place, census results create public policy, determine which communities are most over-crowded, or underserved, which areas have experienced population growth or shrinkage. The Census meant government money and resources. Second, the Census has political ramifications in terms of representation in Congress, since the number of representatives is based in large part on population density of geographic areas. Connected to this is the more inchoate quality of political clout. Census reports and projections of rapid growth in the Latino population throughout the U.S. has meant shifts in public policy, as well as the development of reactionary political movements to ban bilingual education and enforce "English-only" rules.

Opposition to the "multiracial" category was based in more than economics and electoral politics, however. One objection came from African American civil rights groups, which feared that since so many black people were of mixed race due to the long history of slavery and intermarriage with Native Americans, a change in classification would in effect erase huge portions of the black population ("Poll Finds Few"). This was of particular concern since employment discrimination suits have often invoked census data when certain populations are seriously underrepresented in certain jobs compared to the proportion of those groups nationally.

By the middle of 1997 the debate had been upgraded to a controversy, even as the Federal task force assigned to study the possibility of adding "multiracial" to the 2000 Census was arguing against the change ("Panel Balks").[4] The Census Board had changed its tune. Rather than providing a more accurate picture of the racial constitution of the nation, the new category would "add to racial tensions and further fragmentation of our population"

("Panel Balks"). The task force came up with a compromise – Census form-fillers could check more than one racial category – and again invoked Tiger Woods as the perfect candidate for such a system (he could check four categories: black, white, Asian, and Native American). This method would allow Census-takers to distinguish between different kinds of multiracial people: black/white, Asian/Hispanic, white/Native American, and so on.

"There was a strong sentiment," explained task force co-ordinator Sally Katzen (not, coincidentally, an official at the Office of Management and Budget), "that some groups were necessary, but proliferation of groups was not particularly healthy at this time" ("Panel Balks"). So do mixed-race people constitute a group or not? Plenty of things are unhealthy but they still happen, after all. How does one decide which groups are "necessary" (whether healthy or not) and which are incidental? What, too, does the clear desire of racial groups to hold on to single identities reveal about the construction of racialized selves living with the legacy of the "one-drop" rule that for so long defined any person with African descent as black and subject to laws of segregation? Or the constitutional clause that forbade nonwhite immigrants from becoming naturalized citizens? Moreover, why would recognizing a group that embodies the most intimate kind of racial togetherness cause an *increase* in racial tension?

To put it bluntly, according to the Federal Government, multiracial people do not *per se* exist. Their bodies are evidence not of a new kind of racial identity, but the combination of pre-existing, knowable classes.[5] Had the task force come up with the opposite recommendation, they would. They do not exist *not* because there are not people of mixed race who personally identify as multiracial walking around in the U.S., but because they will not be counted. For the Census, racial identity is brought into being for the purposes of quantification, not the other way around. It is the job of a census to reduce the population into collations of numbers and figures that then take on independent meaning, whether or not they are accurate. "Multiracial" as a category is too difficult to shape into a series of statistics; hence it is not.

These conflicts over quantifying racial populations are not new, although they have changed shape over time. Currently, racial identity is explicitly defined and quantified through parentage on the one hand and self-identification on the other (what Werner Sollors has called the tension between descent and consent identities). At the end of the nineteenth and beginning of the twentieth centuries, however, genealogy, appearance, and self-declaration jockeyed for definitional primacy. The categories of racial identity for people of African descent kept changing: in the 1890 Census, forms made a distinction between "Negro" and "mulatto," whereas in 1920 "mulatto" was dropped as a category, leaving "Negro" as the only choice. For a while, "colored" indicated both or either mixed race between African and European and/or lighter skin, until it became a euphemism (although not integrated into the structure of the Census) for all African Americans, whether racially mixed or not (Davis, 1991: 6).

Even more challenging, the 1890 Census required enumerators to "record the *exact* proportion of 'African blood'" in the counted, "relying on visibility" (Davis, 1991: 12). Not only were they to count how many black people there were; they also had to quantify *how* black they were in measurable fractions. How census-takers were expected to derive a complex calculus of genealogy simply by looking at skin tone, hair texture, facial features, and other indicators that had for the entire nineteenth century defined "race" is not clear. The "one-drop" ideology that classified all people of African descent, however intermixed with other kinds of people, as black, proved a burden for the official registrars of the nation's racial composition (although not as much as for "Negroes" themselves).

How, then, was one supposed to tell who was what, particularly in the face of increasingly harsh segregation legislation that was being established throughout the post-Reconstruction South? The shifts in the census during the most brutal years of racial repression are a hint of the search within white supremacy for a hard-and-fast methodology to identify black bodies, count them, and fix them in place. As Michel Foucault has argued, with modernity came the idea of "'docile' bodies," subjected to systems of surveillance and interpretation, "described, judged, measured, compared with others ... trained or corrected, classified, normalized, excluded" (1979: 191).[6] The legal ramifications of Jim Crow and restrictive legislation against Asian immigrants on the West Coast intensified the importance of these processes: when questions of enfranchisement, property, and social access were at stake, accurate classification was of more than just theoretical relevance.

I bring censuses separated by more than a century into the inauguration of my discussion of reading the body as evidence for a variety of reasons. First, reading bodies is what the census does: it looks at individual people, gathers them together in a single document, and presents them as material to be interpreted as evidence arguing for various official and unofficial policies (government funding, electoral districting, educational programs, equal opportunity litigation, anti-immigration initiatives, to name a few). The census also adumbrates a major thematic of my work in this book: the massive trend in the nineteenth century that has extended so effortlessly beyond the end of the twentieth, the urge to count, measure, quantify, record.

Benedict Anderson has traced how European governments used the census to limn the boundaries of their colonial holdings and all the people that the colonies held. The census could reveal the realities of the colonial scene that might otherwise be illegible to Europeans: "the nature of the human beings [a colonial power] ruled, the geography of its domain, and the legitimacy of its ancestry" (Anderson, 1983: 164). It is not by chance that the same jostlings of classification in the 1890 U.S. Census were analogously at work in British and Dutch censuses of their Southeast Asian colonies. Categories based on ethnic identities appeared and disappeared as Europeans struggled to comprehend social, class, and religious differences within India, Malaysia, Indonesia, and other equally diverse locations. The census was more than just a counting tool, it was an instrument of order that rendered colonies and their inhabitants legible, knowable, and controllable.

The census aspires to being a "totalizing classifactory grid ... able to say of anything that it was this, not that; it belonged here, not there" (Anderson, 1983: 184). More significantly, though, this taxonomy is from the outset imagined as hierarchical between sets and substitutable within sets (white is better than black; all blacks are essentially the same). Census classification along the channels of race is not just for convenience; it needs to make a point about order, difference, inequality of faculties, and the need for the subordination of the dominated.

Changes in the style and content of the U.S. census dovetailed with transformations in beliefs about the human place in the evolutionary process (itself a new idea). In the early part of the century, U.S. naturalists moved "from an emphasis on the fundamental physical and moral homogeneity of man, despite superficial differences, to an emphasis on the essential heterogeneity of mankind, despite superficial similarities" (Stepan, 1991: 30). This belief in heterogeneity was imbricated with a sense of human beings as biological and material rather than intellectual, a collection of biological processes rather than removed observers of the natural world (Crary, 1990: 72). Descartes' doubt that he even had a body to perceive with, or that bodies of others had actual material existences, was transplanted by "the progressive parcelization and division of the body into separate and specific systems and functions" (*ibid.*: 79).

The abstraction of the body into a collection of measurable functions renders it legible as a sign of something else, not itself: patterns, qualities, trends, predictable processes. The enormous impact of Darwinism on the intellectual scene in post-Civil War America intersected with these new ways of looking at bodies: not only could bodies tell scientists how they functioned, they could also reveal their origins and development. Experiments with bodies, sciences that took for granted that bodily systems could reveal paradigmatic corporeal configurations, grew similarly to the practice of medicine in the nineteenth century, defining some bodies as normal and others as (socially rather than organically) pathological, deploying a diagnostic gaze that "restor[ed] as truth what was produced in accordance with a genesis ...: reproduc[ing] in its own operations what has been given in the very movement of composition" (Foucault, 1978: 108).[7] For inevitably, the desire to find in the body proof of "difference" *generated* the evidence for such a hypothesis, even though in the guise of searching for it.

Intrinsic to the project of revealing bodies as essentially different from each other through the evidence of visible signs is the belief that "all that is *visible* is *expressible*" (Foucault, 1978: 115). In fact, this need to put the evidence of the body into language was an enormous challenge for the groups of people whom I analyze in this book — eugenicists, jurors, hematologists, military commanders, newspaper reporters, to name a few. Since I am looking most closely at moments when the meanings of the body were at least temporarily in flux, I have often found lacunae in language, inexpressible concepts, or rifts between causes and effects.

That bodies *mean* something other than the accumulations of events through which they have lived is a truism, but one that I focus on in this book. I came to this project through studying the sentimental ethos of the mid-nineteenth century in the United States, a bourgeois aesthetic that assumed (even demanded) bodily transparency; that is, that the face can speak a person's character. As Laura Doyle has argued, "hierarchies of race and gender *require* one another as co-originating and co-dependent forms of oppression" (1994: 21). The valuation of whiteness and of sexual chastity in a racially asymmetrical and hierarchically gendered world was translated into the moral and aesthetic imperative of a lily-white complexion through which the "spotless" soul was easily legible.[8] Behind this belief was an assumption that the body spoke for itself in a language that was clear and manifest.

I became increasingly interested in the development of the idea of bodies as proof of something, evidence of their place in the natural world. For the sentimentalists the body was evidence of the soul's condition, testifying, bearing witness, opening itself up to examination.[9] But these values carried over into a vast array of cultural practices in the United States of the late nineteenth century: the natural sciences, medical research, criminology, psychology, realist fiction, phrenology and other kinds of anthropometry, detective stories, etiquette manuals.

This book chronicles some of the "grandiose assertions" about "the body" that emerged in the U.S. from the end of the nineteenth century to the waning of the twentieth: what it can tell "us" about what bodily phenomena and attributes mean, how different kinds of bodies can be ranked, measured, separated, and interpreted. It traces patterns of scientific theory and practice and legal battles over the information with which bodies have been freighted, and how the processes of abstraction against which Rich warns us have been part of (and have partially constituted) the difficult history of what Donna Haraway has called "the terrible marks of gender and race" in the United States (1989: 1). At the same time, that abstraction has been tied to an insistence that subordinated peoples were little more than their bodies, that their blood and skin made their selves.

In this book, I explore the ways in which bodies were recruited to testify against themselves to support systems of subordination that viewed racially marked bodies as evidence for their own marginalization. These evidentiary moments were often called into being by technological changes − the development of fingerprinting as a criminological tool, for example, or the fine-tuning of blood transfusion − but equally (or perhaps more) often, technological "advances" were summoned by the same forces and at the same time as or even after cultural shifts. As with fingerprinting or the segregation of blood, the technology can pre-exist, dormant, almost invisible, the uses for which it is eventually most noted, and cultural assumptions can take hold well before science or law are anywhere near validating them. [10]

Technology and the Logic of American Racism works chronologically, although not systematically, through a series of what we might call evidentiary crises. These were moments in which the information that bodies could be expected to provide about themselves became unclear, ambiguous, or contradictory. Alternately, they were times in which modes of registering the body shifted, and evidentiary arguments (medical, legal, gendered, raced) had to be reconfigured to shore up the equilibrium of power. Throughout these crises, bodies − both individual bodies and groups of people − resisted being recast as "the body" and grasped the language of blood, skin, and self to render their bodies actual rather than abstract.

Reading the body as evidence

Legibility; visibility; proof. These concepts suffuse writings on race and gender and on legal and scientific evidence from the late nineteenth through to the late twentieth century. As Robyn Wiegman has shown, "the visible has a long, contested, and highly contradictory role as the primary vehicle for making race 'real' in the United States" (1995: 21). Indeed, the word "evidence" itself embraces visibility in its root, convincing us that evidence allows us to see out of an otherwise insoluble conundrum. Evidence is "distinctly visible; conspicuous. ... Obvious to the sight; recognizable at a glance. ... Clear to the understanding or the judgement; obvious, plain" (*OED*). It provides "ground for belief" − seeing is believing − "an appearance from which inferences may be drawn; an indication, mark, sign, token, trace" (*OED*).

Sight itself, though, is not self-evident. To be able to make sense out of what we see, we must "submit [our] retinal experience to the socially agreed-upon description(s) of an intelligible world. ... Between retina and world is inserted a *screen* of signs, a screen consisting of all the multiple discourses on vision built into the social arena" (Bryson, 1988: 91–2). As F. James Davis has shown in *Who Is Black?* (1991), the visible sign of dark skin has very little meaning outside cultural definitions of race and identity. People of African descent in other American countries such as Brazil have been defined (and have defined themselves) within taxonomic systems quite different from the black/white binary that has dominated U.S. discourse on race. Similarly, the classifications of race can supersede what might otherwise be "obvious" or, alternatively, imperceptible visual evidence (for example, the "blackness" of 1940s NAACP director Walter White, who was blond, blue-eyed, and fair-skinned).

The very idea of "obviousness" itself is hardly self-evident either. What feels obvious, what goes without saying, is part of the complexity of culture through which we recognize ourselves, a "peculiarity of ideology that imposes (without appearing to do so, since these are 'obviousnesses') obviousnesses as obviousnesses, which we *cannot fail to recognize* and before which we have the inevitable and natural reaction crying out ...: 'That's obvious! That's right! That's true!'" (Althusser, 1990: 172, emphasis in original). One might even argue that what feels most obvious and intrinsic to us is actually the *most* constructed through ideology. We understand ourselves and our places in the world more acutely through our quotidian interactions with our culture than through some transparent, unmediated knowledge of things "out there." As Raymond Williams points out, "the relations of domination and subordination ... [are] in effect a saturation of the whole process of living – not only of political and economic activity, nor only of manifest social activity, but of the whole substance of lived identities and relationships" (1977: 110).

We have to start, then, at a different place when thinking about how bodies have been deployed as evidence of the systems that have constructed and defined them. The visibility of the body does not determine its meanings, but is determined by them; it's only after we learn to read them that they become visible, something out of which we can see, something we can use to prove that they are workable as evidence after all. And what we read is the often inchoate evidence of "difference," a system of valuation in which the dominant is rendered invisible and the subordinate hypervisible for the purposes of control, and the reverse for the purposes of normalization.

This process is not always purposely malign (although it is rarely benign). We need to make sense out of what we see in the world, so that we do not feel bombarded by chaos. Reality is, as Mark Monmonier has observed in relation to maps, "three dimensional, rich in detail, and far too factual to allow a complete yet uncluttered two-dimensional graphic scale model. Indeed a map that did not generalize would be useless" (1991: 25). But neither generalizations nor foci transparently suggest themselves out of a welter of information. Rather, they "reflect a chosen aspect of reality" (*ibid.*) even as it does not feel like a choice but merely an accurate account of "how things look."[11]

Studying how evidence is invoked, produced, and deployed reveals the "Gordian knot" of culture, "simultaneously real, social, and narrated" (Latour, 1993: 7). We experience the physical world; there is no doubt about that (*pace* Descartes). But that world is mediated by the socius, the arrangement of structures that fix us in relation to each other, and is represented through narratives that allow us to understand those relations discursively. This is particularly true in looking at the scientific studies of evidences of racial and ethnic difference that littered the turn into the twentieth century (and still, occasionally, emerge) that were explicitly designed to reinforce racial hierarchies. Craniometry — the science of measuring skull volume and brain size to come to conclusions about relative intelligence — strikes the contemporary reader as not just racist but as paradigmatic bad science.[12] But behind questions of evidence are questions of epistemology, which are, in the words of Bruno Latour, "questions of social order ... because, when all is said and done, the social context contains as one of its subsets the definition of what counts as good science" (1993: 25–6).

This flies in the face of what has long been considered the calculus of evidence: "facts hammered into signposts, which point beyond themselves and their sheer, brute thingness ... innocent of human intention" (Daston, 1994: 243–4). Such positivism has been under serious revision for more than two decades from several directions: the sociology of knowledge, science studies, poststructural literary criticism, post-foundationalist historiography, critical legal studies, and critical race studies, to name a few.[13] I borrow from all those disciplines in this book, forging connections between "hard science," literature, popular culture, legal procedure, goverment policy, and medical practice.

Moreover, I want to show how these discourses do not exist in a vacuum from each other. Sociologists of knowledge have long argued that a society is "defined by its amalgamations, not by its tools [that is, technologies and disciplines] ... [T]ools exist only in relation to the interminglings they make possible or that make them possible" (Deleuze and Guattari, 1987: 90). From the beginnings of the scientific racism of the nineteenth century up to the genetic research of the present, biology has been a vexed site. As Laura Doyle has shown, science and nature have been imagined in hierarchy, not as coextensive, and "while seeming to privilege the organic world, biological theories ... insidiously turn that domain against itself, using it to give evidence of the supremacy of mind and of the race and sex most skilled in the arts of the mind (including, in a circularly self-authorizing move, the scientific arts" (1994: 7).

Similarly, "science" does not produce a single set of effects, nor can it predict what those effects will be. Developments in DNA technology, for example, both realized an extensive set of fantasies about social and genetic engineering that had been simmering under the surface of, and at times boiling over into, the cultural imagination, and brought to bear a number of previously unimaginable new concerns and opportunities, such as gene therapy on adults. At the same time, the discourses of DNA spread in diverse, even contradictory directions: racial nationalism versus racial integration, extending women's childbearing potential versus the rearticulation of reproductive capacity and economic wealth, agricultural bounty versus the suppression of small farmers through genetically engineered crops and so on.

We cannot separate science, politics, literature, popular culture, economics: they are intimately interconnected.[14] Once a phenomenon has been shaped through expectations that it represents some kind of evidence, it "cannot fail to brush up against thousands of living dialogic threads, woven by socio-ideological consciousness ... ; it cannot fail to become an active participant in social dialogue" (Bakhtin, 1981: 276). In *Technology and the Logic of American Racism* I embrace the heteroglossia of the languages of evidence even as I work to untangle what Walt Whitman called the "many uttering tongues" of surveillance, control, resistance, and change.

Bodies of knowledge, bodies of measurement

In order to be interpellated into an evidentiary role, the body must above all be knowable. Knowability, however, is not a fixed category: different disciplines have various sets of protocols for acceptable information. By the mid-nineteenth century, medicine and the natural sciences offered up what must have seemed like a miraculous welter of information about the insides and outsides of bodies, mainly through advances in surgical technology. Michel Foucault has written about the importance of "open[ing] up a few corpses" – the movement of the medical gaze "from the symptomatic surface to the tissual surface; in depth, plunging from the manifest to the hidden" (1978: 135) – to the contemporary institution of medicine, which still makes dissection and anatomy the center-piece of early medical training. The human body was more than its surfaces and occult interior: it was "deep, visible, solid, enclosed, but accessible" (*ibid.*: 195).

Accessibility to the body at the end of the nineteenth century extended beyond the dissection of corpses. In the final decade of the century, body cavity surgery advanced by leaps and bounds. Midwestern surgeons William and Charles Mayo performed fifty-four abdominal operations in the three years before 1892; by 1900 they were performing 612 annually, and by 1905 they had increased their practice to over 2,000 operations per year (Starr, 1982: 156–7). Surgeons could routinely reach into the body in ways that had been unknown before the 1870s, prior to the development of anti- and asepsis. Functioning human organs, previously invisible except in very rare instances, were available for inspection to any working surgeon thousands of times, expanding the boundaries of corporeal knowability to previously unimagined dimensions. Surgery erased the boundaries between the surfaces and recesses of the body.[15]

Technologies that have allowed the police to render fingerprints from fingers and assemble banks of prints, photographers to capture stable images of people, technicians to store blood outside the body, and geneticists to abstract DNA from that blood, all in the service of producing evidence of identity, find their origins in a basic belief. With its roots in the late nineteenth-century developments I have traced above, an assumption of corporeal knowability rests upon the conception that the inside and the outside of the body are in continual communication (however much time it may take to decipher the language in which they speak), rendering the body legible as long as the reader was in possession of the correct reading skills. At the same time, surface and interior cannot fully correspond. The medicalized body becomes like Dr Who's Tardis: an apparently bounded exterior space that reveals room after room of complex machinery once you are inside the door.

Within judicial law, however, knowability has always been a more difficult issue. Complicated networks of rules of evidence evolved from the early eighteenth century onwards to grapple with what one could see out of evidence within a judiciary context. The answer was, not much. Evidence law, particularly in jury trials, depends upon layers of invisibility: the jury cannot have seen the event at issue, the judge, attorneys, and defendant cannot see the jury doing its work of deliberation, the jury will rarely if ever witness the punishment they recommend. In fact, the rules of evidence take for granted the uncontrollability of the visible. Unable to depend upon a knowable truth (the jury only *hears* eyewitnesses), evidentiary rules are based in the belief that juries must depend instead upon the next-best thing: reason. The language of "reasonable doubt" and "probable cause" is clothed in the assumption that "reasonable men, employing their senses and rational faculties, could derive truths that they would have no reason to doubt" (Shapiro, 1991: 7).

At the beginning of and into the nineteenth century, jurists were drawing explicit parallels between the rationalist principles of legal evidence and the evidentiary needs of other disciplines. The influential Harvard legal scholar Simon Greenleaf argued in his *Treatise on the Law of Evidence* (1842, and going into multiple editions over the next fifty years) that judicial evidence was indistinguishable in principle from the evidence brought to bear within the natural sciences, history, cartography, and even travel writing (see vol. 1, ch. 3). In a formula that will become increasingly familiar over the course of this book, Greenleaf maintained that one of the foundations of evidence was the application of "a process familiar in natural philosophy, showing the truth of an hypothesis by its coincidence with existing phenomena" (quoted in Shapiro, 1991: 38).

Out of this concern for the interweaving of material evidence, eyewitness testimony, and rational deliberation grew rulings about previously amorphous or even quite differently valued types of evidence, most notably hearsay and circumstantial evidence. As Barbara Shapiro traces in her history of Anglo-American laws of evidence, the official U.S. stance of circumstantial evidence changed significantly between the early and mid-nineteenth century. Doctrines about circumstantial evidence developed initially around witchcraft trials in the sixteenth and seventeenth centuries, first in Britain and then in the American colonies. Manuals for examining and trying witches insisted on more than circumstance: instead, they "employ[ed] the language of full proof and half proof, not[ing] the superiority of proof by [at least] two witnesses," although they did authorize circumstantial evidence in support of witness testimony (Shapiro, 1991: 210).

By the mid-eighteenth century, however, what we would now call circumstantial evidence – material information outside the vision of witnesses to a crime – was raised up above eyewitness testimony. Law was envisaged as a process of reasoning about facts, and facts were more reliable coming from inanimate objects than from fallible witnesses (Shapiro, 1991: 233). The jury was imagined perspectively, operating within a disembodied, stable, centered field of vision, "competent to consume vast new amounts of ... information that increasingly circulated" (Crary, 1990: 96). Juries were imagined as bodies of reason that were supremely equipped in viewing, understanding, and weighing evidence.

The nineteenth-century move from rationality to materiality noted above had a powerful impact on the legitimacy of circumstantial evidence. Jurists and jurors were no longer imagined as possessing "an allegedly disincarnated, absolute eye," capable of seeing all within their range of vision (Jay, 1988: 8). Instead, the field of evidence was subject to a more unreliable vision, corporealized and incomplete, "with varying zones of efficiency and aptitude and specific parameters of normal and pathological vision" (Crary, 1988: 37).

Legal theorists in Britain and the United States had lesser faith not in an absolute truth, but in their own ability to locate the truth; as one scholar put it, they were certain that the difference in types of evidence and their relationship to the truth was not "founded on any essential difference in the nature of truths themselves, but [had] reference merely to our imperfect capacity and ability of perceiving them" (Wills, 1872: 2–3).[16] The majority of evidence could produce anything from "probability" to "certainty" about the events it purported to prove, and the concept of probability was complex, interacting with philosophical (particularly from John Locke), mathematical and logical processes. In fact, in an important essay on circumstantial evidence, British lawyer William Wills decisively distanced legal probability from mathematical theorems, arguing that "the nature of the subject precludes the possibility of reducing to the form of arithmetical notation the subtle, shifting, and evanescent elements of moral assurance, or of bringing to quantitive comparison things so inherently different as certainty and probability" (1872: 8).

For Wills, writing in the 1840s, circumstantial evidence was indirect and inferential, inferior to the testimony of an eyewitness. In a direct reversal of eighteenth-century beliefs about the logical nature of legal reasoning,[17] Wills argued that whereas eyewitness evidence "applies directly to the fact which forms the subject of inquiry, the *factum probandum*" (1872: 16) there was "no necessary connection between the facts and the inference [from circumstantial evidence]; the *facts* may be true, and the *inference* erroneous, and it is only by comparison with the results of observation ... that we acquire confidence in the accuracy of our conclusions" (*ibid.*: 17, his emphasis).

By 1875, leading American legal scholar William M. Best was arguing in *The Principles of the Laws of Evidence* that "the farther the evidence is removed from its primary source, the weaker it is," and that eyewitnesses were necessarily closer to the source than juries evaluating circumstantial evidence (quoted in Shapiro, 1991: 200). Juries were caught in a bind: they were forced to use reason in order to determine whether or not evidence was credible, but they leaned towards the visual record of events as more reliable than the objects involved in or resulting from those events.

Most difficult for codifying evidence (and attempts to codify evidentiary rules have stretched from the pioneering work of mid-nineteenth-century legal reformer David Dudley Field up to the present day[18]) have been the multiple exceptions to rules of evidence, particularly the hearsay rule. The *definition* of hearsay has not changed in the 150 years between Simon Greenleaf's definitive *Treatise on the Law of Evidence* and the most recent edition of the *Federal Rules of Evidence*. Hearsay is second-hand information, "that kind of evidence, which does not derive its value solely from the credit to be given to the witness himself, but rests also, in part, on the veracity and competency of some other person" (Greenleaf, 1866, vol. 1: 115). The hearsay rule imagines that the contiguity of bodies is not enough for an accurate representation of truth. In other words, it is insufficient that a witness was close enough to hear someone say something about an event which he or she experienced or saw. Witnesses must instead have actually witnessed an event, seen it with their own eyes: a recourse to visibility as the conduit for truth.

The establishment of exceptions to hearsay inadmissibility came into being at the same time that the hearsay rule was formulated. Greenleaf lists four classes of declarations that can be considered "original evidence" even though reported second-hand: cases in which the fact that a declaration was made, not about the veracity of its content, is at issue; cases in which a witness is reporting "expressions of bodily or mental feelings," and the actuality of those feelings is in question; cases regarding pedigree, that is, family relations and reputation in a given community; and *res gestae*, or excited utterances, in which it is assumed that the utterance is so spontaneous to obviate any risk of deception (Greenleaf, 1866, vol. 1: 148–50).

Throughout the nineteenth and into the twentieth century, exceptions to the hearsay rule increased in both number and specificity. The number of current exceptions (of which there are forty, including "reputation as to character," "dying declaration," "statement against interest," "prior inconsistent statement of witness,") suggests that the rule itself has been evacuated of meaning, oft invoked but equally often countermanded by exception. These exceptions do not simply raise hearing to the status of vision, however. Rather, they presume that the statement heard is so incontrovertible that it is promoted to the position of "positive" or eyewitness evidence.

In *res gestae* exceptions, for example, language is rendered as transparent as and equivalent to the event that caused the excitement. [19] Hearing the excited utterance is *the same* as seeing the exciting event: the declarant (that is, the person making the statement that is reported in hearsay) *becomes* the event and is viewed by the witness. This is underscored by the inadmissibility in many courts of hearsay of excited utterances in narrative form. The utterance must be spontaneous, and spoken "while the declarant was under the stress of excitement caused by the event or condition" (*Federal Rules*, 1990: 128).[20] If the declarant has enough presence of mind to shape an event into a narrative, her or his utterance is no more than a set of signifiers for a given signified. Spontaneous exclamations are not representations of an event – they are part of or can even substitute for the event itself.

Other exceptions to the hearsay rule presume a body in such profound distress, so incapable of presence either through death or distance, or so discredited that hearing its words is equivalent to seeing the events described in those words. In the "dying declaration" exception, the declarant must have believed herself to be close to death, "without hope of recovery ... with the consciousness of a swift and certain doom" in order for her statements to be admissible (quoted in Binder, 1975: 420).[21] One explanation for this exception was traditionally that, as the English judge L. J. Lush conjectured in 1881, no one "who is immediately going into the presence of his Maker will do so with a lie upon his lips" (*ibid.*). I would argue, too, that the dying body and its words become one in a dying declaration: as the body loses materiality, language substitutes for corporeality. Therefore, to hear the declaration is no different from witnessing the circumstances of the death itself.

The hearsay rule needs exceptions, in other words, because some bodies cannot speak for themselves. They are not simply inaudible but invisible, most simply because they cannot appear in the witness box, but more complexly because their own language supersedes their presence – they are rendered transparent by the spontaneity of their own utterances. Alternatively, their speech cannot be trusted, erasing their account of what they saw and did. The witnesses whose hearsay testimony is admitted become greater authorities about the declarants, their reputations, and their motivations, than the declarants are about themselves.

The rules of evidence are, like scientific research and medical practice, a technology of knowledge; that is, they make up a system devised by people to squeeze a certain kind of information out of a situation with specific, predetermined tools. But the comparison is closer and more creepy than that when we juxtapose the expectations of the rules of evidence, particularly the hearsay rule and its exceptions, with assumptions about biological difference, particularly in terms of race and ethnicity, that captured the imaginations of both scientists and laypeople from the mid-1800s onwards. The absent body in the exceptions to the hearsay rule is uncomfortably close to the abstracted body of the fingerprint, or the scrutinized body of the racial passer, or the excluded body of the black soldier, or the atomized bodies of genetics: crucial to the scene of evidence but silenced from it.

The value of the declarant's statement is not that the declarant said it; it is, instead, that the witness heard/saw it (or, rather, that a lawyer can convince the court of that). The statement has become so materialized as to exist outside of and more legibly than the declarant him- or herself. Similarly, the evidence gathered from a body obliterates the living body itself, let alone the person living inside that body. Thus, seeing the evidence that a body bears, like hearing an utterance covered by a hearsay exception, is figured as the originary moment of recognition of a "fact" as proof.

Modern technologies of knowledge deploy what rhetorician Ralph Cintron has called the "discourses of measurement," which constitute "a pervasive set of practices that [seem] to maintain the structures of power, indeed to divide those who [have] more power from those who have less" (1997: 236).[22] Discourses of measurement purport to be about accuracy and "an increase in precision (or the fiction of such an increase) ... an awareness, an understanding, an improvement, something modern" (*ibid.*). Usually, though, they smother previous ways of seeing the world, especially ways that made sense to subordinated people, with the power of the official. Cintron explicitly links the discourses of measurement to processes of social, economic, and political power, arguing that they make way for "the emergence of an expert class nimble in their ability to apply these ordering schemes to individual life and social life in order to manage both better" (*ibid.*: 210). The ultimate goal of discourses of measurement is social stability coupled with self-evident hierarchy: maintaining what Cintron calls (with an explicit debt to Mary Douglas) the rule of the "neat and clean."

Discourses of measurement construct meaning by targeting an arena of "a kind of emptiness, formlessness, or ambiguity. ... [T]hey first invent the emptiness, formlessness, or ambiguity and then systematically fill that emptiness" (Cintron, 1997: 212). Phenomena that were previously unmarked, or perceived as unimportant, meaningless, or outside the realm of human intervention, are redefined as a "problem." Once the problem has been "identified" (that is, created), a discourse of measurement grows up around it, defines it, and constructs a body of knowledge around it, which is then wielded by experts to contain what was previously amorphous and uncategorizable. Simultaneously, these discourses of measurement displace previous ways of knowing about the "problem" before it was defined as a problem: when it was simply an arrangement of events, feelings, ideas, or reactions.[23]

Another characteristic of discourses of measurement is their deployment to counter a sense of wildness or unmanageability: to give the formless form and to control the threat of instability and decay. I would add to this, though, that such discourses are also called into action by a political agenda that needs to sweeten the exercise of raw power that is a little too acrid for the tastes of the professional and managerial classes. The emergence of scientific, legal, or commercial technologies of evidence often accompanied historical moments of brutal violence and political suppression. The proofs of difference that evidentiary technologies promulgated went some of the way towards rationalizing and normalizing inequity by quantifying it as natural superiority and inferiority.

Cintron argues that discourses of measurement have always been with us: agriculture, literacy, arithmetic, money, are all technologies that attempt to tame, systematize and regularize amorphous human and nonhuman activities. While this is certainly true, historical analysis reveals that they took on a distinctive quality in the nineteenth and twentieth centuries: a near-obsession with quantification that masqueraded as Thomas Huxley's much-vaunted and much-quoted "fanaticism for veracity." I detail the growth of this obsession in the late nineteenth century in Chapter 2, but it bears a more theoretical discussion here.

In the late nineteenth century, as David A. Hollinger has shown, science held an exalted place in the cultural imagination of American intellectual life. "Not only" he observes, "was science [considered] noble and pure; its practice was ennobling and purifying" (1984: 43). Hollinger traces the development of the veneration of the sciences (loosely defined, since "sciences" still embraced the natural philosophy of the previous century) from an Emersonian contemplation of nature in order to extract the truth to a more systematic study of natural phenomena, and the attendant professionalization of scientific research (*ibid.*: 145).[24] As science became increasingly defined by the laboratory, and more tied to specific fields of study, scientists represented themselves as searchers after the truth, priests of the religion of knowledge (*ibid.*: 151).

This truth, as Darwin had proved, was much older, much larger, and much more diverse and changeable than earlier scientists had imagined. Rather than formulating general and abstract principles, scientists in the nineteenth century looked to local and specific natural systems. If the paradigmatic figure of the Enlightenment was Linnaeus, taxonomizing all of creation, the model scientist for the American nineteenth century was craniometrist Samuel G. Morton, who specialized in the comparative measurements of human skulls to come to conclusions about racial and national differences.[25]

Comparative quantification – what Stephen Jay Gould has called the "allure of numbers" (1996: 106) – characterized both the natural and social sciences, and gave birth to the struggles over Census-collecting that I described at the beginning of this chapter. The influence of Darwin on the one hand and sociologist Herbert Spencer on the other led to the much-discussed Social Darwinism of the post-Civil War period, and the assumption that "[s]ocial organisms, like individual organisms, are to be arranged into classes and sub-classes" (Spencer, 1873: 53). The battle over the legitimacy of statistics in the 1830s had been settled by the 1860s,[26] largely in statistics' favor, with the work of eugenicist (and later fingerprint expert) Francis Galton, making way for the importation of mathematical methods into the natural sciences. Galton believed that what stood in the way of knowledge was less the lack of data than the way those data were organized. Statistical analysis would render more precision in all kinds of scientific endeavor, illuminating and amplifying human knowledge of natural and mathematical processes.

In his breakthrough book *Hereditary Genius* (1869), Galton derived statistical values for the number of "men of genius" in the British population of 1860, and came to conclusions about the geographic and class distribution of intelligence throughout the British Isles. This work led quickly to his founding of the Anthropometric Laboratory in 1884 that was open to the public as part of the International Health Exhibition. The Laboratory served a double purpose: as entertainment for the Exhibition punters, who lined up in their thousands to have their height, weight, arm span, head circumference and other measurements taken for the cost of a threepenny ticket, and as a source for raw data (and seed money) for Galton in the pursuit of his eugenics work (Kevles, 1985: 14).

In the 1880s, Galton's interest shifted from the mathematics of the general population to the identification of criminals. This is hardly surprising, given the overlap we see between scientific and legal modes of evidence and their analogous deployment of bodies to prove a predetermined set of postulates about what those bodies mean (not coincidentally, Galton's protégé and biographer Karl Pearson moved from studying law to a career in mathematics to developing biometric eugenics methods). Again, Galton deployed a rich array of statistical tools. "Some people hate the very name of statistics, but I find them full of beauty and interest," Galton opined in his book, *Natural Inheritance* (1889). The beauty of statistics was their versatility and agility; they were "the only tool by which an opening can be cut through the formidable thicket of difficulties that bars the path of those who pursue the Science of man" (quoted in Kevles, 1985: 17). Just as modern surgery was allowing doctors to cut an opening into the body itself, Galton proposed statistics as a tool to cut into the information that those bodies were believed to offer up.

Galton's contribution to the natural sciences in the US at the end of the nineteenth century was to shift results analysis from "mere data gathering" to a strictly mathematical model (Kevles, 1985: 17). The study of eugenics, a combination of biology, statistics, "race science," moralizing, and raw stereotyping, certainly benefited from its founder's influence on scientific inquiry. Statistical models themselves became self-evident: not only could the bodies under examination not speak for themselves, but the numbers substituted for any speech at all. [27] More significantly, Galton's successful crusade for quantification changed the way biologists, botanists, astronomers, medical researchers, and a host of other scientists approached the collection and demonstration of evidence.

The combination of these developments soldered together sets of subordinated bodies that were dehumanized and silenced by the joint discursive powers of the law, scientific inquiry, and medical research. Bodies were both de- and hypercorporealized: reduced to elements in a statistical model, and rendered visible only as a collection of physical features (skin color, hair texture, skull size, and so on). Similarly, for the medical profession the body became a Frankenstein's monster *avant le coup*: a collection of parts each one of which the surgeon could detach, reattach, delve into, and bring into view *as* parts.[28] Knowledge became dependent upon the "exposure of physical detail," and the parts did not add up to an integrated whole (Crawford, 1996: 67).

Adding up the evidence

What does the expert do with these pieces? Once a body has been reduced to its constitutive parts, how can the observer transform those parts into as generalized a discourse as "race" or "national character"? Certainly, dissection and detail were key to the processes of creating evidence of identity, and we can see these features in some of the crucial developments of the contemporary era. "A discipline such as psychoanalysis came into being," Carlo Ginzburg has conjectured, "around the hypothesis that apparently negligible details could reveal profound phenomena of great importance" (1989: 124). Focus on evidentiary details – moments in a dream, an odd slip of the tongue or loss of a word – is at the base of psychoanalysis, to be sure. But so is the power of generalization. Psychoanalysis assumes that one can take a seemingly insignificant detail such as the mention of a handbag in a dream (as we see in Dora's case) and expand it into an entire narrative about desire, jealousy, disgust, and sexual competition. Little Hans is not simply throwing a spool out of his playpen: he is re-enacting an Oedipal crisis that affects not just him but all boys.

Like psychoanalysis, other Western and particularly U.S. systems of knowledge that inaugurated the twentieth century maintained this curious equilibrium between the picayune and the universal. An example from popular culture is detective fiction featuring investigators like Sherlock Holmes, who is so adept at picking out the right detail of a welter of material that he even finds evidence in the *absence* of evidence.[29] From this detail, Holmes can reconstruct entire narratives of events that would be invisible to the layperson's eye. In fact, Holmes is paradigmatic of the scientific professional of the late nineteenth and early twentieth centuries, wielding the tools to extricate specialized information where there appeared to be nothing to see, reaching his hands into the cavities of understanding that are closed to non-experts.

The rhetoric of evidence combines seemingly contradictory elements to forge categories of knowable bodies. Evidence is something to be sifted through: columns of figures to be collated, discrete bodily formations to be declared pathological or normal, words to be rendered material or irrelevant. Nothing is too minor to be recorded, compared, and evaluated. But evidence is mute unless it speaks the language of rules. The detail is displaced and redefined by the system to which it gives form. We can look back to the census for another instance of this: a document in which everyone is countable and counted, but simultaneously placed into a network of what Benedict Anderson has called "serialization: the assumption that the world was made up of replicable plurals" (1983: 184).[30]

This dialectical relationship between the detail and the generalization creates, in the atmosphere of the white supremacy of U.S. modernity, an unwieldy synthesis alive to the threats of exceptions (think back again to the problems of hearsay evidence, which works through the same conflict). In fact, statistics has written into it a mechanism that attempts to defang exceptions: the theory of the standard deviation. As long as the standard deviation remains low, the inferences drawn from a collection of numbers can hold; when the ratio of deviations becomes too high, statistical conclusions crumble into a commotion of individual measurements and uninterpretable details.

The challenge for racist statistics, then, is to arrange details into generalizations that will hold them and gird the presuppositions that gave form to the collecting of such details in the first place. The evidence is presumed to be in there: it must be arranged correctly and then decoded along the lines of that arrangement. This is the "double obligation" of the human sciences after the late nineteenth century that Foucault discusses, "that of hermeneutics, interpretation, or exegesis: one must understand a hidden meaning; and the other: one must formalize, discover the system, the structural invariant, the network of simultaneities" (1994a: 4).

Exegetical readings of the body imagine a corpus removed from the world that forms and nourishes it, so that analysis of the evidence becomes an *explication de texte*. Rosalind Pollack Petchesky's work on "fetal images" provides a chilling example of this de- and recontextualization of the body. From its first appearances in *Life* magazine in 1962, in an image that has become hyper-iconic, "the fetus is solitary, dangling in the air (or its sac) with nothing to connect to any life support system" (Petchesky, 1987: 268) — certainly not the woman inside whose body the fetus is lodged. These images construct the fetus as the material evidence of its own humanity, and the pregnant woman as an immensity of empty space.[31] Moreover, the pictures of developing embryos are so insistently material that they destroy any sense of scale. Just as the womb becomes so removed from an actual woman's body (let alone the cultural and personal meanings of pregnancy) that it loses spatial boundaries, the fetus is larger than life, larger even than small children, in the pictures that construct an alternative mode of reproduction: the endless enlarging and photocopying of the same image.

Even as imagining that the body can yield up its "hidden meaning" through close reading ignores the synchronic depth of bodies-in-culture or bodies connected to other bodies, the formalization of evidence erases the chronology of lived human experience. A mark or scar loses its local and historical significance: the silvery trace of surgery, a prison tattoo, words uttered in a moment of terror, are flattened out, assigned new (sometimes reduced, sometimes hyperbolic) meanings within the system. Viewing a collection of bodies as a "network of simultaneities" – a dozen hands of 20-year-old women measured in a day, forty vials of blood frozen at the same moment, ten skin tones laid out like paint swatches on a color chart, the comparative results of the electrophoresis of several different people's DNA – obliterates the processes (levels of nourishment, patterns of physical exercise, regimes of body image, and so on) by which bodies come to look the way they do over time.

Color me resistant

Bodies are not simply acted upon, though. We are not just moved through space by ideology, or discourse, or culture, or whatever name one might give the structures of intelligibility, power, and feeling that make sense of the world for us. Certainly, the smothering power of the Jim Crow South and the economically segregated North and West fixed black bodies in place through debt slavery, political disfranchisement, or the hopelessness born out of poverty. But, as opposed to direct domination, hegemony is not single-voiced, nor is resistance to it.[32] Even within a system of subordination, human relations are active and dynamic: those acted upon also act, in however limited a way. "A lived hegemony," as Raymond Williams observes, "is always a process" (1977: 112).

More importantly, we cannot lose sight of the fact that evidence is not just the result of a search for and corralling and deployment of previously unformed objects. Evidence is *rhetorical* and *dynamic*. It constitutes a way of talking about the world, an argument about the way bodies are arranged and ranked. Like so many rhetorics it does not advertise itself as such, but is cloaked in the language of normalization through either a discourse of common sense or the imprimatur of professions and experts.

The rhetorics of evidence are part of its power: bodies are transformed through language that seems to maintain their materiality. Hegemony depends upon the consent of those whose lives it controls, after all; but the flexibility of rhetoric is that it can be turned against the person who uses it. Tropes can take on double or triple meanings; serious pronouncements can be burlesqued or parodied, sometimes without the initial speaker even knowing; rhetorics can be appropriated, massaged, twisted, reapplied to such an extent that they might be unrecognizable to the person(s) from whom they have been lifted.

Second, evidentiary technologies are not static. They require an interlocutor "who has to accept a meaning for its ascription to ensure power and control: Holmes needs his Watson" (Dubrow, 1996: 16). The same evidence can be stunningly successful at one moment in time, and fall on deaf ears at another. This accounts at least in part for the mercurial career of anthropometry in the twentieth century: the measurements may not have changed, but the audience willing to believe that skull size has a proportional relationship to intelligence certainly has.

Both of these qualities, rhetoricity and dynamism, have also been sites for resistance, as I hope I will show in the chapters that follow. The languages of blood, skin, and bodies have proved to be amazingly mobile and adaptable to any number of agendas. At times, the structures of domination are so adamantine and impenetrable that language and materiality seem merged, and the body can appear to be only a site of subordination (the Tuskegee syphilis experiments were a chilling instance of this, as has been the brutal AIDS phobia that tries to cement the fantasmatic articulation of male homosexuality and disease). But the ways in which bodies resist their inscription as pure legibility are innumerable: subcultural styles of self-presentation, occulted sociolects that rearticulate bodies to languages that the dominant culture cannot read, work slowdowns (both organized and informal), civil dis-obedience, to name a few. Moreover, again and again subordinated people grab the rhetoric of their embodiedness and use it for their own purposes, valuing what has been marginalized, or shifting the relations of margin and center.

Our bodies are densely personal, written over with signs of the lives that inhabit them. It has been one of the triumphs of late twentieth-century feminist and queer activism and scholarship to insist upon the intimate interconnections of body and culture, body and intellect, body, and (dare I say it) soul.[33] Moreover, recent work in queer studies and disability studies, among other fields, has opened up the spaces into which unruly or unorthodox bodies have been squeezed.[34] Too often, certain kinds of bodies have been separated out, held up either for praise or disgust, forced to bear excessive, overdetermined meanings – this kind of body is dangerous, this one lovable, this one grotesque, this one invisible – or combinations of seemingly contradictory qualities.

Technology and the Logic of American Racism attempts a difficult balancing act, chronicling the discourses of embodiedness and evidence that have dominated the public and private spheres over the past century, but being ever conscious of the gingerliness, respect, strength, edginess, and tenderness with which we should approach our own bodies and the bodies of others, whether in words, concepts, or touch. Our bodies are so tightly constrained by the imaginaries of race and sex (both gender and sexuality) that it is hard to recognize them as our own rather than as a series of items to be worked on and worked through.

In writing this chapter, I have come to think of this project as a kind of scar. Scars can be seen in any number of ways: pale and delicate, or rough and weathered, or bundled with keloids, sometimes tougher than the wound it covers, sometimes far more sensitive.[35] A scar covers and reveals past pain; it reintegrates the surface of the body, but is also separate from it. The healing is clearly incomplete, since a scarred body has not managed to reshape itself to the contours of its prior form. This book follows the shapes of the wounds that have been made and attempts to be isomorphic with them without pretending to be identical. By stretching across the damage that has been done, connecting the riven edges but not erasing what has been split open, the scar is a reminder of violence and the destruction it can cause while attesting to the resilience of each individual human body and the myriad processes that help bodies heal themselves.

In his 1845 *Narrative*, Frederick Douglass explicitly conjoins the gashes of scars on his feet with the power that literacy gave him to communicate his life to his readers. Describing the years of sleeping in cold winters that disfigured his uncovered feet, he invites his readers to watch him place his pen into those scars, condensing his struggle for freedom into a single gesture: "My feet have been so cracked with the frost, that the pen with which I am writing might be laid in the gashes" (1987: 271).[36] At that moment his body represents both the ways in which slavery had controlled him, and how he has wrested the power of language from the mouths of slavers as surely as he wrestled the "slave breaker" Covey to the ground.

His feet are broken: nothing will make them whole again. But when he takes his pen and lays it in the deep crevices that slavery has carved into his body, he fills the space, however temporarily, with the evidence of his own life, "written by himself." The physical scar and the literary sign become one. This self-authorship is precious because it has been so rare; it is rare because it prophetically merges two forces that hegemonic structures of race have so long kept apart and unequal: the body, *our* bodies, and the words used to describe them.

2

A show of hands

Establishing identity in Mark Twain's
The Tragedy of Pudd'nhead Wilson

Reading the body

About half-way through Mark Twain's 1894 novel *The Tragedy of Pudd'nhead Wilson*, just as the novel begins unraveling its multiply-tangled knots of identity, crime, and punishment, Twain treats his readers to a parlor game. David "Pudd'nhead" Wilson is entertaining three guests: Luigi and Angelo Capello, Italian noblemen visiting Wilson's adopted hometown of Dawson's Landing, Missouri, and Tom Driscoll, the scion of one of the leading families of the town. Although Wilson was trained as a lawyer, an unfortunate comment he made on his arrival to Dawson's Landing over twenty years earlier has left him largely unemployed:[1] he has "never had a case, and [has] had to earn a poor living as an expert accountant" (*PW* 132). To fill his empty hours, Wilson took up hobbies: palmistry, and one that had no name "which dealt with people's fingermarks," in which he collected impressions of people's fingerprints on strips of glass (*PW* 29).

Although the twins and Tom oblige Wilson by giving him their fingerprints, they are far more interested in his skills in palm-reading. "Why, he'll read your wrinkles as easy as a book, and not only tell you fifty or sixty thousand things that's going to happen to you, but fifty or sixty thousand that ain't," declares Tom, Wilson's antagonist (*PW* 135). The twins, however, are true believers in palmistry as a science: "Four years ago," Luigi recalls, "we had our hands read out to us as if our palms had been covered in print" (*PW* 136). Luigi encourages Wilson to read his palm, and Pudd'nhead accurately interprets a whole host of the count's characteristics, "his tastes, aversions, proclivities, ambitions, and eccentricities" (*PW* 140).

Wilson's *pièce de résistance* is his precise divining of Luigi's greatest secret.

As he is examining Luigi's palm he holds back from revealing one incident which "is too delicate a matter to — to — I believe I would rather write it or whisper it to you" (*PW* 140). Luigi agrees that he and Wilson will both write their versions of the secret and then have someone else read it out loud. Luigi's slip of paper reads, "*It was prophesied that I would kill a man. It came true before the year was out*"; amazingly, Wilson had written "*You have killed some one, but whether man, woman or child, I do not make out*" (*PW* 141, italics in original). Tom responds with appropriate wonder,

> "Caesar's ghost!" commented Tom, with astonishment. "It beats anything that was ever heard of! Why, a man's own hand is his deadliest enemy! Just think of that — a man's own hand keeps a record of the deepest and fatalest secrets of his life, and is treacherously ready to expose him to any black-magic stranger that comes along."
>
> (*PW* 141)

I recount this scene in detail for several reasons. First, it brings to the fore an assumption that underlies *Pudd'nhead Wilson* and my analysis of it: that the body is a surface that is written on and read out of and that the information one can read on a body can provide essential and reliable information about a person's history and character. However, in this novel, these readings are not simply a transaction between the reader and his human text; they are triangulated by the presence of an audience that is initially skeptical of the reading but ultimately authenticates it. The site of reading is transformed into a performance space, and the act of reading into a display of supernatural power somewhere between parlor tarot interpretations and sideshow mind-readings, complete with an audience skeptic (who is, of course, ultimately convinced), a "scientific" methodology, and startling revelations.

This scene also pinpoints Tom's own fear that his body will "expose him." For Tom is not "really" Tom: he is, in fact, the slave Valet de Chambre (otherwise known as Chambers). Early in the novel, Chambers' mother Roxana secretly switched the two when they were infants, to save her own son from the possibility of being "sold down the river." "Tom" grows up in ignorance of his mother's actions; he only learns of his "true" identity in adulthood. After Wilson performs his palm-reading trick with Luigi, he reaches out for Tom's hand: "Now, Tom, I've never had a look at your palms, as it happens; perhaps you've got some little questionable privacies that need —" but Tom "snatched his hand away." His own privacies are more than just questionable; they are, as he himself said, "deep and fatal" (*PW* 145).[2]

Even more striking is Twain's equation of palm-reading and fingerprinting as valid sciences that can tell the trained observer about the hand's owner. In the 1990s, fingerprinting has long been established as an effective and reliable evidentiary technology, while palm-reading has been relegated to the status of superstition, along with séances and astrology. As we shall see, in the late nineteenth century in the United States, "science" embraced a much wider array of knowledge systems, many of which were sited on the surface of the body.[3]

While palm-reading pushes the narrative along – the revelation of Luigi's secret leads in part to his being accused of the murder of Tom's uncle, Judge York Leicester Driscoll (a murder Tom himself has committed) – it is soon pushed out of the spotlight by Wilson's other hobby, the collecting of fingerprints. In this chapter I want to discuss the process by which that displacement occurs and what it means: what is lost and what is gained, what changes and what remains the same. The palm-reading incident in the novel has not garnered much attention from critics, but it is crucial to an understanding of Twain's later use of fingerprints (an element that the novel's readers *have* focused on). Palm-reading represents a particular way of using hands as texts: it presumes that the hand can tell a story, as does Luigi's hand, about a whole personality, "tastes, aversions, proclivities," and so on. Palm-reading reveals *character* – a set of attributes that combine to construct a person. Moreover, palm-reading constructs and performs a narrative: Wilson reconstructs Luigi's life from his palm and Luigi joins in by adding a narrative that explains and deepens Wilson's reading, both for the benefit of Tom, the spectator.

Fingerprinting can tell no such story. It is only a means of identification rather than description. While the palm-reading scene in *Pudd'nhead Wilson* reveals a secret that is framed in terms of an action performed by a human subject – "You have killed someone" – at the end of the novel, fingerprinting reveals a secret *of identity*: Tom is shown by his fingerprints to be an "assassin," "a negro and a slave," and a "usurper" (*PW* 298). In the moment of revelation, Tom is not an active participant in the telling of his story, as Luigi was in the narration of *his* secret. Rather, Tom is rendered mute and immobile, incapable of responding to these accusations, let alone collaborating in their narration. The prints speak for themselves, removed from his body and erasing Tom as a speaking subject.

The move from palm-reading to fingerprinting in the novel represents a larger change that Twain was witnessing in the 1890s – a shift in what information scientists believed they needed to know in order to understand a person or group of people. Twain participated in a number of body-based knowledge systems, occasionally as an amateur practitioner, more often as a subject, and *Pudd'nhead Wilson* is in many ways a meditation on how the language of these systems changed from that of character or temperament to that of identity – a way of thinking about people that is still with us today.

In order to trace these changes, I will not only be exploring these two ways of establishing the evidentiary "truths" of identity through looking at pieces of bodies, but also other methods that were in use during Twain's lifetime and that he believed and even participated in to varying degrees: phrenology, the knowledge system that gathered information about personality by mapping out the shape of the skull, and temperament theory, a closely related set of beliefs that read character through external physical features like hair color, body shape, and skin tone.[4]

Palm-reading was one of a series of occult and body-based sciences that caught the imagination of the middle classes in the United States from the 1850s onwards. While most attention focused on the spiritualist elements of the occult – specifically communication with the dead through "spirit-rapping" and séances, clairvoyance, and mesmerism – palmistry and other forms of fortune-telling (tarot, mind-reading, astrology) also reached unusually high levels of popularity.[5] Palmistry had several manifestations, which went under various names: cheirosophy, a general term describing the information that could be gleaned from reading palms; cheirography or cheirognomy, a more scientifically oriented practice of mapping out palm lines, finger shapes, and so on, to read character and disposition, both emotional and physical; and cheiromancy, the prophetic or fortune-telling element of palmistry.[6] English-language tracts on palm-reading appeared throughout the Early Modern period[7] but it was not until the mid- to late nineteenth century that palm-reading really took off in Britain, France, and the United States, thanks to three major figures: Casimir Stanilas d'Arpentigny, Edward Heron-Allen, and the mysterious (at least according to his own publicity) British palmist, Cheiro.

D'Arpentigny and his French contemporary Adrien Adolphe Desbarolles were responsible for bringing palmistry into the nineteenth century. Both were born at the turn of the century (d'Arpentigny in 1789, Desbarolles in 1801), and both had similar ambitions: to rescue palmistry from its orientalized occult reputation and to rehabilitate it as a science. D'Arpentigny's *Chirognomie* and his *Science of the Hand*, which was translated into English in 1886 by Heron-Allen, were "vastly influential" (Fitzherbert, 1992: 14). D'Arpentigny coined the word "cheirognomy" to separate what he considered a science from the "disreputable" connotations of fortune-telling which the word "cheiromancy" evoked (Gettings, 1965: 202).[8] Edward Heron-Allen took up this strand of palmistry, both in his translation of d'Arpentigny and in his own work. A British intellectual, Heron-Allen went on to write his own compendia of palmistry, *A Manual of Cheirosophy* (1885), and *Practical Cheirosophy: A Synoptical Study of the Science of the Hand* (1887). Heron-Allen was in large part responsible for popularizing French-style palm-reading in Britain and the U.S., thanks to his lecture series, which he brought across the Atlantic during an extended visit in 1886.

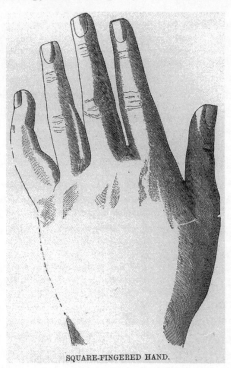

SQUARE-FINGERED HAND.

From *Handbook of Modern Palmistry* by Professor V. De Metz, published by Brentano Brothers, New York, 1883.

The third proponent of palmistry in the late nineteenth century took a radically different approach from that of d'Arpentigny, Desbarolles, and Heron-Allen. "Cheiro" was a palmist to the wealthy and influential in England at the same time that Heron-Allen was touring the United States. Born in Ireland in 1866, Cheiro first shows up in historical records in England in the early 1880s under the name of Louis Warner, which he later changed to Count Louis Hamon. At some point he took on his pseudonym, and by the age of 20 he had established himself as a palmist in London. Cheiro created a whole series of myths about himself that fed into orientalist beliefs about palmistry: he claimed to have been kidnapped by gypsies as a child, and subsequently to have studied palmistry in India and explored Egypt. His first book, *Cheiro's Language of the Hand* (1894) proved his influence: it sold 5,000 copies in its first four months, and went into more than ten editions (Gettings, 1965: 211). After a major success in England he toured the United States in the 1890s, and published several books on palmistry, including *Cheiro's Complete Palmistry* and *Cheiro's Book of the Hand*. In 1912 he published *Cheiro's Memoirs: The Reminiscences of a Society Palmist*, in which he changed his original claims (visits to the East were still mentioned, but the kidnapping gypsies had mysteriously disappeared), and chronicled his encounters with the great and near-great.

Cheiro's popularity represented one way in which palmistry was envisaged: as an ancient art that had its origins in the East, possibly in India or Egypt, an association that was often played out in the public imagination through the correlation of palm-reading, fortune-telling, and gypsies, combined with an inchoate sinister mystery, all of which Cheiro corralled to authenticate himself as a palmist. In *Pudd'nhead Wilson* the Capello brothers invoke palmistry's status as occult knowledge, and the growing representation of it as a science together in their story of the time their palms were first read: they consulted a stereotypical palmist "in the Orient," but the results convinced them that cheirosophy "is ... a science, and one of the greatest of them, too" (*PW* 136).

Certainly, palmistry had a fair number of sciences to compete with in the mid-nineteenth century, and its European and U.S. proponents constructed it along similar methodological lines. In *Practical Cheirosophy*, Edward Heron-Allen assumes the same Darwinian theories of evolution that his phrenological counterparts made an essential part of their work. Hands themselves were a sign of human evolution, and Heron-Allen maintained that "we find an ascending scale of intelligence among animals which are gifted with the nearest approach to, and best substitutes for, hands" (1887: 18). Dexterity, fineness of hands and other physical specifics were homologous to particular personal characteristics, all of which had their place on the evolutionary scale: narrow hands attested to timidity, over-refinement, feeble-mindedness and moral instability; thick and meaty hands showed an underevolved "tendency to brutality" (*ibid.*: 49). These character readings ranged from taxonomy on a broad scale, in which hands were "spatulate and creative" or "square and useful" (*ibid.*: 67, 71), to the micro-level of quirks and peculiarities: the owner of a square hand has "leading instincts [of] perseverance, foresight, order and regularity," but "unless your joints are well developed, it is quite possible that your drawers and cupboards may be untidy" (*ibid.*: 71–3).

Like their emulators in the world of cheirognomy, phrenology and temperament manuals were not complete without a host of illustrations. [9] Phrenologists would provide a diagram of the skull that mapped out the specific locations and meanings of all the "regions" of the head, first identified by German phrenologist Johann Spurzheim. Practitioners would learn to identify these regions by touch, and then to analyze their subjects' characters by feeling their skulls for bumps and depressions in various regions. [10]

Temperament theory, too, relied upon copious illustrations to prove its legitimacy. This knowledge system was devised by Spurzheim's disciple George Cooke, who based his theory on Classical and Early Modern ideas of humors and temperaments, but updated them for the nineteenth century. There had long been strong disagreement over the causes of temperament: for some the roots of temperament lay in the metabolism; for others it was a combination of environmental factors such as climate, diet, and emotional crises both in the womb and outside; some believed it was congenital and hereditary. Cooke used much of the same terminology of his predecessors, such as the names for the temperaments: sanguine, bilious, lymphatic, and melancholic (which later temperament theorists called "nervous"). However, rather than locating the signs of these temperaments in the bodily fluids that gave them their names, such as blood and lymph, Cooke sited them on the surface of the body.[11]

Temperament theory is primarily a way of identifying a person's character, predispositions, compatibility with others, and possible aptitudes. It is not, however, concerned with psychology as we understand the term. Temperament is not read through the psyche but from the surface of the body: from hair and eye color, head shape, proportion of limbs, the distribution of facial features, skin tone, and so on. Some phrenologists identified these physical manifestations as *causes* of what we might call "personality," and to which they often referred as "character." According to Alexander Stewart, author of *Our Temperaments: Their Study and Their Teaching* (1886) – a book that was so well received that it went into several printings and a second revised edition over the course of six years – it was not just that "observers may know the temperament of anyone by looking at him; and associate it with certain mental qualities and traits of character" (pp. vii–viii), but that temperament is physical, first and foremost. Temperament represents the "organization" of the body (a term that explicitly invokes the physical), a physiological arrangement that is more determinate than simply "character" or "personality" (Stewart, 1892: 239).[12]

The widespread acceptance of phrenology and temperament theory – dozens of guides, handbooks, outlines, and encyclopedias appeared between 1850 and 1900 – is borne out by the popularization of these practices through sideshows and itinerant practitioners.[13] P.T. Barnum's American Museum featured a "professor of phrenology"; Twain himself consulted a phrenologist more than once in his life – his last visit was at the turn of the century[14] – even as he poked fun at the charlatans who passed themselves off as the genuine article (for example, in his burlesque of the Duke as a phony phrenological practitioner in *The Adventures of Huckleberry Finn* (1997a: 169–70)).[15]

Nonetheless, Twain sustained a level of faith in phrenology and temperament theory from the early 1850s through to the end of his life that was constituted, at least in part, by the desire to understand what people's bodies meant, what they could say about the identities they housed.[16] As Alan Gribben argues, "he earnestly wished to believe in the existence of an infallible means of character detection and psychological remedy" (1972: 67).

Phrenology was not necessarily a deterministic system, however. For Twain (as for Spurzheim himself), it was also a site in which he could place his desires for human self-improvement, since it was an odd mix of biologism and liberal humanism. By the mid-nineteenth century, "the practitioners of phrenology held that the self-knowledge it afforded could result in the diminution (or at least the control) of undesirable tendencies and the expansion of praiseworthy traits" (Gribben, 1972: 52). Moreover, Spurzheim had considered phrenology "not a determinist science. ... Rather, it was a device by which the human race might perfect itself by developing its strong points" (Gossett, 1997: 72). Phrenology, anthropometry, and other related knowledge systems represent the interweaving of mid-nineteenth-century bourgeois sentimental beliefs (and growing ambivalence) about the transparency of personal affect, liberal evangelical faith in the reformability of even the most degraded, and an aggressive scientism that flourished in the second half of the century.[17]

Many of the pre-Civil War texts on the temperaments doubled as scientific compendia and as how-to manuals: their copious illustrations and examples enabled readers to analogize from the faces of the great and near-great to those of family, friends, and even themselves. In fact, Twain's first discussion of phrenology in his notebooks in 1855 focuses on his analysis of his own temperament (sanguine), and how his features and character conformed to George Sumner Weaver's analysis in his 1852 *Lectures on Mental Science*. Almost thirty years later, in 1882, Twain uses unambiguous phrenological language about Whitelaw Reid, the editor of the *New York Tribune*, whom he despised. Reid's "selfish organs" he writes, are "so heavy they weigh down the back of his head and tilt his face upwards"; Twain accompanied this phrenological insult with a rough speculative sketch of Reid's skull (Paine, 1935: 441).[18]

Similarly, palmistry manuals both before and after 1865 stressed the scientism and applicability of palm-reading, with titles like *Practical Palmistry, Practical Cheirosophy*, and *Palmistry and Its Practical Uses*. Moreover, palmistry's mid-nineteenth-century practitioners often analogized their craft to a number of contemporary knowledge systems, particularly physiognomy and phrenology. British palmist Louise Cotton included a lengthy epigraph from palmist Henry Frith in *Palmistry and Its Practical Uses* (1890), which listed phrenology, physiognomy, and cheirognomy as sister sciences, all of which could provide accurate analyses of a person's character. In *Practical Cheirosophy* Heron-Allen invoked by name Franz Joseph Gall and Johann Spurzheim, the founders of phrenology, and Johann Lavater, father of physiognomy, explicitly comparing their scientific work to that of cheirosophy. In fact, as Francis Galton did for fingerprints less than a decade later, Heron-Allen claimed that palmistry was superior to those sciences in reliability and consistency:

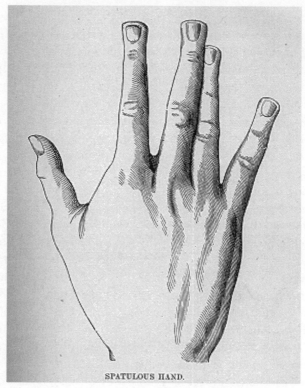

SPATULOUS HAND.

From *Handbook of Modern Palmistry* by Professor V. De Metz, published by Brentano Brothers, New York, 1883.

The phrenologist may be deceived by the growth of hair; the physiognomist may be led astray by a fixed and unnatural expression of the face; but the cheirosophist finds in the hand an unvarying and unalterable indication of the character, a mirror whose images the bearer is powerless to distort.

(Heron-Allen, 1887: 47)

Here, Heron-Allen challenges assumptions about palmistry and rates it as more accurate than other knowledge systems. Not only is "cheirosophy" *not* unscientific, it is more reliable because it is both quantifiable and practically applicable. Phrenology is far from invincible, and may, in fact, be affected by changes in fashion ("the growth of hair"). Heron-Allen also implicitly sets the scene for fingerprint science a decade later in his representation of the subject of cheirosophy: however much the owner of the palm may want to disguise him- or herself by changing hairstyles or affecting an "unnatural expression of the face," the hand is an infallible mirror that renders its bearer "powerless." It is not surprising, then, that Heron-Allen recommends cheirosophy as a method for the emerging field of forensic science.

Playing to the crowd: the science of spectacle

In the years between 1853 and 1893, that is, from the year in which most of the action in *Pudd'nhead Wilson* is set to the year it was first offered for serial publication, palmistry occupied a transitory space between the sideshow and the laboratory. This liminal position is evident in David Wilson's ambivalent relationship to palm-reading. His attempts at palmistry met with a mixed reception before the arrival of the Capello brothers – the people had "got to joking about it" almost immediately (*PW* 138). Wilson makes modest claims for his own palm-reading abilities, apologizing for his amateur attempts since "I've had no chance to become an expert and don't claim to be one. When a past event is somewhat prominently recorded in the palm I can generally detect that, but minor ones often escape me. . . . [O]n the whole [I] let the future alone; that's really the affair of the expert" (*PW* 138). His rhetoric here is that of the self-effacing amateur scientist who is dabbling in a field of knowledge that requires serious study, even though he recognizes the mixed reputation that palmistry has.

Twain's representation of the scene of palm-reading creates multiple layers of spectacle and science. On the one hand, Twain describes in some detail the procedure behind palm-reading, which for Wilson is a painstaking operation:

> Wilson began to study Luigi's palm, tracing life-lines, heart-lines, head-lines and so on, and noting carefully their relations with the cobweb of finer and more delicate marks and lines that enmeshed them on all sides; he felt of the fleshy cushion at the base of the thumb, and noted its shape; he felt of the fleshy side of the hand between the wrist and the base of the little finger, and noted its shape also; he painstakingly examined the fingers, observing their form, proportions, and natural manner of disposing themselves when in repose.
>
> (*PW* 139)

Despite this aura of scientific inquiry, in many ways the entire transaction also resembles the kind of mind-reading stunts that were pulled off at sideshows and circuses across the country. P. T. Barnum, of whom Clemens was an ambivalent admirer and with whom he enjoyed a short but warm friendship in the 1870s (a relationship that cooled after Twain repeatedly declined the request to write advance copy for Barnum's travelling circus in a

Barnum-funded newspaper), often featured "gypsy" palm-readers and fortune-tellers in his museums. When Angelo recalls the accuracy with which his palm was first read "in the Orient," Tom exclaims, "Why it's rank sorcery!", affirming the connection between palmistry and gypsy magic (*PW* 137). Barnum's first museum in 1842 included a "mysterious and beautiful gypsy fortune teller," who combined various occult skills such as palmistry and crystal ball-gazing (Kunhardt *et al.*, 1995: 37). In 1865 he advertised the services of "Madame La Comte, Soothsayer and astrologist, niece to the celebrated Mlle Le Normand," who had been palmist to Napoleon (*ibid.*: 172).

In form, the palmistry episode in *Pudd'nhead Wilson* is very similar to a genre that Barnum (in his influence as a showman) indirectly spawned: "mind-reading" performances in traveling medicine shows that emerged as a major form of popular entertainment in mostly rural areas in the late nineteenth century. Like the palm-reading in *Pudd'nhead Wilson*, mind-reading acts required a skeptical audience and a divination of secrets that was both public and mysterious. Brooks McNamara describes the act of one mind-reader which, although it was clearly a racket (as the following narrative makes clear), enacts a drama very much like the one which Wilson and the Capello brothers create in Twain's novel:

> The audience was offered a stack of ordinary envelopes. A spectator examined them, chose one, and sealed in it a slip of paper on which he had written a question. The envelope was given to [the mind reader] who placed it in the drawer of a small "spirit cabinet." As she slid the envelope into the drawer she swiftly rubbed its face with a sponge dipped in alcohol. The alcohol made the envelope transparent for a few seconds so that the message could be easily read before the drawer closed for a moment, ostensibly to allow the spirits to do their work. After a suitable amount of hocus-pocus, the drawer was opened and [the reader] held the letter against her forehead, stalling to let the alcohol fumes disperse. Then the still-sealed envelope was handed back to the volunteer, the question answered, and the audience considerably impressed.
>
> (McNamara, 1976: 144)

Needless to say, this act is a complete scam, whereas Wilson's palm-reading is treated with respect as a meaningful science. However, the structuring elements of this performance have a great deal in common with those of the palm-reading scene that Twain constructs. Tom Driscoll makes the connections between Wilson's palm-reading and the fortune-telling and mind-reading acts in traveling shows explicit, invoking the showbusiness-like challenge that Wilson's skill is "worth twice the price of admission or your money's returned at the door" (*PW* 135). In order for the reading to work in both environments, there must be an audience (even if only of one) and a way to "prove" that the reading is legitimate. The effectiveness of the performance depends upon the relationship between the reader and the subject – they must be strangers, first of all (the audience would hardly be impressed by a mind-reader divining her assistant's thoughts; instead they would – understandably – suspect collusion). Second, there must be some external proof of mind-reading, something more permanent than verbal affirmation after the fact, since participants could either be paid off to confirm the reader's claims, or deny it out of a desire to prove the reader wrong, no matter what. Hence the use of slips of paper on which questions are written before the mind-reading takes place: incontrovertible evidence of a pre-existing thought. Finally, the reader/performer tells the subject/audience something he/she already knows but that remains concealed. The mechanics of revelation here are almost identical to the performance that Wilson puts on, down to the use of written proof. In this scene and in *Pudd'nhead Wilson*, palm- and mind-reading are *not* fortune-telling, but methods of exposing the body's secrets to an audience beyond the reader/subject dyad.[19]

Wilson's palm-reading "act" does not take place in a theater or a sideshow, however; it is firmly ensconced in the interior space of the home. Admittedly, Wilson's home is not the typical bourgeois site: he is single, acknowledged to be at best an eccentric and at worst a "pudd'nhead," and the scene of palmistry takes place in Wilson's workshop among a group of men. The tension between the public exterior space of performance and the private interior space of the home is intrinsic to the meanings of palm-reading in the novel. Palmistry itself reveals the interior of its subjects, their innermost thoughts by an examination of the outside of the body. It is a practice that merges intimacy and showbusiness.[20]

Twain's own experience with palm-reading came out of at least two incidents of reading in which the home space and the marketplace merged. The first was his visit to Cheiro during the latter's trip to the United States. Cheiro did not keep a separate office for his work, but received clients in his parlor or read "at at-homes and garden parties, where it is impossible to count the numbers that consulted me" (Cheiro, 1912: 101). During his U.S. tour, Cheiro conducted readings either in the homes of his guests, or in his hotel suite, a home away from home. Twain was, needless to say, extremely skeptical of Cheiro's abilities, but he was sufficiently impressed by his accuracy that he wrote a signed affidavit, affirming that "Cheiro has exposed my character to me with humiliating accuracy. I ought not to confess this accuracy; still, I am moved to do it" (*ibid.*: 133).

The second incident is not identifiable by date. Twain recorded it in his notebook just after the death of his daughter Susy in 1896. He remembered that his family had attended a party that featured a palmist, either one of the other guests or a professional whom the hosts had hired as entertainment (she is identified by Twain as "a lady at a party"). "The palmist ... told [Susy] she would have an unhappy life and that with all her gifts she would fall just short of success. She would be a failure. It distressed her for days" (Paine, 1935: 320). This episode is notable not simply for the seriousness with which Susy took the reading – not only did she not laugh the prediction off, but she was preoccupied with it – but for the striking combination of showbusiness and intimacy of that moment. The palmist had clearly offered her skills as a kind of parlor game, an extension of the charades and theatricals that were wildly popular among the middle classes in the second half of the nineteenth century, whether for pay or simply for the entertainment of her fellow guests.[21] The party was not organized around occult activity, unlike the séances and spirit-rapping sessions in which middle-class people were participating during this

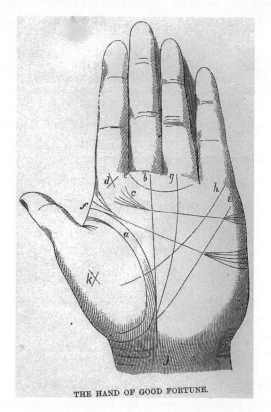

THE HAND OF GOOD FORTUNE.

From *Handbook of Modern Palmistry* by Professor V. De Metz, published by Brentano Brothers, New York, 1883.

same period; rather, palmistry in this instance was a diversion, not the focus of a meeting of like-minded spiritualists.

At this social occasion, then, at a moment that should have been one of light-hearted enjoyment, the palmist reached into a part of Susy Clemens's life so intimate that even she did not have access to it – as Twain said of his own reading by Cheiro, the palmist "exposed [Susy's] character ... with humiliating accuracy" (Cheiro, 1912: 133) – and transformed that interiority into a proof for other party-goers of palmistry's evidentiary veracity. Unlike the personal details revealed during Twain's visit to Cheiro, however, this palmist's readings could not be immediately verified or disproved. But the fact that Twain brings up this episode in reference to Susy's premature death from meningitis implies that he reads his daughter's fate as connected to the predictions from the party.

We can see the traces of these two moments in Twain's representation of palm-reading in *Pudd'nhead Wilson*. Like the Capello brothers, Twain was a skeptic about palm-reading until an encounter with a palmist who combined the exoticism of the "Orient" with the apparent methodological rigor of science: "what was told us of our characters was minutely exact – we could not have bettered it ourselves" (*PW* 137). We also see Twain in Wilson himself, a cynic, a free-thinker and an ironist, as the epigraphically quoted entries from "Pudd'nhead Wilson's Calendar" at the head of every chapter exemplify: far from credulous. The site of reading itself is a remarkable mix of public and private, occupying the space of leisure and carving out a space of performance, merging the interior self and the society event, very much like the party the Clemenses attended, or like the parlors in which Cheiro plied his trade.

Through palm-reading, the parlor and the circus meet and the audience is shrunk down to a single character, Tom: the skeptic who is thoroughly convinced. The role of audience here is not passive and receptive but active and participatory. Tom is an essential part of the performance of palm-reading; he must witness and legitimate it. But Tom is not the only member of this audience. We as readers enter the space of spectators, waiting in our putative parlors for the act of palm-reading to transpire before us as entertainment. Just as Tom holds the written text that Wilson reads out of Luigi's hand, we hold the text that will reveal his secret. The moment of Tom's discovery is the same moment of our discovery that Luigi has killed a man.[22] Reading this scene moves us into identifying with Tom only a few pages after he has learned what the reader already knows: that Roxy is his biological mother and that he is "really" black, a knowledge that Wilson and the Capello brothers do not share.

In many ways, *Pudd'nhead Wilson*'s plot revolves around information shared and withheld – who knows what and when – particularly information to which Tom has access. After Tom learns that Roxy is his mother, the plot takes a specific turn; it twists again when he does or does not know the status of Judge Driscoll's will that either favors or disinherits him. For most of the novel, the reader is far ahead of Tom. We have witnessed Roxy's baby switch; we see Judge Driscoll tear up or rewrite his will; we are even a step ahead of Wilson in his investigation into Judge Driscoll's murder and his use of fingerprints to unmask the killer. But at this moment of palm-reading we know no more than Tom does, and we learn about the Capello brothers at the same time. Even as Twain turns his readers into not just his audience but Wilson's as well, he aligns us with Tom. If we are skeptical of palm-reading, so is Tom; if we are amazed by its results, he is as well.

The reader's identification with Tom is brief and glancing, but not insignificant. Audience is crucial to the climactic scene of the novel, in which Tom is exposed as both "really" black and as Judge Driscoll's murderer. More importantly, during that scene, Tom is transformed from audience member to spectacle, from white subject to black object (and object of exchange in the system of chattel slavery). This is a long way from the Tom of the palm-reading scene, the Tom who is an active participant in a performance that depends upon him for verification.

This transformation is signified and mediated by a switch in evidentiary technologies, from palm-reading to fingerprinting. By the time Tom Driscoll is revealed as his uncle's murderer, we have witnessed David Wilson's unfolding of multiple mysteries through the magic of fingerprinting: who has been responsible for the burglary raids on the households of Dawson's landing, the innocence of the Capello twins in Judge Driscoll's murder, and, perhaps most importantly, the childhood exchange of Tom Driscoll for Valet de Chambre.

The initial courtroom scenes are standard fare, laying out witnesses, testimony, and occasional comments from onlooking townspeople. Wilson's opponent, Pembroke Howard, traces a chain of circumstantial evidence to convict the brothers. Luigi is a "confessed assassin" (*PW* 209); the twins own the knife with which Judge Driscoll was murdered; they were found standing over his dead body only hours after the Judge had announced that Luigi, in the aftermath of kicking Tom and participating in a dishonorable duel with Judge Driscoll (dishonorable because Luigi, as an "assassin," had insulted a gentleman like the Judge by dueling with him), had been "warned that he must kill or be killed the first time he should meet Judge Driscoll" (*PW* 267).

Like Pembroke Howard's, Wilson's case is constructed of "certain circumstantial evidence" (*PW* 269), all of which is based on actual events, but none of which has much probative value. Certainly we as readers recognize its truth value, since we are, in some ways, eyewitnesses to Tom's murder of Judge Driscoll while disguised as a woman, but appearances, however "accurate," are too deceptive here. Wilson's problem is that he is missing a crucial piece of evidence that goes beyond eyewitnesses: he is, as Tom Driscoll says, "grubbing and groping after that woman that don't exist, and the right person [is] sitting under his very nose all the time!" (*PW* 271).

Wilson fills in the central piece of the puzzle through his use of fingerprints. As we have seen through the course of the novel, Wilson has collected the "finger marks" of every resident of Dawson's Landing over the course of twenty-three years, and he "liked to have a 'series' of two or three 'takings' at intervals during the period of childhood, these to be followed by others at intervals of several years" (*PW* 35). The night before his final presentation in defence of the Capello brothers, he is poring over the prints of women in Dawson's Landing, hoping he will find the "mysterious girl" who has been raiding houses and whom Wilson suspects of murdering Judge Driscoll. Tom Driscoll pays him a visit and leaves his own print on the piece of glass – with Roxy's print – that Wilson had been examining. As Wilson takes the strip of glass and holds it up to the light, he sees the fingerprint he has been searching for: Tom's. In addition, in studying the series of prints he took from Tom and Chambers as infants onwards, he recognizes the baby switch that took place.

The "revelation" of this "extraordinary mystery ... riddle ... puz[zle]" (*PW* 277) is not complete until the courtroom scene, however. As readers, we have witnessed all of the "mysteries" that Wilson reveals. However, we are still captivated by the process by which he uncovers each twist of plotting. As Susan Gillman observes, for the reader "the only real suspense in the novel has been waiting not for the identity of the murderer (which we've known all along) but for the moment when Wilson would discover the means of proving it" (Gillman, 1990: 99). Wilson is the consummate showman, drawing his audience into the excitement of discovery. Throughout Wilson's presentation of evidence, Twain interpolates the reaction of the jury and other townspeople, which develops from skepticism to amazed faith. Wilson's declaration that "he should probably not have occasion to make use of [his witnesses'] testimony" arouses "an amused murmur. ... 'It's a clean back-down! He gives up without a lick,'" but his claim that "'I have other testimony – and better' ... compelled interest and evoked murmurs of surprise that had a detectable ingredient of disappointment in them" (*PW* 280). Wilson's audience wants the conventional show of the courtroom drama: impassioned questioning, steely (or, depending on who is doing the questioning, quivering) witnesses, weepy confessions, "legal ambushes and masked batteries" (*PW* 281). What they don't realize is that Wilson is going to give them a very different kind of performance.

At first, Wilson engages only the evidence that has been presented so far: why, for example, the brothers remained in Judge Driscoll's parlor after they had supposedly murdered him, rather than running away; why they would lie about the loss of the knife that was the murder weapon; what the motive of the murder was ("robbery, not murder" (*PW* 285)). At this point, though, he changes tack, introducing his series of fingerprint records as evidence. This is also the moment at which Twain makes explicit the parallels between this scene of reading from the body and that of palm-reading earlier in the text.

Just as the twins aver the scientific value of palm-reading, Wilson speaks in technical and specialized language about fingerprints, calling them a person's "physiological autograph" (*PW* 286). Moreover, he implicitly compares fingerprint technology's efficacy to that of the similar sciences of phrenology and physiognomy. In language strikingly like that of Edward Heron-Allen in his cheirosophy manuals, Wilson maintains that

> this autograph can not be counterfeited, nor can [its owner] disguise it or hide it away, nor can it become illegible by the wear and mutations of time. This signature is not his face — age can change that beyond recognition; it is not his hair, for that can fall out; it is not his height, for duplicates of that exist; it is not his form, for duplicates of that exist also, whereas this signature is each man's very own — there is no duplicate of it among the swarming populations of the globe!
>
> (*PW* 287)

This claim has a noticeable effect on the audience, who were "interested once more" (*PW* 287). As Wilson walks them (and us) through the theory behind fingerprint reading, they participate as though they were a sideshow audience. Wilson explains that every finger has "various clearly defined patterns, such as arches, circles, long curves, whorls, etc.," and invites them to "look at the balls of your fingers," at which "every man in the room had his hand up to light, now, and his head canted to one side, and was minutely scrutinizing the balls of his fingers; there were whispered ejaculations of 'Why, it's so — I never noticed that before!'" (*PW* 287–8). At every point in his explanation, Wilson calls upon the audience to prove it to themselves on their own fingers, and the fingers of the twins, just as the mind-reading audience McNamara described was invited to examine the soundness of the envelopes that held secret questions.

Half-way through his lecture Wilson makes use of an old oratorical trick, one that Twain himself was not above using in his own speaking engagements: "Wilson stopped and stood silent. Inattention dies a quick and sure death when a speaker does that. The stillness gives warning that something is coming" (*PW* 289). Wilson's showmanship is explicit here, as he "waited yet one, two, three moments, to let his pause complete and perfect its spell on the house [until] through the profound hush he could hear the ticking of the clock on the wall" (*PW* 289). Twain's use of the term "house" invokes multiple meanings.

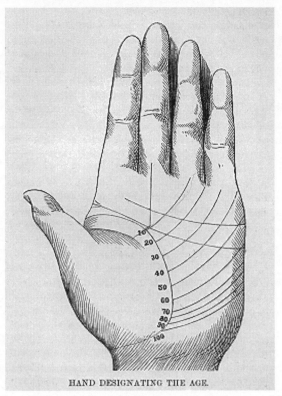

HAND DESIGNATING THE AGE.

From *Handbook of Modern Palmistry* by Professor V. De Metz, published by Brentano Brothers, New York, 1883.

Certainly, it refers literally to the courthouse. However, like any great performer (as, according to all reports, Twain himself was), Wilson has a full house; he is playing to the house. The theatricality of this moment is intensified by Twain's ambiguous terminology, in which courtroom and stage are interspliced.

As the performance continues, the audience's responses become increasingly animated. Their reactions grow from murmurs and whispers to exclamations, applause, and "sensation − confusion − angry ejaculations" (*PW* 298). Wilson constructs elaborate tests to prove the veracity of his act, asking, for example, both the brothers and other townspeople to impress their fingerprints on the glass of the courtroom window while he turns his back. Wilson's correct identification of the prints is met not just with "a deafening explosion of applause"; "The Bench" himself declares that "[t]his certainly approaches the miraculous!" (*PW* 292).

Having won his audience over with this preliminary exercise, Wilson raises the stakes, reconstructing the story of first Judge Driscoll's murder and then the exchange of babies. The foreman of the jury takes over the role that Tom played in the palm-reading scene: skeptic who is convinced by the physical evidence. Moreover, the foreman's responses to Wilson's questions about the identities attached to various fingerprints grow more emphatic over time. His initial replies are declarative and restrained, directed at the judge. As the performance continues, however, the foreman's statements are in response to Wilson himself, and are represented at a much higher pitch, in italics and then accompanied by exclamation marks.

At the same time, Twain constructs Wilson as a kind of audience as well. In the course of his own performance, Wilson keeps a constant eye on Tom to monitor his reactions.[23] But Wilson is a very different audience from that of the throng at the courthouse. While they are wondering and awed at what they see, Wilson is a knowing spectator, watching the correspondences between Tom's emotions and his external reactions. At his announcement that "we will produce [the murderer] before noon!" Wilson observes Tom "flying signals of distress," which the rest of the audience (mis)reads as a sign of the "hard ordeal for a young fellow who has lost his benefactor by so cruel a stroke" (*PW* 289–90). Similarly, when Wilson proves that the twins' fingerprints are not on the knife and declares that "[w]e will now proceed to find the guilty," the narrative turns immediately to Tom, whose "eyes were starting from their sockets – yes, it was a cruel day for the bereaved youth, everybody thought" (*PW* 296). Twain interpolates Wilson's display, the larger audience's reactions, Tom's responses and the audience's misreading of those responses as constitutive elements of a larger performance in which Tom, although a putative member of the audience, is defined as separate from it.

Through Wilson's demonstration, Twain transforms the court into a performance space. Unlike the performance of palm-reading that we saw earlier, this does not take place in a parlor or a private home but in a public space, in the presence of the whole town. Both performances hinge on the revelation of a murder, but where the palm-reading exercise was an attempt to construct a narrative and was executed among supposed equals, this display is designed to establish identities by separating out innocent from guilty and, as a consequence, white from black, legitimate citizens from chattel slaves.

To maintain the mystery, Wilson interpolates two sets of fingerprints, which he labels "*A*" and "*B*." Wilson has prepared pantographs – geometrically enlarged drawings of the prints – and he quizzes the jury foreman on them. He presents pantographs of the fingerprints of "*A*" and "*B*" at five, seven, and eight months: at five and seven months, the foreman observes, the prints correspond, but at eight months they have been exchanged. "This produced a vast sensation," Twain reports, but even more sensational is the lengthy description Wilson articulates to explain these anomalies:

"*A* was put into *B*'s cradle in the nursery; *B* was transferred to the kitchen and became a negro and a slave [sensation – confusion of angry ejaculations] – but within a quarter of an hour he will stand before you white and free! . . . From seven months onward until now, *A* has still been a usurper, and in my finger-record he bears *B*'s name. Here is his pantograph at the age of twelve. Compare it with the assassin's signature upon the knife-handle. Do they tally?"

The foreman answered –

"*To the minutest detail!*"

(PW 298)

As he identifies "Valet de Chambre, negro and slave, falsely called Thomas à Becket Driscoll," Wilson challenges "Tom" to "make upon the window the finger-prints that will hang you!" (PW 298–9).

"The test of measurement": Francis Galton and the establishment of identity

Twain had used fingerprints as a way to identify criminals briefly in *Life on the Mississippi*, but he knew little about them until the publishing house of Chatto and Windus sent him a copy of Sir Francis Galton's *Finger Prints* in 1892.[24] Twain wrote to the publishers, promising that "I shall devour" the book, and decided to integrate fingerprints into his current work in progress, *Pudd'nhead Wilson* (Gribben, 1980: 251). Galton's influence is everywhere, from the thank-you letter Twain wrote to Chatto and Windus, which he "signed with eight fingerprints," as Galton signed his book (Wigger, 1957: 518), to the lengthy explanations of fingerprinting as a forensic tool, which are taken almost word for word from Galton's work.[25]

Francis Galton's life project was not fingerprints, however; he was "the father of eugenics," and was responsible for coining and popularizing the term (Rogin, 1990: 78; see also chapters by Gillman, Sundquist, and Cox in Gillman and Robinson, 1990). Galton's eugenicist work of the 1870s and 1880s was primarily concerned with "hereditary ability," as the titles of his books *Hereditary Genius: An Inquiry into Its Laws and Consequences* (1879), *Inquiries into Human Faculty and Its Development* (1883), and *Natural Inheritance* (1894) suggest. It is not clear how much Twain knew of Galton's background, although he did make a striking parapraxis in a discussion of the book. In an 1897 letter to an acquaintance in London, discussing the sources and accuracy of his fingerprint material, Twain wrote: "The finger mark system of identification . . . has been quite thoroughly and scientifically examined by Mr. Galt" (quoted in Gribben, 1980: 251). Twain conflates Galton's name with that of Franz Joseph Gall, one of the founders of phrenology, which implies an at least unconscious association between Galton's work and that of the body-based sciences that took so eagerly to the eugenicist principles that Galton propounded.

Twain's debt to Galton is clear throughout *Pudd'nhead Wilson*. Galton devised the practice of oiling the hand by passing it through one's hair and then pressing the fingertips on glass – the method Wilson uses in the novel – although he did not think this was as efficient as using ink or smoke collected on paper. He called fingerprints "self-signatures" (Galton, 1892: 168), a phrase quite similar to Twain's "natal autographs," and the book contains a lengthy discussion of the individuality of fingerprints that Twain retooled in the courtroom scene of *Pudd'nhead Wilson*.

Given his interest in hereditary intelligence, Galton investigated the "tendency to hereditary transmission" of fingerprints, but came up with conflicting results. He found that patterns of prints were passed down genetically, not as whole prints, but certainly as manifested in elements of compound prints. In a side note that must have piqued Twain's interest, he asserted that there could not be "the slightest doubt as to the strong tendency to resemblance in the finger patterns of twins" (*ibid.*: 186), although no two people could have *identical* prints, and "the number of cases is too few to justify quantitative conclusions" (*ibid.*: 189). As a eugenicist, Galton was determined to find a correlation between racial difference and fingerprints: he wanted to prove in particular, that types of prints and patterns were peculiar to specific "races" (he examined English, Welsh, "Hebrew," black, and Basque hands) and distinguishable from others. However, he was disappointed to find that even though "the patterns are hereditary ... we have seen that they are uncorrelated with race or temperament" (*ibid.*: 209). Attempting to follow studies of phrenology and physiognomy, which recommended or condemned marriage between various head patterns and temperaments, Galton came up short, finding that fingerprints "cannot exercise the slightest influence on marriage selection" (*ibid.*).[26]

Galton was clearly disappointed that there was "no particular pattern that is special to any one of them, which when met with enables us to assert, or even to suspect, the nationality of the person on whom it appeared" (*ibid.*: 193). In fact, he ended up grasping at straws, asserting that

> [t]he impressions of Negroes betray the general clumsiness of their fingers, but their patterns are not, so far as I can find, different from those of others, they are not simpler as judged by ... their contours [although] they give an idea of greater simplicity, due to causes I have not yet succeeded in submitting to the test of measurement.
>
> (*ibid.*: 196)

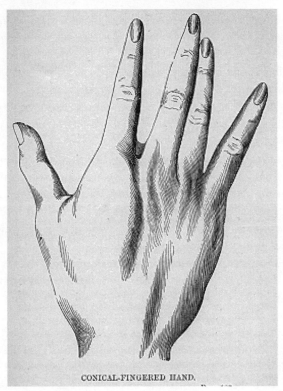

CONICAL-FINGERED HAND.

From *Handbook of Modern Palmistry* by Professor V. De Metz, published by Brentano Brothers, New York, 1883.

Clearly, this "idea of greater simplicity" was far less convincing than what Galton was looking for. It was also opposed to the methodology of *Finger Prints* itself. The book did not depend upon "ideas" but, as Galton himself suggests, on "the test of measurement." Galton documented every step of the fingerprinting process. He recommended the most efficient methods of print collection, and very specific directions about how to gather the prints, endorsing particular kinds of ink and paper, describing how to apply each finger to the ink and detailing the best technique for committing the print to paper. He drew up multiple charts of different kinds of prints, dividing them into their constitutive parts of arches, whorls, and loops, and going into each category in almost numbing detail. Galton used 500 subjects in his study, generating 5,000 prints, and the book is full of tables, charts, reproductions of prints, and highly technical language.

As Stephen Jay Gould has commented, in his eugenics work (1996: 107), "[q]uantification was Galton's god." Galton's obsessive quantification also applied to his research on fingerprinting. Moreover, he disliked having to adapt the taxonomies he set up to exceptions – or, perhaps more accurately, he only established systems that had clearly distinguishable classes of things and could not admit hybrids. He resisted having to classify "compound" prints that contained combinations of arches, whorls, and loops, preferring his "threefold system of classification ... [which,] while in some degree artificial, is very serviceable for preliminary statistics, such as are needed to obtain a broad view of the distribution of various patterns" (*ibid.*: 79–80). As a result, Galton was often hard-pressed to deal with prints that did not conform to his system of classification; ultimately he realized that "[a] little violence has of course to be used now and then, in fitting some unusual patterns to some one or another of these few symbols [used for indexing prints]" (*ibid.*: 144). Galton's inability to deal with anomalies in his system betrays a mind so preoccupied with taxonomy that he is willing to employ violence, albeit metaphorical, to squeeze atypical prints into his program.

It is this focus on the programmatic, the systematized, the taxonomic, that is at the heart of Twain's use of fingerprints, and of the move from reading palms to reading fingers for the evidence which the body can provide both analytically and criminologically. The refusal to incorporate the mixture of elements is played out in what the prints reveal in the final court scene: not just that Tom Driscoll murdered his supposed uncle, but that he is "negro and slave." This classification may be, as Twain maintains, "a fiction of law and custom" (*PW* 33), but as with his mother, "Tom"'s racialized fraction, encapsulated in the "system of deceptive mathematics" (Gillman, 1990: 90) of his one-thirty-second-part black "outvoted the other ... parts and made [him] a negro" (*PW* 32–3). This voting power, introduced at the beginning of the novel, is reinstantiated by a show of hands at the end of the text[27]– first Tom's and Chamber's prints, then the unanimous vote of the jury – a demonstration that denies the possibility that mixture carries meaning. More than "a little violence" ensues from this forcing of a compound identity into a singular category.

Ironically, Galton's obsession with system is what initially blinds Wilson to the truth of the murder mystery. Convinced that the murderer is the "mysterious girl," he searches through his "great array of the finger-prints of women and girls, collected during the last fifteen or eighteen years, but he scanned them in vain" (*PW* 258). When he finally recognizes Tom's print on Roxy's glass as the same one from the knife-handle and looks through the series of Tom's "impressions," he is "stupefied with astonishment" that the series is interrupted:

> "It's no use; I can't understand it. They don't tally right, and yet I'll swear the names and dates are right, and so of course they *ought* to tally. I never

labeled one of these things carelessly in my life. There is a most extraordinary mystery here."

(*PW* 276–7)

Wilson's ability to resystematize the fingerprints and reclassify them as "*A*" and "*B*" allows him access first to the mystery itself, and then to its successful rearticulation in the courtroom. It is only when he can imagine fingerprints as separate from the bodies that bear them, or the meanings he thinks those bodies carry, that he can solve both the murder of Judge Driscoll and the mystery of the nonmatching prints.

The irony that Wilson cannot see what is before his eyes is deeply significant for the interrelations of identity, character, and performance that I have been tracing here. Informed by Judith Butler's theories of performativity, Peggy Phelan argues that "the visible real is employed as a truth-effect for the establishment of ... discursive and representational notions of the real" (1993: 3). That is to say, Wilson cannot construct a meaningful narrative of "that woman that don't exist" because he cannot imagine the woman as simply a "truth-effect," rather than actually *real*. Tom represents himself as female (much as he, for a long time unknowingly but no more or less convincingly, represents himself as white), and his audience believes what it sees because Tom's performance conforms to the discursive conventions of femaleness (or whiteness). Wilson is stumped because he is faced with a narrative that seems to him incoherent: only when he can "see" the "truth" of the mysterious woman's role in the story of Judge Driscoll's death can he mount a convincing performance for the jury.

The desire for coherent and legible identities is rooted in the study of fingerprints. In *Finger Prints*, Galton identified one important use of fingerprint evidence "in civil as well as in criminal cases": in the colonies (or, as he called them, "our dependencies"), "where the features of natives are distinguished with difficulty" (1892: 14). The inability (or, perhaps, refusal) of the colonizers to put identities to the faces of the colonized necessitated a technology that did not rely on eyewitnesses or personal description but could instead abstract the self into a series of patterns, each of which was – with a little magnification – totally distinguishable. Fingerprinting could thus achieve apparently opposite goals: unambiguously pinpointing individual indigenous people and depersonalizing native people as a group.[28] Fingerprints may "defeat masquerade, disguise, doubling and counterfeit identity," since no person can have more than one print and no print can belong to more than one person (Rogin, 1990: 80). However, far from "identify[ing] the true and unique individual 'character,'" they subordinate "character" – the term used, as we have seen, by palmists and phrenologists alike to describe what their work uncovers – to "measurement" (*ibid.*). Fingerprints only have meaning in relation to other, precollected prints. They have no transparent or independent value outside an entire system of taxonomy, classification and record-keeping. As Susan Gillman has pointed out, "Fingerprints appear theoretically to be the one measure of unique, noncontingent, individual identity, but are in practice relational indices that must be read in and against the context of other sets of prints" (1989: 91).

In *Pudd'nhead Wilson*, the townspeople of Dawson's Landing also have difficulty distinguishing the features of two "natives" – children who were born in the town on the very same day – but it is whiteness that makes distinction impossible, not blackness. As Ruth Frankenberg has argued, the dominance of whiteness means that white people are both invisible and hypervisible; it makes its subjects visible *as* subjects but illegible as *raced* subjects. Only their fingerprints can tell them apart after Roxy exchanges them, suggesting to the reader that "the light mulatto [acts as] an uncanny reminder that blackness both *was* and *was not* visible and whiteness both *was* and *was not* a form of property with legal significance [during slavery]" (Sundquist, 1990: 64). However, by the time we find out their "real" identities, both Tom and Chambers (in whichever configuration) have lost the ability to inhabit the selves that their fingerprints claim for them. The former Tom is totally evacuated of self: through a juggling of property rights, he is reduced not just to a state of slavery but to the status of "inventory," both incapable of crime and capable of sale as a piece of property.[29] The former Chambers, on the other hand, has more identities than he can handle. The law has given him back his "real" self, but he finds himself "in a most embarrassing situation":

> He could neither read nor write, and his speech was the basest dialect of the negro quarter. His gait, his attitudes, his gestures, his bearing, his laugh – all were vulgar and uncouth; his manners were the manners of a slave. Money and fine clothes could not mend these defects or cover them up; they only made them the more glaring and the more pathetic. The poor fellow could not endure the terrors of the white man's parlor, and felt at home and at peace nowhere but in the kitchen.
>
> (*PW* 301–2)

In the courtroom scene, Tom is reduced from audience member to object of surveillance to spectacle to lifeless body (at the moment of exposure the eyes of the audience turn to Tom, who "turned his ashen face imploringly toward the speaker, made some impotent movements with his white lips, then slid limp and lifeless to the floor"; *PW* 299) to object of exchange. In its aftermath, however, Chambers cannot occupy the space that Tom has left empty: only his fingerprints can. The "character" of Tom has been emptied out, since the person who had that character (or temperament, or disposition) really had the "identity" of Chambers, and "new" Tom does not have enough content to fill up his identity.[30]

Michael Rogin has claimed that "[a]lthough Pudd'nhead uses palmistry to tell the twins' history, his success is left over from the farcical story and irrelevant to the racial tragedy" (1990: 80), but I would argue quite the opposite. The move from palm-reading to fingerprinting as a way to understand what hands can tell us about the bodies to which they are attached dramatizes a major trend in scientific inquiry in the U.S. at the end of the nineteenth century. Palmistry depends upon representations of the body, as does phrenology – we see the hands, faces, skulls. Phrenology, temperament, and palm-reading manuals represent parts of actual bodies: they are full of portraits of faces, models of heads, engravings of whole hands. In the palm-reading scene in the novel, Wilson holds Luigi Capello's hand to study it. Twain describes the scene as highly tactile: Wilson reads Luigi's past by "tracing life-lines, heart-lines, head-lines and so on ...; he *felt* of the fleshy cushion at the base of the thumb ...; he *felt* of the fleshy side of the hand" (*PW* 139, emphasis added). In fact, the illustration to this scene in the original American Publishing Company edition of 1894 shows Wilson, Tom, and Angelo standing in a semicircle around Luigi, Wilson holding and gazing into Luigi's hand. At the final court scene, however, Tom does not even have to be present to be exposed. His fingerprint has been abstracted from his body, and is only of probative value in relation to other disembodied prints.

In fingerprinting, Galton reduces embodied fingers into inky prints, and abstracts the prints into items on charts and tables. Each individual print is simply an exemplum, a sample that only has meaning within the larger structure. While palm-reading manuals did include hand prints, and Cheiro and his peers occasionally read from prints rather than actual hands, the majority of palmistry occurred as an interaction between palmist and subject. Fingerprint analysis is almost impossible to effect on the physical hand: a print is a clearer and easier subject of study. Palm-reading and, in particular, phrenology require physical contact between two people. Phrenologists had to touch the head of the person being read, had to feel the texture of the bumps and depressions. This actual presence, contiguity, and mutuality of bodies hampers fingerprinting.

This reading requires a couple of qualifications, however. After all, palm-reading does not represent a positively anti racist, or at least nonracial, way of reading bodies, nor does fingerprinting somehow stand in for the massive repression of African Americans that was taking place as the technology was developed (in fact, given fingerprinting's supposed neutrality, one would imagine quite the opposite relationship). First of all, palmistry was hardly unencumbered by the white supremacist worldview that produced so many of the knowledge systems which flourished in the nineteenth century. Certainly, the palm-reading manuals of the mid- to late nineteenth century made no such claims to racial neutrality. As we have seen, they participated in discourses of evolutionary racism, orientalism, "the exotic," "the criminal type," and the like. Scientific palmists drew up diagram after diagram of different types of hands and what they represented: their books were full of hand prints of celebrities and murderers as well as people from Eastern and Southern European countries, who were inevitably picked to exemplify "the Elementary Hand: Denoting the lowest grade of intelligence, sloth, dulness and coarseness" (Heron-Allen, 1887: 62). Moreover, palm-reading became popular in the U.S. at the same time as the rise of polygenism, a theory that understood racial differences as divisions of species, and believed that those differences were readily legible on the surfaces and in the crevices of the body itself.

But the move to fingerprinting in this novel represents a different way of thinking about identity. *Pudd'nhead Wilson* shows us how the language of racialization changed, and how we can read those changes through the kinds of science that existed to "prove" racial difference, and the methodologies those sciences adopted. Methodologically, palmistry, phrenology, and temperament theory are quite different from fingerprint analysis, eugenics and IQ testing, the heir to body-based theories of racial and ethnic hierarchy. One set of ways of reading hands and heads was replaced by a different array of methods of reading those same hands and heads, and those *methods* themselves carry ideological meaning even apart from the results they evinced.

Nor am I arguing that this change was singular, immediate, and unambivalent. Raymond Williams' work on culture has shown that "new conditions ... [are] neither uniform nor static" and that culture itself "is a process, not a conclusion" (1958: 295). As Eve Kosofsky Sedgwick has pointed out in a different context, arguments that call into being a "Great Paradigm Shift" can obscure both the partial and resistant ways in which cultural change occurs and the heterogeneity of what followed such change (1990: 44–5). Williams has proposed a tripartite division of cultural phenomena around this idea: dominant, residual, and emergent, all of which coexist in an uneasy dynamism. I do not want to propose a "unidirectional narrative of supersession" in tracing the shift in *Pudd'nhead Wilson* from palm-reading to fingerprinting (Sedgwick, 1990: 46); rather, rules of prohibition, classification and racialization that we might categorize as belonging to different historical and cultural moments can and do coexist synchronously, or simply survive relatively unchanged within different contexts. In Williams' words, "in cultural production both the *residual* – work made in earlier and often different societies and times, yet still available and significant – and the *emergent* – work of various new kinds − are often equally available *as practices,"* as well as dominant cultural formations (1982: 204, emphasis in original).[31]

We can see this push/pull of cultural shifts in *Pudd'nhead Wilson* itself: as Twain is chronicling a new way in which his contemporaries are conceptualizing identity through the body, he is also − by setting the novel in slavery time − acknowledging how little hegemonic discourse about blackness has changed in its effects on African American people themselves. In addition, anthropologists and criminologists did not, for example, suddenly stop using portraits as a tool for identifying types, particularly the "criminal type." The work of Italian criminologist Cesare Lombroso, which centered around equating people who manifested certain physical (and especially facial) features such as large jaws, long arms, low foreheads, or even tattoos, with members of a hereditary genetic criminal class, was actively deployed in the U.S. in both police investigations and court trials through the first decade of the twentieth century (Gould, 1996: 168).

However, Twain's transposition of the terms of reading hands was more prescient than he could have imagined. As he was writing *Pudd'nhead Wilson,* the shift from looking at bodies to looking at abstracted information about bodies that the book synecdochally represents was already taking place in the work of people like Galton and the endless graphs of brain size and weight of craniometrist Paul Broca. Moreover, as Mark Seltzer argues, "the conversion of individuals into numbers and cases and the conversion of bodies into visual displays" was part of a *fin-de-siècle* obsession by naturalist novelists with what Seltzer terms "statistical persons" − fictional identities that were distillations of quantifiable elements that, once composed, could hardly be described as "characters" (Seltzer, 1992: 100). The portraits of faces and hands that were the mainstay of phrenology and palmistry manuals, the analyses of character and analogies of types with celebrities, were replaced by tables of anonymous numbers. Just around the corner (and within Twain's lifetime) was the soon-to-be national obsession with another set of abstracted numbers: the IQ.

The story of the Intelligence Quotient (IQ) in the United States is a chilling illustration of the process I have identified above. IQ was devised by French psychologist Alfred Binet. Although he dabbled briefly in craniometry, he was soon disillusioned with the inaccuracy of skull size and brain weight as a method of precisely assessing intelligence. Following (ironically) Francis Galton, Binet turned instead to psychological techniques. He devised tests of reasoning that might measure the limits of intellectual ability, which he equated with "mental age": that is, "the youngest age at which a child of normal intelligence should be able to complete a task successfully" (Gould, 1996: 179). The mental age was then divided by the chronological age of the person, and from that computation came the intelligence quotient.

Binet did not see IQ as a free-standing, absolute test of a person's intellectual ability. Rather, he considered it to be a "rough, empirical guide constructed for a limited practical purpose," that is, identifying children who might need extra help and attention in keeping up with their peers in school. Binet did not consider intelligence to be "a single, scalable thing like height" (Gould, 1996: 181), but a complex of abilities and limits that IQ could only approach in assessing. Most importantly, he resisted identifying intelligence as an inborn quality that the IQ could ferret out, and refused to use it for ranking students by "mental age."[32] IQ was simply a diagnostic tool, not a self-signifying quantity.

When IQ arrived on U.S. shores, however, Binet's caution was tossed aside. As Thomas Gossett has argued, by the beginning of the twentieth century, proving racial difference through bodily phenomena had lost much of its scientific legitimacy. Here, instead, was "a method ... which seemed to prove all nonwhite races are *intellectually* inferior" (1997: 364; emphasis added). American psychologists such as H. H. Goddard, L. M. Terman, and R. M. Yerkes transformed IQ into *the* measure of a race-, ethnicity- and class-specific, hereditary, reified, unitary attribute called intelligence. Individual scores could locate a person along a fixed numerical scale that ranged from "genius" (above 145 points) to "average" (100 points) to "high-grade defective" (that is, fit only for unskilled work: 75 points); the scale ended at "feeble-minded." A wide variety of physiological, cultural, and behavioral phenomena were classified as "general low-level." By the end of the 1910s, IQ had such cultural cachet that all 1,700,000 men who joined the US armed services in World War I had been tested (in part to identify those men "intelligent" enough to qualify for officer training).

IQ continues to be invoked as a putatively meaningful way to measure ability and rank individuals accordingly. The cult of the number that developed at the end of the nineteenth century, best exemplified by the science of fingerprinting, has lasted a remarkably long time and has done inestimable damage to both individuals and whole groups of people based on race, class, gender, or ethnic difference. *Pudd'nhead Wilson* is one of the first texts to register the onset of this cult, and Twain, simultaneously distrustful of and seduced by the blandishments of "objective evidence," writes his ambivalence into this tragicomic narrative. The "little violence" that Francis Galton felt compelled to exercise in order to make his filing cabinets full of fingerprints all align to the tripartite classification of arches, whorls, and loops; the transformation of Tom Driscoll from a scoundrel with "questionable privacies" written into his palm (*PW* 145) to a fingerprinted piece of "erroneous inventory" (*PW* 303); the roots of the United States' love affair with numbers as positive proof of personal identity: Twain exposes them all in a seemingly farcical but ultimately cataclysmic show of hands.

3

Fixing identity

Reading skin, seeing race

Over the years that I have been teaching Nella Larsen's *Passing*, my students have commented on a common experience they have when reading the much-analyzed scene in which girlhood friends Irene Redfield and Clare Kendry Bellew reunite after more than a decade's separation. Irene has been whisked by a taxi from the "sweltering" August streets of Chicago to the roof of the Drayton. Arriving at the rooftop cafe is "like being wafted upward on a magic carpet to other world, pleasant, quiet, and strangely remote from the sizzling one she had left below" (*P* 147).[1] Irene's serenity is broken by the arrival of a "sweetly scented woman" who takes the table next to her, and soon fixes her with a steady stare (*P* 148–9). Irene checks herself for smudged make-up, misplaced clothing, or other reasons why this woman might be looking so intently at her. Finally the thought strikes her: "Did that woman, could that woman somehow know that here before her very eyes on the roof of the Drayton sat a Negro?" (*P* 150).

My students, whatever their race or ethnicity, are always taken aback by this moment. They certainly had not guessed Irene's identity as "a Negro"; the novel seems to lead from its outset in other directions. They often report feeling deceived, as though the text has perpetrated an act of passing upon/against them, as though Larsen does not trust her readers enough to let them in on the secret from the very beginning.[2] Moreover, the paragraph following the "revelation" of Irene's race seems to accuse them even further, lumping them in with a category of perhaps willfully naive white observers:

Absurd! Impossible! White people were so stupid about such things for all that they usually asserted that they were able to tell; and by the most ridiculous means, finger-nails, palms of hands, shapes of ears, teeth, and other equally silly rot. They always took her for an Italian, a Spaniard, a

Mexican, or gipsy. Never, when she was alone, had they even remotedly seemed to suspect that she was a Negro. No, the woman sitting there staring at her couldn't possibly know.

(P 150)

Of course, as re-readers of the novel already know, the staring woman, the former Clare Kendry, is herself "a Negro" – something Irene is unable to see – passing as white and married to a wealthy white businessman, Jack Bellew, in order to escape racism and poverty. Indeed, in a later conversation with white writer Hugh Wentworth, Irene argues that "Nobody can [tell someone's race]. Not by looking" (P 206).[3] Irene's inability (or refusal) to see the world around her accurately is at the center of the novel, and as she is the central consciousness of the text, it is not surprising that readers fall into that same mode of perception. Moreover, as I discuss in greater detail in Chapter 4, to be racially unmarked and to be white are often conflated: since Irene is not explicitly *identified* as black in the opening pages of the novel there is no reason to assume that she is anything but white.

However, students (usually but not exclusively African American) occasionally comment on their sense that there was "something" about Irene that struck them as "different." It is, they argue, her acute sense of observing and being observed: the layering on of adjectives in narratively still moments, for example. A sentence that stands out is the description of Clare eating a melon on the roof of the Drayton before Irene knows who she is: Irene "saw the silver spoon in the white hand slit the dull gold of the melon" (P 149). Similarly, at the beginning of the novel, Irene remembers Clare as a "pale small girl sitting on a ragged blue sofa, sewing pieces of bright red cloth together" – a rhythmic series of adjectival phrases.[4] The depth of detail seems almost baroquely unnecessary. The narrative voice must have a reason for looking so intently.

Many critics have pointed to the centrality of the visible in *Passing*.[5] The novel, like the phenomenon of passing itself, "is about specularity: the visible and invisible, the seen and the unseen" (Ginsberg, 1996: 2). So much in the novel depends upon what is seen, noticed, perceived, or not. The "not" is crucial here; as Robyn Wiegman argues, the passage quoted above reveals that "the seeming veracity of the flesh can fail to register itself, and it is significant that Larsen represents this failure by foregrounding corporeal signs that do *not* appear" (1995: 21). Passing, after all, is about what cannot be seen, or at least cannot be seen by those whom passing is designed to fool. Or, rather, what is seen does not register, but is mistaken for something else, just as Irene is mistaken for "an Italian, a Spaniard, a Mexican, or a gipsy" (P 150).

Less discussed in *Passing*, however, is the intense "color consciousness" – a phrase with multiple and interlocking meanings – throughout the novel. This attention to color is a byproduct of the recognition of the permeability of racial boundaries through the vehicle of light skin. As Shirlee Taylor Haizlip illustrates in her family memoir *The Sweeter the Juice*, passing is part of the family story of innumerable African Americans.[6]

> Currently, one of the country's major black political figures is married to a woman whose sisters pass for white in Tennessee. In Buffalo, there is a man who lives as white but frequently returns to his black high school reunions in Washington, D.C. . . . A woman I knew as black when I was young is now white and no longer speaks to me. Multiply these instances many times over and the footprints of those who have crossed the color line become infinite and untrackable.
>
> (1994: 34)

This kind of subtle analysis is beyond the white characters in Larsen's novel. Jack Bellew, for example, can recognize that his wife is "gettin' darker and darker" but states unequivocally that there are "No niggers in my family. Never have been and never will be" (P 171). Similarly, Hugh Wentworth is charmed by the fact that some of the light-skinned revelers at the Negro Welfare League benefit dance might actually be black. Hence, *Passing* is more than a meditation of visibility, sexuality, race, and identity, although it is all of those things. It is also an analysis of the simultaneous codes of color that black people live with in both black and white worlds. While racial identity to whites seems clear-cut, the African descent characters in the novel, and in U.S. culture, have long recognized that it is anything but black and white.

In this chapter I want to explore the multiple meanings of skin color in the 1920s, and the intensity of concern that circulated around skin as a mode of racial evidence. *Passing* provides one flashpoint for this concern, as does Wallace Thurman's mordant *The Blacker the Berry*. These novels interrogate the layerings of color and race both within African American communities and the ways in which members of those communities represent themselves to the dominant culture. The politics of skin extended beyond the realms of fiction, however. Juxtaposed with these literary representations are the numerous newspaper articles, investigative reports, and exposés of passing that littered the press in the 1920s. The most sensational of these, to which I will be paying particular attention, is the court case brought in 1925 by Leonard Kip Rhinelander, the heir of a prominent New York family of Dutch descent, to annul his marriage to Alice Jones, the working-class daughter of a black West Indian father and white English mother.

By allowing these texts to collide with each other, I want to dissect how the racial assumptions that white spectators, readers, watchers, and – not least – juries in the 1920s brought with them to their experiences of perceiving skin color and making meaning out of it were often less complex than, usually totally unaware of, and almost always anticipated by African American observers. Quite different codes of skin and race were at work in black discourse. At the same time, the Rhinelander trial suggests a cross-pollination of these perceptions, and a subtle reworking of the kind of evidentiary content skin might have. Most importantly, all these texts enact the intersections of racial identity, gendered (that is, female) sexual and economic vulnerability, and class mobility that passing both pushes into the foreground and attempts to conceal.

Color coding, codes of color

It is a truism in the criticism of *Passing* that Irene looks at Clare with an interest that approximates obsession.[7] The sexual forcefields in the novel surround the relationship between the two women. Both their marriages have been thoroughly desexualized: Irene's because of the profound differences between herself and her husband Brian, not least because he thinks sex is a "grand joke, the greatest in the world" (P 189), and Clare's because she cannot risk the possibility of another pregnancy and a dark child.

Irene's looking at Clare outstrips sexual desire, though. Her gaze is a peculiar combination of mastery and abjection (a state in which she often finds herself). Looking at Clare before they set out for the Negro Welfare League dance, Irene is "choked" by her desire for Clare, "exquisite, golden, fragrant, flaunting, in a stately gown of shining black taffeta, whose long, full skirt lay in graceful folds about her slim golden feet" while she herself feels "dowdy and commonplace" (P 203). Nonetheless, Irene's gaze is also policing, causing her to "[regret] that she hadn't counselled Clare to wear something ordinary and inconspicuous" (P 203). Clare invites people to look at her, to desire her, to compare themselves to her, but her "flaunting" is, as Irene warns her, "not safe. Not safe at all" (P 195). Irene scolds Clare while she desires her; she feels a certain control over her through knowledge of her "secret" even as she is incapable of revealing that secret to someone to whom it might matter (Bellew, for instance).

Looking at Clare, Irene wants to consume her but cannot – she is "choked"; wants to understand her but cannot; wants to disavow and distance her but cannot. It is not simply that Clare's passing thwarts what Robyn Wiegman has termed "our cultural trust in the objectivity of observation and the seemingly positive ascription we grant representation" (1995: 9), or that the novel destabilizes what we take for granted as visibly "true." Rather, *Passing* reveals the kind of struggles a viewer needs to go through to see anything, and the ways in which what that vision means is profoundly predetermined by racial group membership.

"Passing" is a term sited within a matrix that has as its vectors both time and space. It is both a temporal metaphor – time passes, after all – and a spatial one (we pass down a road). Throughout the novel, Larsen establishes oppositions between black and white identity that highlight how movement within time and space are constructed through racial and gendered identity. For example, Irene's habitual lateness is understood as a product of her membership in the leisure class but also as generated by her identity as a black woman. In this she contrasts in terms of gender with Brian, and in terms of race with white people.

After receiving the letter from Clare that begins the novel, Irene shows it to Brian rather than reading it to him "so that he might be occupied while she hurried through her dressing. For she was late again, and Brian, she well knew, detested that. Why, oh why, couldn't she ever manage to be on time?" (*P* 183). Brian, on the other hand, "had been up for ages, had made some calls for all she knew, besides having taken the boys downtown to school" (*P* 183). Irene is late at all the social engagements in the novel. She is the last to arrive at Clare's tea-party in Chicago; she is late for her own tea-party as well as for the party at the Freelands. Much of this lateness is linked to Irene's femininity, usually through dressing, fixing her hair, and applying make-up. Brian, on the other hand, whom the narrator distances from the fate of being "pretty or effeminate" (*P* 183), is always already dressed and immersed in activity.

At the same time, Irene explicitly links her lateness to race, invoking "C.P. [Colored people's] time" as the larger reason for her inability to be on time (*P* 233). The expression "C.P. time" suggests that the ease with which people move through time is conditioned by a minoritized identity, and that blackness cannot necessarily be contained by or conform to temporal limits.[8] On the one hand, "C.P. time" implies a lateness forged in racial solidarity, a way of carving out a rebellious identity in the face of temporal conformity: it declares that white people will just have to wait. On the other hand, Irene's lateness is both caused by and a continual source of anxiety. By the end of the novel her lateness puts her at a serious disadvantage in heading off what she imagines is an affair between Brian and Clare: "She must hurry or she would be late again, and those two would wait for her downstairs together, as they had done so often since that first time" (*P* 232). For Irene, then, lateness is a sign not of leisured superiority, or racial tricksterism, but of vulnerability. She cannot comfortably inhabit the subordinated discourse of "colored people's time," nor move in the rhythms of the dominant order. Just as her passing is incomplete and circumstantial, her passage through time is fitful and out of step.

Passing also requires smooth movement through space. Lauren Berlant has linked this mobility to dominant culture's disavowal of the body, and the hyperbolic embodiment of subordinated groups. According to Berlant, Irene's desire to "[go] native ... for the sake of convenience, restaurants, theatre tickets, and things like that" (*P* 227) is connected less to wanting "to pass as a white person, but [more] to move unconsciously and unobstructed through the public sphere" (Berlant, 1991: 111). When Irene passes at the Drayton, she feels as though she has been "wafted" – lifted effortlessly, bodilessly, to the space of whiteness. Likewise, Clare is described as subtly but continually in motion. When we first see her, she is in a "fluttering dress of green chiffon" (*P* 148); at the tea-party with Irene and Gertrude, she is in "a thin floating dress"; at the Negro Welfare League dance Irene only "catching glimpses of Clare in the whirling crowd" (*P* 204). She makes small movements throughout conversation, "pass[ing] her hands over the bright sweep of her hair" (*P* 195), or "reach[ing] out and [giving] Irene's hand an affectionate squeeze" (*P* 210). Her very conversation "floated" (*P* 221).

The passing body must remain in motion over time and through space in order to sustain its (in)visibility. As Ann Game argues (1991: 95),

> A moving body occupies successive positions in space, but the process by which it moves from one position to another is one of duration which eludes space. ... Motion itself, the act, is not divisible, only an object is; space which is motionless can be measured, but the motion of bodies cannot. Movements cannot occupy space, they are duration. ... To think of a body occupying points in space is to do so from a perspective outside the body, not from the perspective of the moving body.

In motion, the body cannot be subjected to the "frenetic twenties ... mania for category-making: this passion for creating and identifying human types" that we saw growing out of the nineteenth century and reaching one of its apexes in IQ testing (Kaplan, 1997: 151). The passing body represents a double threat, always moving effortlessly through both time and space. In order to be seen, measured, understood, the passing body must be *fixed* and looked at in stasis. [9]

It is this fixing in time and space that creates the illusion of knowability. And illusion it is. The different elements of this matrix both intersect and contradict. Passing denotes ongoing movement in what Gertrude Stein called the "continuous present" (1972: 31). But the observer of the passing cannot *see* both the spatial and temporal properties of passing happening simultaneously. For, as quantum physics has shown us, we cannot look at a body without either stopping its movement or changing its trajectory, or both. We cannot look at it without shaping it to fit our gaze. So the questions we need to ask are not whether a viewer constructs what she sees, for that is inevitable, or whether vision is subjective or objective (how can it be objective when the moving body is *made* into an object by the viewing subject?), but rather, who sees what? How do cultural texts show us how vision is segregated by race, by gender, by class?

Larsen gives some pretty clear answers to these questions in *Passing*, most of which focus on how racial status constructs racialized vision. Larsen represents the double consciousness with which black women writers wrestled throughout the 1920s, a "politics of resistance ... to counter representations of blackness and black female sexuality created by racism" (McLendon, 1995: 4). Moreover, *Passing* reveals a profound awareness of the split between white and black understandings of the cultural (and chromatic) shadings within African American communities, working through "the theory that blacks were despised, not for their lack of education or money or manners, but simply because they were 'colored': light or dark, ignorant or intelligent, cultured or not, black people living among hatred and bigotry shared a common problem" (*ibid.*: 7).

At the same time, Larsen complicates this solidarity of oppression. In *Passing*, black people may share a common problem in relation to whites, but they do not feel the kind of fellowship Jacquelyn McLendon sees as a hallmark of Larsen's fiction in her claim that "despite differences of skin color, education, and economic status [her characters] suffer the same inequalities and injustices that other blacks living in white America suffer" (1995: 93). One phenomenon that is a byproduct of unjust racialization is the discrimination on the basis of color and class through which the urban black New Yorkers of *Passing* experience their lives. One might ask how far Brian Redfield's disgust at his patients, "their stupid meddling families, and smelly, dirty rooms, and climbing filthy steps in dark hallways" (*P* 186) is from John Bellew's racist outburst against "black scrimy devils" (*P* 172), for instance.

Moreover, the black characters in *Passing* are, in Wallace Thurman's phrase, highly "color conscious." Inanimate objects are insistently described by color, particularly at the beginning of the novel: Clare's dresses, of course, as well as the melon and spoon cited earlier; the green glass from which Irene drinks her tea; the blue tie worn by Clare's escort to the Drayton; the blue draperies and chocolate-colored furniture of Clare's apartment in Chicago, to name just a few. Larsen also describes the various skin tones and textures of all her black characters: Irene's face is a shade of "warm olive"; Clare's mouth is "like a scarlet flower against the ivory of her skin" (*P* 148); their tea companion Gertrude's face is "large [and] white" (*P* 167); Brian Redfield's skin is "of an exquisitely fine texture and deep copper colour" (*P* 184); the Redfields' servant Zulena is "a small, mahogany-coloured creature" (*P* 184), and so on.

Passing's black characters are deeply concerned with color and what it means. Even a dark-skinned character like Irene's friend Felise Freeland is well aware of the mechanisms of passing that the variations in skin tone allow some African Americans, as well as the in-group calumny implicitly aimed at dark skin. After she and Irene run into Jack Bellew, she comments sardonically, "Aha! Been 'passing' have you?" (*P* 227). At the excruciating tea-party in Chicago, Gertrude Martin takes for granted that "nobody wants a dark child," even though she knows Irene lives as part of the black community in Harlem (*P* 168). The leisured and economically privileged Irene recognizes that race is not a static category, and that it is continually recombining in relationship with other identities. In fact, color itself is not a single defining characteristic – not only are all black people not the same color; even those who *are* the same shade bring different gendered and classed meanings to their coloring.

These complications of color are most fully worked out at the Chicago tea-party that Clare hosts for Irene and their former schoolmate Gertrude Martin, and at which Jack Bellew makes his entrance. As happens so often in the novel, this scene's meanings multiply before the reader's eyes. All three women grew up in or around a bourgeois black community in Chicago's South Side; all are light-skinned enough to pass for some kind of white, at least on occasion. Both Gertrude and Clare are married to white men, causing Irene to feel "outnumbered ... in her adherence to her own class and kind; not merely in the great thing of marriage, but in the whole pattern of her life as well" (*P* 166). But such alliances and separations are not simple: as Cheryl Wall argues, "[p]assing for white ... is only one way this game is played" (1995: 89). Shortly after this sense of exclusion, Irene internally reasserts her connection to Clare through her class-inflected judgment of Gertrude: [10]

> Gertrude, Irene thought, looked as if her husband might be a butcher. There was left of her youthful prettiness, which had been so much admired in their high-school days, no trace. She had grown broad, fat almost, and though there were no lines on her large white face, its very smoothness was somehow prematurely ageing. Her black hair was clipt, and by some unfortunate means all the live curliness had gone from it. Her overtrimmed Georgette *crêpe* dress was too short and showed an appalling amount of leg, stout legs in sleazy stockings of a vivid rose-beige shade. Her plump hands were newly and not too competently manicured – for the occasion, probably. And she wasn't smoking.
>
> (*P* 167)

Gertrude is no less white than Clare, and certainly lighter-skinned than the olive-complexioned Irene, but even her color cannot save her from being a fat butcher's wife, and looking like it. Larsen is acutely aware of the intersections of class, gender, and color that are in motion in urban black communities, and that Irene, moving among those same poles, both labors under and manipulates to her own advantage. Cheryl I. Harris' claim that "whiteness and property share a common premise – a conceptual nucleus – of a right to exclude" hints at an organizing principle to Irene Redfield's social life: not only is whiteness property, but property and class status dovetail with light skin to produce the "right" kind of whiteness that should exclude people like Gertrude, even though she passes for white (Harris, 1993: 1714). The implication of the passage above is that Gertrude has squandered her whiteness. Unlike Clare, who found a wealthy financier, Gertrude married down the class ladder. She is static – even her hair has lost its "live curliness." Her cultural capital as a "white" woman is dissipated.

Perhaps the most damning indicator of Gertrude's loss of status, more than her "sleazy stockings" and "overtrimmed Georgette *crêpe* dress [that] showed an appalling amount of leg" (that is, what contemporary Americans would call her "trashiness") is the fact that she has let her body get out of her control. Whereas Clare has transformed her adolescent "thin body" (*P* 144) into an adult slenderness that extends all the way down to her feet (*P* 203), Gertrude is "broad, fat almost," her legs "stout" and her hands "plump" (*P* 167).

This fatness is explicitly linked to Gertrude's drop in class status, which outranks her rise in racial status: it is the sign that she "look[s] as if her husband might be a butcher" (*P* 167). Her lack of sophistication, signaled by her clumsy manicure and the fact that she is not smoking, is of a piece with her physical size. Both represent her inability to use her body to her advantage, as do Clare and Irene. Ann Douglas has linked the obsession with thinness in the 1920s with a desire on the part of modernists to destroy the mother-centered culture that pervaded bourgeois life in the nineteenth century (1995: 248–9). While the brittle knowingness of *Passing* resembles at least stylistically the modernist sophistication of Larsen's New Negro peers, it is telling that all three women in this scene identify themselves primarily as wives and mothers. In fact, the complexities of their status emerge out of this identification, the lightness of their husbands, and the (putatively undesirable) darkness of their children.

Passing is as much about class as it is about race, and class constructs what color means for the black characters in the novel as powerfully as does race. Philip Brian Harper has suggested that *Passing* dramatizes "the particular desire the standard racial pass is supposed to fulfill – the desire not just for a reliable means of subsistence, but for access to such material comfort as is conventionally seen as being precluded by black identification in the U.S.

context" (1998: 387). Certainly both Clare and Irene pass for reasons of access, and class mobility is a powerful motivator in the passing narrative. However, class, color, and race do not line up quite so neatly in this novel. Rather, "passing for non-black allows these women to wear their gender according to a particular class style" (Berlant, 1991: 111). Clare initially passes so that she can be more like her affluent *black* friends who "had all the things I wanted and never had had. It made me all the more determined to get them, and others" (*P* 159). So although Irene passes to get access to the bourgeois accoutrements Clare now takes for granted, Clare passes to more closely resemble Irene (who is, at the moment when Clare confesses her motivation for passing, herself passing for white at the Drayton, without which act she and Clare would never have reunited).

Conversely, Gertrude's pass effects the opposite set of movements to Clare's, even though on the surface they may seem to be cognate to them. Ironically, Irene represents the standard against which this scene implicitly encourages the reader to measure both Clare and Gertrude, and to ask, has each woman's pass been a success? Irene's unselfconscious class privilege is a status to which Clare has aspired (and that she has achieved), and from which Gertrude has declined. [11]

In this scene, then, identifications slip and slide, spliced and merging, never simply one thing at once, nor the same thing all the time. Color as an indicator is unmoored from the surface of the skin, resited within a variety of bodily meanings, its visibility defined by the assumption of changeability rather than knowability (when asked whether Brian is dark, Irene replies that "her husband ... couldn't exactly 'pass'"[*P* 168]). Reading identity out of the external evidence of skin is a task of formidable complexity. [12]

Given the multiple signifiers that the reader of this scene must learn, apply, and see in relation to each other, the entrance of John Bellew and his starkly polarized view of racial difference is particularly shocking. Certainly he seems at least partially aware of the distinction between race and skin. His use of the nickname "Nig" for Clare acknowledges that a dark complexion does not necessarily equal membership in the class "Negro." In fact, it relies upon the belief that Clare is not "really" black. Explaining why he calls Clare "Nig," Bellew says:

"When we were first married, she was as white as – as – well as white as a lily. But I declare she's gettin' darker and darker. I tell her if she don't look out, she'll wake up one of these days and find she's turned into a nigger."

(*P* 170)

However, for Bellew, this transformation is impossible. After Clare baits him (although he doesn't recognize it as such), asking, "What difference would it make if, after all these years, you were to find out that I was one or two percent colored?" Bellew reacts with a confidence close to violence: "Oh, no, Nig ... nothing like that with me. I know you're no nigger, so it's all right. You can get as black as you please as far as I'm concerned, since I know you're no nigger" (P 171).

In some ways, Bellew's racial consciousness is the inverse of the black characters' understanding of race and color. Bellew recognizes that whiteness can come in an assortment of shades, an assumption that allows Irene to pass as Spanish or a gypsy. But he implicitly holds on to the one-drop rule: "one or two percent colored" means "nigger," absolutely and without exception. To be white means not just to look white or claim oneself as white, since "allowing physical attributes, social acceptance or self-identification to determine whiteness would diminish its value and destroy the underlying presumption of exclusivity" (Harris, 1993: 1741). Rather, to be white is to be everything, anything but black, even dark-skinned, or untraceable genealogically. Whiteness can have depth, diversity, variety; blackness is singular, impermeable, the point of no return.

For Bellew, to be a "nigger" is irreducible and fixed. One does not have to have met any black people to know them "better than they know their black selves" (P 172). They are intrinsically criminal, "robbing and killing people. And ... worse" (P 172). The irony of Bellew's pronouncements is, of course, that, as Irene phrases it internally, "you're sitting here surrounded by three black devils, drinking tea" (P 172). But it is also that Bellew is speaking a totally different language of blackness from the one in which his tea-party companions are fluent. To be black is to be a "nigger," undifferentiated by color, class, or region. For Bellew, blackness is *not* borne out on the skin. It is not an evidentiary category but an ontological one.

While Bellew's racial classifications obviously devolve from an unreconstructed racism, his ignorance of the nuances of the meanings of skin seem to be shared by even well-intentioned whites like Hugh Wentworth, a character based on Larsen's supporter, Carl Van Vechten. The significance of color is a topic of conversation at the Negro Welfare League dance that Irene has helped organize, an event characterized by the intermingling of shades, types, sizes, classes:

Young men, old men, white men, black men; youthful women, older women, pink women, golden women; fat men, thin men, tall men, short men; stout women, slim women, stately women, small women moved by.

(P 204)

Surrounded by this movement, Wentworth wants to fix the people he sees. He engages Irene in a conversation on passing, after noticing Clare dancing with a dark-skinned "Ethiopian." His first question is to inquire about the "name, status, and race of the blond beauty out of the fairy tale" that is Clare as she whirls by (P 204–5) — to see her is to want to pin her down. He recognizes that he may not be an accurate reader of his surroundings, but cannot resist the power of the dominant class to place what he sees into knowable categories.

In addition, Wentworth's racial sophistication extends to understanding that "lots of people 'pass' all the time" (P 206), but not that racial crossings are not equally easy. Hinting at the close attention which African Americans pay to the meanings of color and race, Irene argues that "It's easy for a Negro to 'pass' for white. But I don't think it would be so simple for a white person to 'pass' as coloured" (P 206). It is not simply that white people would hardly want to pass lower down on the social ladder; rather, black people are attentive readers, minutely aware of how color, class, and race intersect with self-presentation in a way that white people, assuming the transparent binary of racial difference, do not feel the need to be.

These two scenes suggest that the toughest audience for racial passers is not the white mainstream, but the black communities from which the passer comes. White spectators cannot hold the passing body still enough to read accurately the messages inscribed on it. They assume a stasis of identity that is evidentiarily transparent and limpidly legible. Black spectators accumulate readings over time, paying attention to detail, never assuming they know. Irene's example of Dorothy Thompkins is instructive here. Irene admits that it took her "four or five times, in groups and crowds of people, before I knew she wasn't a Negro," but that after talking to her "less than five minutes, I knew she was 'fay.' Not from anything she did or said or anything in her appearance. Just — just something. A thing that couldn't be registered" (P 206). Irene's acknowledgment that the passer cannot be "registered" as an object, but more as an inchoate accumulation of "somethings" is a direct challenge to John Bellew's evidentiary claim that whites know blacks "better than they know their black selves" (P 172); it is, in fact, a rethinking of what there is to be known in the intersections of race and color.

These shrewd and subtle interpretations of the passing figure in motion come at great cost, however. One of the penalties of attentive reading is the understanding that those in power have not been trained in such astute interpretations: indeed, that their ignorance is what allows them to maintain their dominance. What Amy Robinson calls the "in-group clairvoyant" is both superior in her reading and silenced by it, aware that the act of passing "requires a speaker and *two* audiences: one audience that's ignorant and another that knows the truth *and remains silent about it"* (Rabinowitz, 1994: 205; emphasis in original). Moreover, Clare's elusive movements, her sinuousness and refusal to be pinned down as an evidentiary specimen bear the double burden of liberatory movement and the injunction, to paraphrase Ralph Ellison, to "Keep That Nigger [Girl] Running" (1952: 33).

A jury of peerers: showing some skin in the Rhinelander case

As *Passing* shows us, racial differences in reading the evidence of skin are hardly neutral, and are intimately connected to patterns of power and dominance that are unequally portioned out both between and within racial groups. Larsen makes it painfully clear that "the violence done to ... oppressed groups results from the law's refusal to acknowledge the negotiated quality of identity" (Harris, 1993: 1766). And, the novel indicates, the very inequity between these systems of reading means that the John Bellews of the world need not even be aware of what they are not seeing, and simply understand that it is not there.

However, as occurs at the end of the novel, that protective membrane of ignorance is occasionally rent by the brief but traumatic vision of the possibilities color affords to passers. The first rip in the fabric of John Bellew's racial arrogance is made by his running into Irene on the street. She is out shopping with Felise Freeland, her dark-skinned friend. The shock of seeing Irene in the company of a visibly black person prompts Bellew's recognition that Clare, as Irene's childhood friend, is not all he assumed, since "if [Irene and by extension Clare] associates with blacks, she becomes black, where the sign of blackness is contracted, as it were, through proximity, where race itself is figured as a contagion transmissable through proximity" (Butler, 1993b: 171). It is a short step to Bellew's final statement of his racial/racist truth: "So you're a nigger, a damned dirty nigger!" (*P* 238).

In *Passing*, then, it seems that Bellew's analysis of the situation wins out. He retains the power of interpellation, calling out to Clare after she falls/jumps/is pushed from the window, "Nig! My God! Nig!" reinstantiating the nickname that has served both to dramatize and deny the intricacies of racial identification among which Clare has remained in motion. But he cannot return to the ignorance he did not even know he had – his own daughter is, by his logic of all-or-nothing blackness, "a damned dirty nigger" as well. As the ending of the novel tells us, "everything was dark" (*P* 242).[13]

While the ending of *Passing* is dramatic, it draws on a fascination with passing that pervaded both the fiction and the newspapers of the 1920s. The story of the passing figure who marries a white person and is revealed by whites to be "really" black was a popular one during this period. A cursory glance through the black and white press of the 1920s reveals a wealth of stories from around the country that feature young women and men who unknowingly married partners of African descent.[14] More importantly for our purposes, many of these cases raise similar issues of visibility, class, motion, and group-defined reading practices that are so decisive in Larsen's novel.

The highest-profile case of passing in the 1920s was one that even earned a mention in *Passing*. The so-called "Rhinelander case," an attempt to annul the marriage between Leonard Kip Rhinelander and Alice Beatrice Jones,[15] was splashed on the front pages of newspapers all over the United States, and even internationally, for more than two years.[16] Even the staid *New York Times* put the Rhinelander case on the front page throughout the annulment trial, and racked up eighty-eight stories on the issue from 1924 to 1925 (Madigan, 1990: 525).

The facts of the case are hardly shocking to current readers, but they caused an enormous stir in New York in the mid-1920s, not least because one of the protagonists was from a wealthy and powerful old Dutch New York family. Briefly, Leonard Kip Rhinelander, heir to a substantial fortune and influential family name, met Alice Jones in 1921 when his car broke down in New Rochelle. Jones was working class: her father worked as a chauffeur and cab-driver and she had been employed as a chambermaid. After a passionate courtship, punctuated by an ongoing correspondence and culminating in trysts at the Marie Antoinette Hotel in New York City, the 22-year-old Rhinelander waited until he inherited much of his fortune (over $400,000 in 1920s currency, according to some sources), and married Jones in October 1924.[17] Within weeks of the marriage, however, Rhinelander had returned to his parents and was suing for annulment on the grounds of fraud. Rhinelander alleged that Jones had deceived him as to her racial heritage, that she was really black, and he would never have married her had he known. The case went to jury trial the following year, and lasted about two months. The jury found for Jones, leaving her open to sue for divorce and a substantial financial settlement.

This sketch of the events cannot communicate the intensity with which this case was watched by the black and, more obsessively, the white public. The mainstream newspapers were full of the case, far more so than the black press, which reported on it sparingly. As well as articles, the case spawned editorials, satirical cartoons, mentions in Broadway revues and the Yiddish theater,[18] and even found its way into a major novel of the New Negro Renaissance, *Passing*.[19]

Larsen's mention of the Rhinelander case is brief. Irene is indulging her paranoia that Brian and Clare are having an affair, and wondering "[w]hat if Bellew should divorce Clare? Could he? There was the Rhinelander case. But in

From *New York World*, November 25, 1925.

France, in Paris, such things were very easy. If he divorced her — If Clare were free —" (*P* 228). For Irene, the Rhinelander case represents both the precedent of passing and the difficulty Bellew might have in ridding himself of Clare, as Rhinelander had experienced in his failed annulment from Jones.

A closer examination of the case, however, shows that the links between Larsen's novel and the Rhinelander case are much closer than such a cursory mention would suggest. The patterns of reading skin that I have traced so far are at the center of the case, particularly in terms of the differing expectations of race and color that separate black and white spectators. Indeed, the questions of power and perception are even starker in the Rhinelander case, explicitly mediated by the judicial system, filtered through significant differences in class status as well as racial difference. In newspaper reports on the case, readers can see the struggle between competing discourses of race, class, and color that were at the heart of the trial, and the ways in which those discourses collided with and informed each other. While I do not mean to suggest that white supremacy was ever in danger throughout the case, the Rhinelander trial does reveal that dominant discourses were not homogeneous, and in fact different streams of white supremacist rhetoric occasionally came into conflict with each other, curiously mirroring African American recognition of the multiplicity of racial meaning and the fluidity of color.

There are several moments of friction within the lengthy story of the Rhinelander case, which was reported on extensively in the mainstream press from within a month of the marriage for a year and a half into the conclusion of the trial itself, and beyond, into the Rhinelanders' divorce and Leonard Rhinelander's premature death at age 34. These occur at the initial discovery of the marriage by the press in November 1924, and reports of its immediate fall-out, the detailed descriptions of the adversaries and their witnesses, the testimony and cross-examination of Rhinelander and Jones (as well as the revelation of their love letters to each other), and, finally, the jury's decision and press analysis of that verdict, along with substantial interviews with several jurors analyzing the outcome. At each of these moments, the white press attempts to unravel the interwoven meanings of race, color, and class; simultaneously, marginal voices extrude from the mainstream narrative, suggesting other ways of reading color and race that are remarkably close to those intimated in *Passing*. The all-white, all-male jury's final verdict, exonerating Jones of fraud, and the ways in which jurors defended their decision, are particularly worthy of analysis in the way jurors articulated a commonplace racism with a more sophisticated reading of skin clearly picked up from the experience of the trial.

In the Rhinelander case we see the struggle between the genealogical definitions of racial identity (also filtered through social class) and the understanding of race as inflected by skin color, and color less empirical than interpretive. Throughout their discussion of the case, mainstream newspapers [20] focused on Leonard Kip Rhinelander's class and family background. His mother, long dead at the time of the trial, was "Adeline Kip, another of the New York families that go back to the days when the Dutch called this city New Amsterdam," and his father was "prominent in many clubs, and is a member of several historical societies, membership in which is confined to the descendants of those who settled America" ("Society Youth Weds Cabman's Daughter").[21]

The definition of racial identity by association that we see in *Passing* was in play at the beginning of the reporting on the Rhinelander case. While Alice Jones was initially identified only by class affiliation – the *Times* described her as the "daughter of a Pelham taxicab driver and odd-job man" ("Society Youth") – her racial identity was called into question by her affiliation with black people. Rhinelander's attorney Isaac Mills argued in his opening statement that "we will introduce photographs that show [Alice's sister] Grace consorted with Negroes, and we introduce proof that Alice kept company with a Negro before she met Rhinelander" ("Rhinelander Annulment Suit"). The *New York Times* brought the affiliation in its earlier coverage of the case, just after the marriage was announced. A detective hired by Philip Rhinelander, Leonard's father, found that Grace Jones "is the wife of a butler employed in Pelham ... [by] Mrs. Joseph Arthur, whose housekeeper said yesterday that the butler was a Negro" ("Society Youth").

The fact that a woman, whatever her class status, might be related to someone who would marry or even keep company with "a Negro" is presumed, however implicitly, to constitute some kind of evidence about Alice Jones' racial identity, the inverse of John Bellew's hysterical claim that there are "no niggers in my family. Never have been and never will be" (*P* 171). The presence of "niggers in [the] family" disarticulates color and race. Just as Clare can get "as black as you please ... since I know you're no nigger," Alice Jones' complexion is not even mentioned as an indicator of her race; having a black ex-boyfriend and a Negro brother-in-law is enough (*P* 171).

It was a short step from the discovery of a black brother-in-law to the claim that Jones herself was a Negro. Until and even beyond Jones' acknowledgment that her father was West Indian of part-African descent, much was made of official documents from employment records to immigration certificates to marriage licenses, recording members of the Jones family's racial identity in a variety of terms: "white," "mulatto," "colored," "Negro," depending on the context or circumstance. At these moments we get a glimpse of the unwieldiness of the taxonomy of color and its imbrication with race in dominant U.S. discourse. The terms "white," "Negro" and "colored" execute a particularly awkward dance with each other, articulating as they do the discursive and etymological overlaps between race and skin.

Several examples stand out. The first emerged as part of the investigation financed by Rhinelander's father Philip and reported by the *New York Times* (the early *Times* reports are firmly in the Rhinelander family's camp). Jones had been working in a laundry in New Rochelle during the Great War with

a number of Italians of swarthy complexion [who] were employed at the laundry ... and the [employment agency] inspector asked them whether they were "white" or "black" ... [The inspector then went on to mark

Jones down as "mulatto"]. Miss Jones asked [a co-worker] what "mulatto" meant. "When I told her it meant that she was colored ... Alice began to sob and warmly denied that it was true."

While it is hard to believe that a teenager growing up in suburban New York in the second decade of the twentieth century would not know what "mulatto" meant, this story reveals a series of discursive instabilities. Jones aligns herself with the Italians (whether Italian nationals or Italian Americans the story does not make clear) in her exteriority to the U.S. codes of racialization and ambiguous shading. The dark skin of the Italians complicates what is "white" and "black" to such an extent that the report itself must put the terms in quotation marks. Not only is the inspector (an oddly Dickensian *cum* Foucauldian figure) unclear as to whether the Italians are black or white, they do not seem to have an answer to the question. Such a lack of taxonomic confidence can only reflect upon the inspector's decision to inscribe Alice Jones as "mulatto."

Moreover, this story gestures towards the changes in racial labeling that Walter Benn Michaels argues was characteristic of the 1920s: the rise of the nomenclature of the "Nordic" in sharp contradistinction to other kinds of people of European descent, particularly Southern and Eastern Europeans.[22] The terminology of "white," "colored," "Negro," and the like is also explicitly identified as nationally specific to the United States by Alice Jones' sister Grace, who claimed that although their father George had been marked as "colored" in his immigration papers, Jones *père* "isn't colored but is of West Indian descent" ("Rhinelander Bride's Family Speaks").[23] Similarly, Jones himself located his identity through geography: "my mother ... was a Caucasian of pure English descent. The only information I have about my father is that he was a native of one of the British colonies" – a racially ambiguous statement, given the deployment of "native" in 1920s U.S. discourse to mean American-born white Protestant ("Rhinelander Bride Fights for Alimony").[24]

Despite the claims by Rhinelander's lawyers, ranging from implications to asseverations that any American would recognize any of the African-descent Jones family as Negro, Grace Jones (although described by several newspapers as darker than her sister Alice and hence "obviously" or "clearly" black) was labeled "white" on her marriage certificate. Isaac Mills, one of Rhinelander's attorneys, asked her "how it was that her marriage license gave her color as white, and she said that the clerk merely looked at her and 'put me down as white'" ("Says Rhinelander Knew of Girl's Race"). The ingenuousness of this statement belies its power to destabilize Mills' rhetoric of epidermal obviousness. If an agent of the state charged, in part, to prevent illicit unions

– as cross-racial marriages were defined in New York in the 1920s, by custom
if not by law[25] – constructed a different racial identity for Grace Jones from the
one Mills asserted was "obvious" to any viewer, then the "obvious" was
clearly less self-evident than it might pretend to be.

At the beginning of the publicity, Alice Jones seemed unsure of what tack to
take. Initially, she denied, in her words, having "colored blood." Yet the terms
in which she couched this denial were not necessarily racially specific. Her
evidence for whiteness was as much linked to class as to anything else: "We
have always been quiet people. . . . [W]e own four houses. . . . Father is a retired
real estate man. . . . We've been a decent family" ("Rhinelander's Wife Denies
She Is Negro"). Her racial sense of self was subordinated to her claim to
"decent" class identity; one might say she was resisting the status of a
Gertrude Martin and trying to take on the rank of an Irene Redfield.[26]

By early December 1924, Alice Jones was no longer denying an identity as
"colored," but still insisted that there was no deceit ("Rhinelander's Bride
Replies to His Suit With Complete Denial of Deceit Charge"). However,
despite the fact that the issue in the case was fraud – whether Jones attempted
or succeeded in convincing Rhinelander that she was white – the questioning,
testimony, and newspaper reports maintained their focus on color and what it
might mean. Rhinelander's lawyers took an explicitly genealogical tack in their
complaint: that "the former Miss Alice Jones . . . has negro blood in her veins,"
and that she fraudulently represented herself to Rhinelander as white
("Rhinelander Bride Fights for Alimony"). Rhinelander's lawyers, not
coincidentally hired by his father, were so certain that their discourse was
hegemonic that they requested a jury trial, in the implicit belief that, as the
reporter from the New York *World* put it, "a jury of twelve white men would
not compel Rhinelander to maintain the responsibilities of husband to the
daughter of a mulatto taxi driver" ("Betting Is 5 to 1").

But that is not how the case turned out. Instead, much of the testimony
hinged on what Rhinelander could or could not see, whether racial identity was
visible or invisible. On the one hand, the complaint that Rhinelander's lawyers
entered explicitly used the language of blood to signify an essential racial
difference between black and white: "the defendant represented to and told the
plaintiff that she was white and not colored, and had no colored blood, which
representations the plaintiff believed to be true" ("Bride's Color Starts Suit").
Nonetheless, they rhetorically split the difference between race as genealogy
and as appearance, asking the jury to consider "Is the defendant colored or of
colored blood?" ("Calls Rhinelander Dupe"). What initially reads as a
redundancy – wouldn't being "colored" mean she was "of colored blood"?
Wouldn't having "colored blood" make her "colored"? – is a way for the
plaintiffs to cover both taxonomies at once. Taking advantage of the plaintiff's

need to speak two different rhetorics at the same time, the defense pursued a much more narrow line of questioning. What could Rhinelander, or any of the jury, *see* in Alice Jones' face or her father's that would unambiguously indicate blackness, Jones' lawyers asked.

All the mainstream press reports seem to be peering hard at Jones, her father, and her other defenders, as well as at Rhinelander, although to a much lesser extent. In fact, Rhinelander's face was often described, particularly in the New York *World*, as "a mask" and "colorless." Demanding that a jury look at Alice Jones' face for evidence, Rhinelander himself presented "a complete mask, hiding all emotions" ("Rhinelander an Alert Witness"). No longer trusting his vision, Rhinelander "religiously averted his eyes from his wife" throughout the trial, and refused the gaze of others, making of his face "an impenetrable mask" ("Rest from Ordeal for Rhinelanders").

Alice Jones Rhinelander's appearance is described again and again in newspaper reports. In order to bolster his argument for fraud, Isaac Mills asserted in his opening argument that the jury could "see by looking at her [that] the trace of Negro blood in Mrs. Rhinelander is almost imperceptible" ("Rhinelander Annulment Suit"). Jones was represented, however, in a wide variety of ways. All the newspapers carried large, usually front-page photographs of her. But not all these photographs looked alike. Particularly before the beginning of the court case, and before Jones had "admitted" her racial background, she appears lighter-skinned in newspaper pictures. Some of the early photographs even seem touched up, softening her features and lightening her complexion. [27]

Jones' appearance in photographs also depended upon where the sympathies of the publication in which the photograph was printed lay. The sensationalist *New York Evening Journal*, which characterized Isaac Mills' opening argument as "a sketch — 'in sepia'" and represented Alice Jones as a temptress along the lines of Salome, printed a large photograph of a noticeably dark Jones (Rex, 1925: 1). A *Daily News* editorial that saw the case not as "a subject for ribald jests or sub rosa comment," but instead as a "great drama upon the most tremendous central theme of which we have knowledge," illustrated the text with head shots of both Jones and Rhinelander that were almost identical in shading and tone: in fact, Jones' skin seems lighter than Rhinelander's ("Greek Tragedy — Not Bedroom Farce").

By printing large photographs of her, the press implicitly encouraged its readers to scrutinize Jones' face for clues, to make the pictures speak for themselves. But the photographs do not tell a single story. The oddest experience in analyzing this case is the extent to which the reader finds herself complicit in the racist economies of skin and blood, looking at Alice Jones' face, trying to determine whether she could pass convincingly. The tacit editorial

Alice Jones Rhinelander. From *New York American*, 1925.

content blended into the process of photograph production, shading, even juxtaposition (in one photograph she looks lighter than Rhinelander, in another darker), means that our eyes cannot be trusted.

Moreover, when we look at Alice Jones in a photograph, we cannot appreciate the extent to which her appearance changed over time in aschematic ways. The New York *World* described Jones after one of her lawyers, Lee Parsons Davis, announced that "she has colored blood in her veins": "the lines from her high cheekbones to the corners of her mouth softened. Her face, as a result, did not appear so long and, relieved of a large part of the strained look, her features seemed much more attractive" ("Mrs. Rhinelander Admits Her Color"). In this passage Jones becomes more humanized, more feminine, more attractive than before: her face rounds and softens, her cheekbones are de-emphasized. As she acknowledges her racial background Jones looks more *white*, her features rearrange to appear more like an idealized white female face that is soft, round, relaxed. Here the link between white supremacist discourses of racial identity and the passer's rhetoric of proliferating meaning is severed, even reversed, to the extent that "colored blood" is the *cause* of more "Caucasian" features.

This shifting in appearance, and the meanings of appearance, becomes especially clear in Lee Parsons Davis' cross-examination of Rhinelander. Examined by his own attorney, Rhinelander testified that Jones claimed to be "of Spanish extraction" (just as Irene Redfield is occasionally taken for/passes for Spanish) and denied being "colored."[28] Rather than depending upon Rhinelander's account of what Jones told him, or on the terms of racial identification that are instantiated by an appeal to either blood or association, Davis focuses on what Rhinelander *saw*.[29] However, this strategy betrays many of the subtleties of passing and color coding that Alice Jones must have had to master in order to move through the world. While rejecting an argument grounded in racial essentialism, Davis substitutes a color essentialism in which the "visible economy of race" is transacted in the hard currency of black and white (Wiegman, 1995: 21), a system of exchange that masquerades as a self-evident "natural reading of skin" (*ibid.*: 10).

In his opening argument, Mills claimed that Rhinelander "became so utterly infatuated he reached a condition where he didn't know black from white." Jones' lawyers countered with ridicule, sarcastically mimicking and discrediting Rhinelander's claim to ignorance: "Had no suspicion there was colored blood in the family! He must have been blind!" ("Rhinelander's Wife Admits Negro Blood"). Throughout his cross-examination of Rhinelander, Davis returned again and again to questions of visibility, and "[brought] up color at every opportunity, for his contention is that Rhinelander could not have helped knowing that the Jones children and Mr. Jones were negroes" ("Rhinelander Trial Suddenly Halted"). He "made member after member of the Jones family stand up so that their dark color might be seen, and demanded how it could be possible that Rhinelander did not suspect that his wife had colored blood" ("Rhinelander Says He Pursued Girl"). According to a headline in the New York *World*, Rhinelander had the "opportunity to see color" ("Mrs. Rhinelander Admits Her Color").

Davis forced Rhinelander to stare at Jones and members of her family and define their color. Interestingly, unlike the various shades of white, brown, yellow, and black that Larsen lists Irene seeing at the Negro Welfare League dance, the only terms of definition which Davis introduced and Rhinelander used were "dark" and "light" — a repolarization of the racial divide that Alice Jones breached in her marriage. When Davis asked Rhinelander to describe Jones' color, the following interchange ensued:

> "Dark," he replied.
> Q. [Davis] How dark? A. [Rhinelander] Fairly dark.
> Q. Very pronounced, is it not? A. It isn't any darker than the arms of
>   women I've seen in Havana.
>   ("Save Me from the Gutter")

As Rhinelander resorted to the nonspecific racial discourse of "looking Spanish," Davis focused on the *un*ambiguousness of skin. A large part of Davis' strategy was to force Rhinelander to admit that much of his complaint was false, that he was not "deceived as to her color" since her color and that of her family was so obvious. "Does your wife look the same now as when you met her?" Davis asked. "No inquiry arose in your mind as to her color?" ("Rhinelander Says He Pursued Girl").

The yardstick of color in Davis' cross-examination was George Jones. Photographs show him to be dark-skinned, and newspapers portrayed him as "an unmistakable negro" ("Rhinelander Trial Suddenly Halted"), although his features were, as Mills pointed out to the jury, "strictly Caucasian, point[ing] out the aquiline nose, small nostrils, narrow, long face, and high cheekbones" ("Rhinelander Plea").

Q. Did you see the color of her father, Mr. Jones? A. Yes.
Q. How does the color of your wife compare with that? A. About the same.
    Mr. Jones is decidedly dark. Rhinelander said he was not colorblind but that his wife's color and her father's had not created the slightest suspicion that she might have colored blood.

                                        ("Save Me from the Gutter")

Leonard Rhinelander testified that he never suspected George Jones might be racially as opposed to simply epidermically "colored," insisting that he had believed Jones' explanation for his dark skin, that he was "an Englishman suffering from jaundice" ("Rhinelander Near Collapse"). When asked whether Jones was "the same color as now when you met him in his own home," Rhinelander replied, "He looks darker now" Q. [Davis] "What did you think he was when you first saw him?" A. "I didn't know what he was" ("Trial to Go On"). Davis' questioning approached the absurd; he asked whether lights were on in the house when Rhinelander and George Jones first met, and whether Rhinelander was "surprised by his color" ("Rhinelander Shifted").

On the one hand, Rhinelander seems to be grasping at straws, offering weak denials in the face of the obvious. Yet he sounds strangely like John Bellew: someone who sees and does not see the racial meanings of skin right in front of him. Rhinelander's insistence that Alice Jones' and even George Jones' dark skin did *not* speak race to him has an odd consonance with Bellew's blustering claim that Clare "can get as black as you please as far as I'm concerned, since I know you're no nigger" (P 171).

In all this, Lee Parsons Davis is an ambiguous figure. He certainly takes the charge of constructing a zealous defense seriously. However, he was perfectly willing to practice a defence of reductiveness in terms of racial logic, even to the point of humiliating his clients. The most surreal moment of the trial was initiated by Davis to prove that Jones' skin was unambiguously "colored":

> Mr. Davis dramatically called on Justice Morschauser [the presiding judge] to clear the courtroom of all men in it not having business there so that he might have Mrs. Rhinelander partially disrobe and show the jury how dark her skin was. . . . [S]he bared her body to the waist.
>
> ("Rhinelander's Wife Cries Under Ordeal")

This "color test" was not part of Jones' testimony ("Rhinelander Completes Case"); it was an illustration of Rhinelander's claim that "his wife's skin was now the same color as it was when before their marriage they lived in the Hotel Marie Antoinette" (" 'Threat' Defied by Rhinelander"). Since powder and make-up could lighten her face, and the sun could darken her arms, the only way to get an "accurate" view of her skin, the defense argued, would be to look at her torso.

The image of an all-male white jury scrutinizing Alice Jones Rhinelander's body for evidence of its racial pedigree is uncomfortably close to the iconography of the slave auction block. This parallel both intensifies Jones' vulnerability as a black woman and "ungenders" her. As Hortense J. Spillers has powerfully argued, the black female body during and beyond slavery was not seen as "body" but rather as " 'flesh,' that zero degree of social conceptualization that does not escape concealment under the brush of discourse, or the reflexes of iconography" (Spillers, 1994: 457). For Spillers, enslavement transformed a culturally specific, gendered African body into undifferentiated, laboring flesh marked not by gender but by the whip or the bill of sale: "These undecipherable markings on the captive body render a kind of hieroglyphics of the flesh whose severe disjunctures come to be hidden to the cultural seeing by skin color" (*ibid.*: 458).

In many ways, Alice Jones becomes flesh rather than body. Like the slaves who were used as canvases for medical experiments, her body is subjected to "a total objectification," transformed into a "living laboratory" (*ibid.*: 459). In proposing that Jones strip for the male jury, "we lose any hint or suggestion of a dimension of ethics, of relatedness between human personality and its anatomical features, between one human personality and another, between human personality and cultural institutions" (*ibid.*). This evacuation of ethics — an absence of the sense that humanity endows every person with a modicum of integrity and selfhood — is part of Davis' *modus operandi* in dealing with his client (a shocking breach of legal professional ethics as well).

Nonetheless, this is not the whole story. While Jones' status as black woman reduces her to an expanse of skin to be examined and evaluated, the very lightness of that skin and the class privilege that lightness has brought with it protect her as a "lady" and shape the way in which the examination is framed. First of all, the fact that Davis insisted the Judge "clear the courtroom of all men in it not having business there," and that Morchauser complied, suggests that both men assumed that Jones had some right to privacy and modesty – both prerogatives of bourgeois women – however abbreviated. Moreover, the press represented Jones as distraught and humiliated by this process, weeping both during and after she was ordered to undress ("Rhinelander's Wife Cries Under Ordeal"). The very use of the word "ordeal" implies that being forced to strip to the waist was exceptionally arduous, something that a woman like Jones would not usually be expected to do and would suffer greatly from. Davis and Morchauser's treatment of Jones and the representation of that treatment by the press reveal the overlapping and often contradictory discourses at work in this case, and the powerful effect which the destabilization of codes of skin color and race had on both actors in and viewers of the action.

The ironies of this case are many and painful. On the one hand, Alice Jones Rhinelander seemed to be well aware of the codes of passing that interwove class mobility, the adoption of an ambiguous "Spanish" racial identity, and the delicate balance of the private and the public. Her vehement denial of her racial background may seem in contrast to her openness with Rhinelander about her black family members. But the line between private and public is crucial here. Indeed, privacy was invoked several times during the trial.

The *New York World* editorialized that the case should never have come to open court but should have been "handled privately by men of understanding and of honor" ("The Rhinelander Case"). But privacy is a deeply conflicted concept, tied particularly to a racially specific sense of ownership of self that leans heavily on white privilege. Privacy is in part being left alone to associate with "one's own kind," that is, to practice racial exclusion; passing itself "can be seen as a paradigmatic invasion of privacy" – an infiltration of the territory of "men of understanding and honor" (Robinson, 1996: 246). The passer moves unnoticed into private spheres that would otherwise be closed to her, but seriously compromises her own sense of personal and cultural boundaries.

The need to present an acceptable public image in a racist world can fundamentally warp a sense of self. As Lauren Berlant points out, "the whiteness of blackness ... requires the light-skinned African-American woman to produce some way to ameliorate the violation, the pain, and the ongoing crisis of living fully within two juridically defined, racially polarized bodies" (1991: 111). Alice Jones' amelioration required a decisive split between inside and outside worlds, but the series of identities she must assume "ensure social survival but result in psychological suicide" (Wall, 1995: 89). Jones' frequent dissolution into tears throughout the trial is a bodily sign of the crisis into which the annulment case threw her.[30]

Moreover, unlike the characters in *Passing*, who can use the conflicting codes of race and color to their (occasional) advantage, Alice Jones Rhinelander was turned into an object, a spectacle. Where Clare Kendry managed to remain always in motion, even at the moment of her death, Alice Jones was fixed by a series of white men: her own attorney, the jury, the mainstream press. The white male gaze at the black female body was literalized both in Rhinelander's testimony and the forced stripping which Jones had to perform in front of the jury. Yet, in the final analysis, even the jury was not sure what it was looking for, what it was looking at. The trial went through the motions of racial degradation and sexual exploitation, transforming Alice Jones into a "sepia" temptress, a racial and class interloper, a woman whose identity could be revealed by the exposure of her flesh. But those discourses were interrupted by doubt that the "visible economy of race" really depended upon an ontological and epistemological gold standard. When the jurors looked at Alice Jones, what did they see?

On the one hand, they were clear that she was "really" "colored," but then had trouble defining what that meant. They heatedly insisted that although Isaac Mills' closing argument was a "frank appeal against miscegenation" – "there is not a father among you," he insisted to the jury, "who would not rather see his son in a casket than wedded to this mulatto woman" ("Lays Son's Plight") – "[r]ace prejudice didn't enter into the case at all" ("Rhinelander Loses"). The logic they used was oddly paradoxical, though: the jury decided that "Rhinelander had not only not been deceived by his wife as to her color, but that he would have married her even if he had known she was colored" ("Rhinelander Loses"). This formulation seems internally contradictory: if he was not deceived, how can we speculate about what he would have done "if he had known"? Being undeceived, how could he not have known? It seems that the jury is affirming the success of Jones' pass, but in the absence of actual passing. In fact, this decision makes more sense if reformulated with Jones at the center: she didn't pass to Rhinelander, but she could have if she had not wanted him to know her background; she didn't have to because he didn't care.

In the jury's decision, passing is tacitly acknowledged for what it is: an act of necessity that depends upon striated layers of trust and deception. Nonetheless, the all-white jury did not quite recognize the meaning of its decision. Instead, jury members dodged questions of race and color and couched their decision in the normalizing discourse of heterosexuality and the objectifying language of visibility: "We decided it merely as a case between a man and a woman, and in reaching our verdict considered Rhinelander as a normal man with a normal sense of perception" ("Rhinelander Loses"). This raises the question of what constitutes a "normal" sense of perception – is it normal to "notice" racial difference and make decisions according to a strict racial binary? Or is it normal to assume that everyone is white unless explicitly labeled otherwise? What if those labels conflict, as they did for the Jones family?[31]

In interviews with jurors after the decision, what becomes clear is the taxonomic chaos that this case generated.[32] Their verdict was in part based on the analysis that "Mrs. Rhinelander is not a Negro but a 'colored woman and only partly Negro.' All the discussion centered about this definition of the word 'colored'" ("Jurors Say Facts Beat Kip"). Even as they lined up to condemn miscegenation and avow that "if we had voted according to our hearts it would have been a different story," the jurors did not follow juridical understandings of racial identity, most often defined by the "one-drop" rule. Indeed, when one juror held out against finding for Jones, the rest of the jury convinced him with a direct reversal of the one-drop system:

> when another juror asked him if he would call a quart of clear water "whiskey" after a small glass of whiskey had been poured in and altered the color of the water, [juror Max] Mendel admitted he would not call such a dilution "whiskey."
>
> ("Jurors Say Facts Beat Kip")

This argument affirms by inversion the logic of passing. Clare Kendry recognizes that her light skin is not the same as a legal right to whiteness; the jurors acknowledge that darker skin is not quite the same as blackness. Except, of course, that by law Alice Jones is *both* "a colored woman" *and* "partly Negro" – these two things reinforce each other rather than canceling each other out.

Reading about this case creates a vertiginous feeling. Certainly, a postmodern reader is hardly surprised by the destabilization of codes of identity, or of the disarticulation between the visible and systems of self-identification. What is so dizzying is that having been destabilized, the discourses of color and race are up for grabs, deployable simultaneously in both racist and (at least putatively) anti-racist schemata. As the Rhinelander case amply illustrates, sometimes the most effective defense of African American people can incorporate, or even foreground, racist methodologies. It is easy to see that white and black people read and represent race through different structures; that is a lesson which *Passing* teaches with chilling efficiency. But even when they are speaking the same words, those words combine quite differently: they are spoken in different accents, to a markedly different effect.

The most poignant part of this story is that although Alice Jones won her case (and went on to settle for a significant chunk of money), she was unable to anticipate how flexible and adaptable the structures of white supremacy were. She expected that her case would somehow thwart "[a]ll the Rhinelander millions" ("Rhinelander Sues to Annul Marriage"). In part she was right: she successfully defeated Rhinelander's attempt to convince the courts to say their marriage never happened and that it never would, should, or could have happened. But her victory was deeply pyrrhic. Her lawyer spoke the complex language of racial identification rather as blackface minstrels "spoke" black English: vulgarizing cultural difference for the benefit of a white audience, working within a framework that only white people would define as "Negro," reaffirming white power in the guise of representing black reality.

Negro skin, black mask

The Rhinelander case illustrates what happens when dominant and marginal discourses about race and skin are forced to cross-pollinate in a limited space. However, it would be a mistake to imagine that, compared to white beliefs about the interaction of race, color, gender, and class, African American discursive structures are necessarily more liberatory or, in the final analysis, anti-racist. A hierarchy of color that privileges movement, ambiguity, disconnection between the identity of race and the evidence of skin, inevitably privileges light skin over dark. Alice Jones may have been able to pass as "Spanish," but her father was "unmistakably Negro"; like Brian Redfield, George Jones "couldn't exactly 'pass'" (P 168).

Moreover, gender is a crucial term in this mix. While both *Passing* and the Rhinelander case suggest that women may have more class mobility, particularly through the vehicle of racial passing, that mobility is not just one-way, and it is fragile, to say the least (Gertrude Martin is a fine example of this). A woman who cannot remain in motion, who is, or at least feels fixed by color, can be reduced to a piece of evidence for racial identity.[33]

An understanding of how color might be negotiated and manipulated can devolve into a paranoid "color consciousness," in which rather than being a vehicle for motion, color becomes a self-evident sign of identity, rather as we saw in the Rhinelander case. This kind of "color consciousness" is dangerous in the hands of the white ruling class: Lee Parsons Davis used color as a heavy object with which to cudgel a frozen and weeping Alice Jones Rhinelander. But it is most damaging when it is internalized within an African American context and replaces a strategic conceptualization of color as a tool with a static belief in color as status.

"Negro society," wrote Y. Andrew Roberson in his essay "Color Lines Among the Colored People," "is, like Caesar's Gaul, divided into three parts: Yellows, Browns, and Black, in the order named so far as social importance goes. ... There are eight recognized shades [of brown], namely: *high, pleasing, teasing, tantalizing, bronze, chocolate,* and *stovepan*" (1922: 43–4).

While Roberson's taxonomy has a certain satiric flavour (teasing and tantalizing?), the concept of color prejudice within African American communities was not new to the 1920s. Charles W. Chesnutt's "The Wife of His Youth" features an almost exclusively light-skinned social organization nicknamed the "Blue Vein Society." The Blue Veins deny any color prejudice, and "declared that character and culture were the only things considered; and that if most of their members were light-colored, it was because such persons, as a rule, had better opportunities to qualify themselves for membership" (2). The story's climactic moment occurs when it is revealed that Mr Ryder, "one of the most conservative" of the Blue Veins and most typical of the light-skinned bourgeoisie – thrifty, a homeowner, conversant in English poetry – was married in his youth to Liza Jane, a dark-skinned former slave who has spent twenty-five years searching for him. Having heard Ryder's story as a hypothetical tale, the Blue Veins avow that Liza Jane's constancy deserves the reunion of the light-skinned man with "the wife of his youth" (23). Although the narrative ends at the moment of revelation, it suggests the possibility of reconciliation both between Ryder and Liza Jane and between the couple and the Blue Veins.

Other early-twentieth-century African American texts dealt with light-skinned black characters: Pauline Hopkins' *Contending Forces* and Frances E. W. Harper's *Iola Leroy* are notable examples. But they were as, if not more, often about the black character's *own* discovery of his or her racial heritage as they were about self-conscious passing. The dissection of the color line through an anatomy of passing was a particular fascination for the New Negro Renaissance. Given the intense racial consciousness of the white working and ruling class and the success of the Nativist movement, black writers were caught in an awkward bind: both resistant to an essentialist understanding of race and (in part at the encouragement of their white sponsors) inclined towards an analysis of an atavistic black identity that moved to the beat of the tom-tom. [34]

The commodification of blackness went hand in hand with the de-emphasis of race as a term of analysis since, as Ann Douglas has argued, "for the New Negro to allow race to be the dominant category was to permit whites to call the shots" (1995: 343). Passing "highlights an illusory sense of certainty in what is actually an area of social ambiguity and insecurity" (Sollors, 1997: 250): it de-essentializes race to the extent that it can be defanged. No wonder, then, that the passing figure was so popular to Negro Renaissance writers, since he or she fulfilled both black writers' yearning towards a nonracial reality and catered to white readers' scopophilia while remaining always in motion.

What, then, of the person who "[can't] exactly 'pass,'" who *does* register as visually knowable as black? What if she is a woman, unable to propel herself into the middle classes through professional status? Larsen gives us the character of Felise Freeland to suggest that brown-skinned women were not excluded from the high cultural maelstrom of Harlem, as long as they had money (after all, let's not forget the Redfields' "mahogany-colored" servant Zulena). In *The Blacker the Berry*, however, Wallace Thurman offers an acidulous dissection of the ways in which dark skin is constructed as not simply inferior, primitive, or even just unattractive, but as a repository for black animosity about the seeming impermeability of the color line. The dark-skinned woman bears integumental evidence of the racial difference which both "old" and "new" Negroes wanted to downplay and even erase.

First published in 1929, the same year as *Passing*, *The Blacker the Berry* is a caustic indictment of "color consciousness."[35] Its central character, Emma Lou Morgan, is the dark-skinned child of a light-skinned black family in Boise, Idaho. She is the only black student in her high school, a member of a small and highly stratified black community. Emma Lou's dark-skinned father abandoned her and her mother early on, leaving them in the care (or at the mercy) of Emma Lou's maternal grandmother, "the founder and the acknowledged leader of Boise's blue veins," so-called because "all [the blue vein society's] members were fair skinned enough for the blood to be seen pulsing purple through the veins of their wrists" (*BTB* 28). In the "blue vein"'s conception of race, blood (that is, genealogical racial identity) is always contained by and read through the scrim of skin.

The novel begins in Emma Lou's last weeks of high school as she is contemplating her future. While for many students this would represent a coming of age, Emma Lou's growing maturity is constituted through an intensification of color consciousness. As Thurman tells us in the very first paragraph of the novel:

> More acutely than ever before Emma Lou began to feel that her luscious black complexion was somewhat of a liability, and that her marked color variation from other people in her environment was a decided curse. Not that she minded being black, being a Negro necessitated having a colored skin, but she did mind being too black.
>
> (*BTB* 21)

For Emma Lou, color is both causally connected to race and in excess of it. In some ways, color substitutes for race in Emma Lou's understanding of hierarchy: being "too black" is evidence of a different identity from "Negro." It separates her from her community and even her own family. The language of "curse" cannot help but resonate with another curse which a father visits upon his child: the racist myth of the curse Noah set on his son Ham that marked his face black and condemned him and his descendants to be "the slaves of slaves." Certainly, the story of Ham weaves in and out of analyses of racial difference in the nineteenth and twentieth centuries, and makes its appearance in many texts of the 1920s: Clare Kendry refers to herself as "a daughter of the indiscreet Ham," for example (*P* 159).[36] Thurman calls upon this rhetoric of an originary curse to expose the deep divides within Emma Lou and between herself and the rest of her community.

In *The Blacker the Berry*, the difference of race is dislodged by the difference of color. After her high school graduation, Emma Lou execrates her own abilities and invokes the brisk business that cosmetics companies were doing in skin-lightening products for black women: "High school diploma indeed! What she needed was an efficient bleaching agent, a magic cream that would remove this unwelcome black mask from her face and make her more like her fellowmen" (*BTB* 23).

Appropriating and signifying on the discourse evolved by the previous generation of black writers and intellectuals, particularly W. E. B. DuBois and Paul Laurence Dunbar, Thurman reworks the classic statement of black double consciousness: "we wear the mask." In Dunbar's poem of the same name, the mask is invisible to the white viewer. Its purpose is to disguise the pain that white supremacy visits upon the black self, since to reveal that pain would be to evoke more violence. The mask "hides our cheeks and shades our eyes. . . ./ With torn and bleeding hearts we smile,/And mouth with myriad subtleties" (Dunbar, 1965: 167).

Dunbar's mask is caused by racism, not race, and certainly not by color – it is to the genuine African American self as the minstrel's burnt cork is to authentic dark skin (and let us not forget that Dunbar's contemporary, the great black comedian Bert Williams, had to cork his light skin up to make him sufficiently "black" for a white audience). Emma Lou's mask, by contrast, is the surface of her skin itself. Nonetheless, she sees her organic exterior as artificial, or at the very least imposed. Rather than being the accepted sign of Negro identity, black skin becomes the exception, evidence of Emma Lou's separation not just from white people but from her own community and family.

For Emma Lou's grandmother and the rest of the "blue veins," the "motto must be 'Whiter and whiter every generation,' until the grandchildren of the blue veins could easily go over into the white race and become assimilated so that problems of race would plague them no more" (*BTB* 29). This attitude takes the logic of passing to an almost absurd conclusion. In order to pass successfully, the passer must remain in motion, and not allow her- or himself to be fixed and examined. The blue veins imagine passing as working diachronically, with each generation effecting a more convincing pass until, after three generations, the family simply moves out of visual range altogether, disappearing into undifferentiated whiteness. What's interesting here, though, is that it is not whiteness as a *racial* category that is being privileged here, at least not explicitly. Rather, it is whiteness as a *color* – or, perhaps more accurately, since "being a Negro necessitated having a colored skin" (*BTB* 21), an *absence* of color – that the blue veins are angling for.

Emma Lou's Uncle Joe is the lone dissenting voice in this (d)evolution towards the invisibility of whiteness. Unlike the intensely color-conscious blue veins, Uncle Joe is what his contemporaries would have called a "race man" – someone who saw his task as a light-skinned Negro to "uplift the race." He insists that "Negroes were Negroes whether they happened to be yellow, brown, or black, and a conscious effort to eliminate the darker elements would neither prove nor solve anything" (*BTB* 36–7). In her first days at the University of Southern California, Emma Lou emulates his values, seeking out black friends of all colors, and working to prove to her family and herself that "a dark-skin girl could go as far in life as a fair-skin one. ... What did the color of one's skin have to do with one's mentality or native ability? Nothing whatsoever" (*BTB* 53).

Emma Lou is proven to be overly ambitious in her analysis of the politics of skin. In large part her problem is that those politics are too often unpredictable, interleaved with class, region, self-presentation, and opportunism. Having been brought up to imagine herself coming from "a family of the best people," Emma Lou seeks out Negro students who share her class status (*BTB* 42). But she is uniformly rejected by them because of her dark skin. The black sorority will not pledge her because she is not "high brown or half-white" (*BTB* 56). [37]

However, color is not all here. For example, the sorority does pledge Verne Davis, who is dark-brown-skinned. When Emma questions her friend Grace Giles about this, Grace "sneers. 'Verne, a bishop's daughter with plenty of coin and a big Buick. Why shouldn't they ask her?'" (*BTB* 56). At the same time, money is not exactly the key either. Another wealthy dark-skinned student, Hazel, is even more rejected than Emma Lou. Although her father is an oil baron in Texas, Hazel is unacceptable because she is "vulgar" and "country." She is loud, speaks non-standard English, and has not learned the understatement that is the personal style of the leisure classes. Of course, Emma Lou judges Hazel as harshly as do her light-skinned classmates, and in noticeably racial language: "Negroes always bedecked themselves and their belongings in ridiculously unbecoming colors and ornaments. It seemed to be part of their primitive heritage which they did not seem to have sense enough to forget and deny" (*BTB* 44). In the context of Emma Lou's appraisal of Hazel and her "kind," "Negro" is no longer a blanket racial definition but a set of intersections between color, behavior, clothing, and class: all external signs, not genealogical determinants. Her judgment of Hazel distances Emma Lou from Negrohood, even though she, as dark-skinned, is most visibly marked as Negro.

The tragic irony for Thurman is that Emma Lou "had a vague idea that those [black] people on campus who practically ignored her were the only people with whom she should associate" (*BTB* 59). She has been raised in a family that does not see its racial identity as Negro but as always already passing or preparing its younger generations to pass. Emma Lou herself careens between two equally fictive identities: disassociating herself from blackness and hyper-identifying as the most degraded kind of black. She longs to be affirmed as a dark-skinned person even as she wants to affiliate herself with people for whom blackness is rendered contingent (at least within the black community) by either skin color or socioeconomic class. Most of all, Emma Lou wants to disappear.

Since she cannot disappear into whiteness, Emma Lou chooses to disappear into Harlem – like hundreds of thousands of real and fictional African Americans – where she imagines she will dissolve in the variegated sea of Negro life. In the Harlem scenes, Thurman effects a layered set of parodies and satires: of gender relations, class conflict, the phenomenon of whites "slumming" at cabarets and rent parties, and of intra-community black debates about the meaning of race, color, and identity. He shows, in particular, how the meanings of skin are manipulated for a variety of reasons, of which genealogical racial identity is just one (and only a minor one, for that matter).

Two scenes in the novel, actually collages of scenes, are particularly notable in Thurman's re-evaluation of how and what skin signifies. The first covers Emma Lou's work as a dresser and personal assistant for a white stage starlet Arline Strange, who plays "a mulatto Carmen in an alleged melodrama of Negro life in Harlem" (*BTB* 104). The featured performers are all white in various shades of blackface, and many of the minor character actors and all the chorus girls are black. Emma Lou is amazed by the play:

> She never tired of watching the dramatic antics on the stage. She wondered if there were any Negroes of the type portrayed by Arline and her fellow performers. Perhaps there were, since there were any number of minor parts played by real Negroes who acted very different from any Negroes she had ever known or seen. It all seemed to her like a mad caricature.
>
> (*BTB* 105)

Arline inhabits a "Negro" world that is in fact constructed by, performed for, and consumed by whites. She goes to cabarets in Harlem like the Cotton Club, reserved for whites only (fulfilling Brian Redfield's prophecy that "Pretty soon the colored people won't be let [into Harlem] at all, or will have to sit in Jim Crowed sections" (*P* 198), and the more racially mixed and hotter Small's Paradise (Ogren, 1989: 74). Most ironically, Arline is amazed that Emma Lou, as a genuine Negro, does not go cabareting, since "I thought all colored people went" (*BTB* 105).[38]

While Arline is "deepening the artificial duskiness of her skin," she entreats Emma Lou not to "let on to my brother you ain't been to Small's before. Act like you know all about it" (*BTB* 105). This scene is ironic to the point of burlesque: a working-class white woman (class in this novel is most often indicated by use of standard or non-standard English) darkens her skin to further her career, while a middle-class black woman tries to lighten her skin to advance hers. The white woman enacts a black identity that could not be further from the blackness which the black woman inhabits but that is more stereotypically black: going to cabarets, speaking in slangy, urban English, spending her work day in a fictionalized Harlem quite different from the Harlem that Emma Lou actually lives in.

The grandest irony is that Arline's character is a "Negro cabaret entertainer," but Arline does not really attempt to imitate black performance style. As Emma Lou observes, "Arline was being herself rather than the character she was supposed to be playing. ... [The white audience's] interest seemed genuine. Arline did have pep and personality, and the alleged Negro background was strident and kaleidoscopic" (*BTB* 106). Arline's audience consumes a Negro-ness that is, in fact, simply Arline's personality blacked up for cosmetic effect. Arline's make-up is *less* a mask than Emma Lou imagines her organic skin to be. The "Negro background" may be no more than an allegation, but the evidence of self that Arline brings to bear suggests that she can substantiate the "charge" of a stereotypical negritude more than Emma Lou, who has never been to a cabaret.

The visit to Small's Paradise, an actual nightclub of the 1920s, brings into even sharper focus the disjuncture not just between actual black experience and the theatrical blackness Arline represents on stage, but in Emma Lou's recognition that the blackness on display at Small's is no less theatrical than the near-minstrelsy of Arline's character. Emma Lou's dark skin is imagined by whites to mean that she has access to the vibrant Harlem underground, since, as Kathy Ogren has argued, black urban culture "was immediately associated with the carnal pleasures of the cabaret" (1989: 5). By contrast, her class position means that she is more a stranger to nightclubs and rent parties than the white cultural tourists she is supposed to be guiding. Watching the floor show at Small's – two singers and dancers, "one light-brown skin and slim, the other chocolate-colored and fat," singing "Muddy Waters ... their bodies undulating and provocative" – Emma Lou is "mesmerized" (*BTB* 108). She "forgot herself," but this forgetting is not into blackness. Instead, she "gaped, giggled and applauded like the rest of the audience. ... Idiot, she berated herself, just because you've had one drink and seen your first cabaret entertainer, must your mind and body feel all aflame?" (*BTB* 109).

In losing her sense of self, Emma Lou's consciousness merges with that of the rest of the audience – the almost all-white audience. This reaction contrasts with Zora Neale Hurston's much remarked-upon description of seeing nightclub performers, which draws heavily on the primitivism that coursed through the New Negro Renaissance. Listening to jazz, Hurston reports:

> I follow those heathen – follow them exultingly. I dance wildly inside myself; I yell within, I whoop; I shake my assegai above my head, I hurl it true to the mark *yeeeow*! I am in the jungle and living the jungle way. ...
> My pulse is throbbing like a war drum
>
> (Hurston, 1979: 154)

Whereas Hurston's experience is atavistic, throwing her back to an ancestral African past full of tom-toms and jungle rhythm, Emma Lou's reverie is identified through the newness and strangeness of the blues singers. She is struck by how *different* they are from her, and, by association, how similar she is to her white companions.

The cabaret scene does not represent a "real" blackness in the way Hurston implies it does, however. Emma Lou is "conscious of a note of artificiality, the same as she felt when she watched Arline and her fellow performers cavorting on the stage in 'Cabaret Gal.' This entire scene seemed staged, they were in a theater, only the proscenium arch had been obliterated" (*BTB* 110). The blues singers at Small's are not just performing their act; they seem to be playing at being "cabaret gals" in this Harlem nightclub as much as Arline does on Broadway, or even to be imitating the appearance of the cabaret performer that white actresses like Arline initially popularized among white audiences. The same holds true for the audience members, who are also playing roles they may even have *learned* from watching shows like "Cabaret Gal" (or, for that matter, reading Negro Renaissance novels like this one, which are full of party, dance, and cabaret scenes): throwing down drinks, handing the performers dollar bills as tips, dancing with Negroes. Arline's brother sees enough of Small's to know that her show is "all wet," that is, not an accurate representation of the cabaret scene. But Emma Lou recognizes, however inchoately, that the cabaret itself is just as much a performance, another mask constructed for white people's vision.

The connections between the commodification of "authentic" blackness and the black community's color consciousness are discussed at length in a set piece in the novel that one might read as an amplification of *Passing*'s conversation between Irene and Hugh Wentworth at the Negro Welfare League dance. Emma Lou's boyfriend Alva asks her to join him in taking a racially mixed group of writers to a rent party. The group is a thinly disguised who's who of the Harlem literary élite: Tony Crews/Langston Hughes, Cora Thurston/Zora Neale Hurston, Truman Walter/Thurman himself, and Ray Jorgensen/Carl Van Vechten.

The writers engage in a heated discussion about "pink niggers," and the origins of color prejudice in black communities. Truman Walter is the straight man in the argument, pointing out that "all the standards are the standards of the white man, and ... almost invariably what the white man does is right and what the black man does is wrong, unless it is precedented by something a white man has done" (*BTB* 144). The closer to white, the more favored by both white and black he maintains, since "the Negro with a quantity of mixed blood in his veins ... finds adaptation to a Nordic environment [rather] than one of pure blood" (*BTB* 144). Thurman does not let this apparently "reasonable" argument stand, however. Crews counters: "you seem to forget ... that because a man is dark, it doesn't necessarily mean that he is not of mixed blood" (*BTB* 145). In other words, while light skin indicates that there *is* at least one white forebear, dark skin does not mean that there is *not* (Emma Lou herself is proof of that). So the evidentiary value of skin is partial to say the least — it can only prove what it already makes clear, that lightness indicates whiteness. But dark skin cannot prove the absence of whiteness, only the presence of African descent, which light skin *also* proves.

Truman/Thurman's analysis of color ends up as an examination of "color prejudice," reversing the terms of the discussion. Truman sees it as a manifestation not of race at all, but of a more generalized human nature linked with cultural relativism:

> "In an environment where there are so many color-prejudiced whites, there are bound to be a number of color-prejudiced blacks. Color prejudice and religion are akin in one respect. Some folks have it and some don't, and the kernel that is responsible for it is present in us all, which is to say, that potentially we are all color-prejudiced as long as we remain in this environment."
>
> (*BTB* 146)

Color itself, then, is not the issue; "color prejudice" is. To the extent that color itself matters, it exists only through the pervasiveness of the color prejudice

that perpetuates itself through impersonal institutions and personal commit-
ment – the things that combined make up "environment" – much as religion
does. Color is not a mask, as Emma Lou feels it to be, nor is it evidence of an
authentic Negro identity, as Arline imagines it might be, or a sign of a
degraded class status. Instead, it is a product of a historically outmoded
(Truman makes the explicit link to slavery), culturally specific set of beliefs.
Color carries no intrinsic meaning outside color prejudice, an insight very
much like that of contemporary theorists that slavery and racism constructed
identities of race.[39] Bluntly put: skin proves nothing but that we expect it to
prove something.

Truman may be theoretically astute, but his theory is outmastered by
practical reality. Emma Lou feels herself continually humiliated by the "color
prejudice" of the black community, to such an extent that she takes every
insult of dark-skinned people as personal. When her boyfriend Alva takes her
to a midnight show at the Lafayette theater, a four-hour marathon of motion
pictures, chorus girls, comedians, and blues singers, a particular comedy sketch
incenses Emma Lou. It is a party scene in which "all the men were dark and . . .
all the women were either very light brown or 'high yaller,'" something
Thurman points out is the rule at every "Negro" entertainment from "Cabaret
Gal" to Small's to the Lafayette (*BTB* 173). In the middle of this elegant party,

> a very Topsy-like girl skated onto the stage to the tune of "Ireland must
> be heaven because my mother came from there." Besides being corked
> until her skin was jet black, the girl had on a wig of kinky hair. Her lips
> were painted red – their thickness exaggerated by the paint. . . . Every
> one concerned was indignant that something like her should crash their
> party. She attempted to attach herself to certain men in the crowd. . . . It
> ended by them agreeing to toss her bodily off the stage to the orchestral
> accompaniment of "Bye, Bye, Blackbird," while the entire party loudly
> proclaimed that "Black Cats must go."
>   Then followed the usual rigamarole carried on weekly at the Lafayette
> concerning the undesirability of black girls.
>
>   (*BTB* 174)

Emma Lou is "burning up with indignation. . . . [S]he even felt that all the
people near by her were looking at her and that their laughs were at her
expense" (*BTB* 175). While Thurman implies that Emma Lou takes the sketch
too personally, one could argue that she is absolutely right. Dark skin speaks
for itself in this visible economy of color. The other audience members need
not be looking at her to be laughing at her expense, since the "undesirability of
black girls" is so self-evident that it erases her even as it makes her

hypervisible. Moreover, darkness is presented as going hand in hand with "Topsy-like" appearance and behavior: the exaggerations of minstrelsy, "country" ways (the little girl later turns up riding a mule), and sexual voraciousness. It is clear that the audience at the Lafayette, most of whom, as Alva points out, are "either dark brown or black," use the Topsy figure to distance from themselves the horrors the dominant culture associates with being a Negro at all (*BTB* 179).[40] The child actress is *artificially* black – her blackness comes from burnt cork, not her own skin – as though to suggest that however dark they might get, Negroes are safe from such extremes.

One might also attempt a more sophisticated reading that connects the Topsy character at the Lafayette with the blues singers at Small's and Arline's role in "Cabaret Gal." The performers at Small's see in their white audience what "Cabaret Gal" also acknowledges: that the same thing lies at the bottom of Arline's barely disguised minstrelsy and the "genuine" cabaret performance. The crucial ingredient is what Eric Lott has called "cross-racial desire" (1993: 5), and it serves, as Lott has argued, "as a principal site of struggle in and over the culture of black people" (*ibid.*: 18). At the same time, by the 1920s minstrelsy had become a self-defined style, disarticulated, almost, from racial identity itself. Susan Gubar has identified the various conventions of minstrel style, what she calls the "anatomy of blackface": burnt cork (which "draws attention to its own artifice" (1997: 79)); the grin/grimace; bulging eyes; twitching limbs or the stiffness of body parts – all of which we see in some combination in all three of these performances.

The Topsy figure may be the return of the repressed for the well-heeled, light-skinned party-goers in the skit at the Lafayette, just as Liza Jane is to Chesnutt's Mr Ryder in "The Wife of His Youth." But she is also a parody of a parody, wrapped up in a critique of the white obsession with blackface and the black bourgeois horror of it. The Topsy figure sings a popular Irish American song typical of the sentimental ballads that softened the hearts of minstrelsy's most avid fans, while implicitly pointing to stereotypical Irish American racism.[41] Gubar argues that the Negro's vogue led to the multiplied performances of "blacks impersonating whites impersonating blacks" (1997: 112); Thurman uses this kind of mirroring both to highlight the "color consciousness" of the black mainstream and to mock it. "Topsy," after all, is a fiction made up by a white woman; she is no closer to Emma Lou than the character Arline plays in "Cabaret Gal" or the shimmying blues singers at Small's.[42] The violence of the black audience's response, then, is more complex: is it a rejection of blackness? Of minstrelsy? Of black bourgeois pretention?

Although Emma Lou sees her dark skin as a "mask," she is unable to abstract her darkness from her sense of self – she cannot recognize the "Topsy-like girl" as a parody rather than an indictment. This is not surprising: even her mother describes her as an "evil, black hussy" (*BTB* 177). Emma Lou's avowedly color-blind light-skinned friend Gwendolyn adverts to color as the reason that Emma Lou chooses to live with the working-class Alva and his son by another woman rather than continuing her relationship with the respectable Benson Brown: "Where is your intelligence and pride? I'm through with you, Emma Lou. There's probably something in this stuff about black people being different and more low than other colored people! You're just a common ordinary nigger!" (*BTB* 208). Both Emma Lou's mother and Gwendolyn automatically connect blackness as a color with the most negative beliefs about Negro people as a race and working people as a class: to be black is to be a hussy, a nigger, common. As we saw in her judgment of Hazel at USC, so does Emma Lou herself.

Emma Lou's problem is that she sees blackness as both inside and outside her sense of self, both abjected and introjected, as evidence for the thing she rejects (rural poor or urban working-class "ignorant" blackness) and the thing she represents, the "evil, black hussy" who has sex outside marriage, gets drunk at rent parties and brings men home (all of which Emma Lou actually does). She sees the blackness of her face as a mask, yet she covers her face with a thick layer of powder and rouge that turns her skin an "ugly purple tinge" (*BTB* 128) – a mask covering a mask.[43] Emma Lou believes she knows what blackness means, and it both must and cannot mean her. If passing for white presumes the protection of unknowability, the indeterminacy of the external sign, dark skin represents for Emma Lou an excess of meaning, of *over*determined signs.

Ultimately, in trying to escape what she believes blackness says about her, Emma Lou makes herself untouchable and almost unrecognizable. She removes herself from her co-workers at the public school at which she teaches, "too shy to make an approach and too suspicious to thaw out immediately when someone approached her" (*BTB* 209). She loses the ability to connect with people, growing "more haughty, more acid, and more distant than ever" (*BTB* 210). She intensifies her already elaborate skin-bleaching routine, "drenching [her face] with a peroxide solution, plastering it in a mudpack, massaging it with a bleaching ointment, and then, as a final touch, using much vanishing cream and powder" (*BTB* 128), and thickening the purpling face powder and rouge to the extent that her co-workers write her an anonymous note asking her to "take a hint and stop plastering your face with so much rouge and powder" (*BTB* 214). In trying to disappear, Emma Lou makes herself more conspicuous; in trying to peel off the mask she creates a new one, grotesque and unnatural.[44]

By the end of the novel Emma Lou has left Alva, although it is not at all clear what she will do. Although she decides that "her motto from now on would be 'find – not seek,'" the narrative does not imply much liberalizing of her own self-hatred, only a vow that "she intended to balance things. Life after all was a give-and-take affair. Why should she give important things and receive nothing in return?" (*BTB* 218–19). Thurman ends the novel in cacophony: Emma Lou returns home to pack her things and finds Alva, near death from cirrhosis, and his male lover raucously drunk. The baby's "cries deafened her, and caused the people in the next room to stir uneasily," but Emma Lou does not interrupt her packing (*BTB* 221).

Emma Lou walks out into a screen as blank as the snow Clare Kendry's body lies on·at the end of *Passing*, as silent as the protective veil of obscurity Alice Jones Rhinelander drew around herself after her divorce from Leonard Kip Rhinelander was finalized. That none of these three women could disappear into an undifferentiated whiteness or an embracing blackness says less about the tones of their skin than the codes of color that shaped both their sense of self and the rules by which they were forced to play out their lives. John Bellew's final diagnosis – "So you're a nigger, a damned dirty nigger!" (*P* 238) – applies to all three of them equally, fixes them in space and time, constructs them as objects to be looked at and for judgment to be passed upon. While they could, with varying degrees of success, manipulate the language of color, none of them could beat it either on its own terms or theirs.

4

"Liberty's life stream"

Blood, race, and citizenship in World War II

Blood's Magic for All: from tribe to type

In 1948, the Public Affairs Committee, a left-leaning not-for-profit organization that put out educational pamphlets,[1] published a booklet written by Alton
L. Blakeslee entitled *Blood's Magic for All*.[2] Almost breathless with postwar
optimism, Blakeslee declared that "the blood flowing in your veins is today's
most amazing medicine" (1948: 1). The pamphlet discussed the history of
hematology and went on to list the multiple uses to which blood had been put
during World War II, particularly the use of plasma in reviving wounded
soldiers and reversing the symptoms of shock.

Blakeslee made short work of the racial mythology of blood: under the
subheading "There's no racial difference" he announced that "there is not a
whit of difference in the blood of healthy persons of any racial group or color"
(1948: 9). Instead of representing racial identity, blood was a medical product,
the domain of "blood experts" (*ibid.*), doctors, and scientists. Moreover,
Blakeslee dismissed the articulation of blood as a genealogical or tribal marker.
Blood was a substance that could connect people who were in all other ways
different from each other, conjoined only by humanity in general, and
nationality in particular. Blood and plasma donation created "arteries spanning
the nation ready to meet sickness, accident, disaster, or war" (*ibid.*: 29). The
equivalency between blood and the health of the nation was undergirded by an
illustration on the same page (see illustration): an outline of the continental
United States dotted with blood banks represented by little black boxes
topped with flags. From each box issue the tendrils of arteries and capillaries,
branching across the nation. These arteries also act as highways (a trenchant
image for the late 1940s, since the Interstate Highway System had been
approved by Congress in 1944 and car travel was fast becoming identified

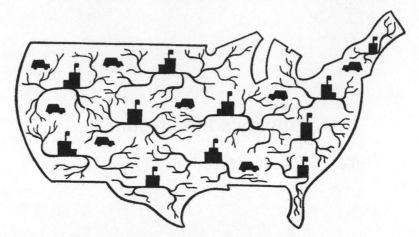

The goal—arteries spanning the nation ready to meet sickness, accident, disaster, or war.

From *Blood's Magic for All*, published by the Public Affairs Committee.

with "being an American"), traversed by silhouetted vans that shuttle blood the length and breadth of the country.

Blakeslee's focus in the pamphlet was to encourage Americans to donate blood, and make "blood's magic" available to all. As we shall see, blood donation had been a major element of the home front war-effort during World War II, and had shaped an array of discourses around blood, American identity, democracy, and citizenship. In the opening maneuvers of the Cold War, Blakeslee sees another blood emergency: "If atom bombs struck even a few American cities, we should need two or three million pints of blood to treat the injured in the first two to three weeks alone" (1948: 25). To encourage donation, Blakeslee reaches for an image that had been constructed and aggressively promoted throughout World War II, an identity for blood that combined national and political identity, hygiene and modernity, deracination and resegregation. Donating blood "admits you to a modern kind of democratic citizenship" (*ibid.*: 31).

How did blood become the signifier for modernity, democracy, and citizenship rather than tribalism, genealogy, and race? In this chapter I will be tracing these changes through a diverse constellation of phenomena: the development of blood typing, transfusion, and storage technologies that culminated in the massive project of the American Red Cross Blood Donor Service in the 1940s; the ongoing segregation of blood donated by African Americans from the mid-1930s to the early 1950s; the dialogue about democracy and citizenship that bounced through U.S. culture, from the intelligentsia to the popular media to black communities to government agencies and beyond, over the course of World War II; the removal of Japanese Americans from the west coast and their internment in "relocation camps" from 1942 until the end of the war; and the ramifications of the shift of focus to citizenship as a defining characteristic of what it meant to "be an American" from the 1940s for African American organizing during that period.

In the United States in the 1940s, something was happening to blood: more than one thing, and on more than one level. What people could and would do with blood was changing both literally and metaphorically. The literal changes are fairly easy to trace: the advances in blood transfusion technology, the development of reconstitutable dried plasma, new analyses of anemia, among other biotechnological work. The metaphorical, cultural changes are a little more difficult to identify, but the popular dissemination of knowledge about the medical purposes to which whole blood and plasma could be put plays a major role.

These scientific advances center around a new capability: that of blood donation, storage and transfusion. Certainly, scientists had been trying to transfuse blood for centuries: the medical textbooks are full of stories, some comparatively gruesome, dealing with primitive attempts at direct transfusion from body to body. William Harvey's publication in 1628 of his treatise on blood circulation launched a series of only occasionally successful experiments in moving blood from one person (or, just as often, animal) to another. Transfusions were usually performed to treat so-called "bad blood" – weakness, sickliness, and so on – and were achieved by transferring the blood of a healthy animal, usually a lamb, by way of glass tubes from donor to recipient (Keynes, 1922: 6–7). Some skeptics feared that transfusees would sprout horns, wool or hooves from lamb's blood, but, on the whole, the procedure was uncontroversial. Except of course for the high percentage of fatalities these procedures caused – something that happened with enough frequency that after "increasing interest and exaggerated enthusiasm" for the procedure in the first half of the nineteenth century, the large number of deaths and near-deaths led to a serious decrease in attempts at transfusion after the 1870s (Kilduffe and DeBakey, 1942: 36). What saved blood transfusion from a place in medical history next to leeches, the water cure, and calomel [3] was Karl Lansteiner's discovery in 1900 of isoagglutinating and isoagglutinable matter in blood, which allowed him and subsequent scientists to organize blood by compatible and incompatible types. [4]

Needless to say, this research cleared up a number of mysteries about blood transfusion, the most pressing of which was why some people were strengthened by transfusions and others died a painful death shortly after them. Lansteiner's work, and the research of other hematologists, explained both why animal blood transfusion was not healthy for humans, and why it did not result in the transfusee sporting horns or developing a pelt. It also struck a blow at blood's symbolic value as the "signifier and signified of race" (Saks, 1988: 41), as the "vital substance that bound families, tribes, and even nations into a biological and communal whole; blood as race; blood as the link that passed on genetic inheritance and connected members of a group to each other" (Love, 1996: 183). Blood *did* come in types, but those types stretched across, and had little or no connection to racial and ethnic boundaries.[5]

Blood as a metaphor for racial identity works only when it cannot be seen, in a world in which blood cannot be scrutinized as such outside the body. As Eva Saks has argued, blood became the ruling metaphor for race in the years after emancipation, a period in which "the value of white skin dropped when black skin ceased to signify slave status" (1988: 47) and, perhaps not coincidentally, the practice of blood transfusion almost completely ceased in the United States. The very *invisibility* of blood made it a potent symbol: race was not what was on the outside, but rather was constituted in the most basic unit of human life, the blood itself. So when white courts and legislatures were establishing the language in which to talk about and prohibit miscegenation, or establish segregation, they abandoned racial categories based on skin and took up a discourse of genealogy, that is, blood. As Saks shows, "by choosing the internal, biological *res* of blood, miscegenation jurisprudence transformed race into an intrinsic, natural, and changeless entity: blood essentialized race" (*ibid.*: 48). The "one-drop" rule summons up the image of an unassimilable blob of blackness that continually circles through the bloodstream, something that can be identified as separate from the millions of other drops even as it contaminates them. It is this one drop, as we see in *Pudd'nhead Wilson*, that outvotes all the others, that, rather than being diluted into nothingness, can become a ruling force in the self.[6]

This way of imagining race – what Hazel Carby has called "the American obsession with 'pure blood'" (1987: 311) – was profoundly undermined by the development of blood transfusion technology. Once blood could be stored outside the body, examined microscopically, typed by elements rather than by racial categories, and transferred not just from one body to another but from body to test-tube and from bottle to body, the conflation of racial and sanguinous purity could not be sustained. The discovery of type O, the "universal donor" type, shredded white supremacist fantasies about the literal entity of "white blood." Genealogy and the discourse of blood could no longer be casually articulated one to the other as part of an ostensibly seamless social formation. As Stuart Hall has argued, "It is not the individual elements of a discourse that have political or ideological connotations, it is the ways those elements are organized together in a new discursive formation" (1986: 55).

Blood had to take on new meanings that corresponded to its new identity: classifiable but racially uncodable.

This issue became pressing in the 1940s as blood took on another meaning, one directly related to the intense need for blood donation on the Pacific and European war fronts. During the 1920s and 1930s scientists found ways to make blood transfusions even more efficient, discovering methods to defibrinate stored blood (that is, to prevent it from clotting outside the body and hence lengthen its shelf life), and reduce contamination in collecting, storing and transfusing serum. They worked out how to separate plasma from blood solids, and how to dry plasma for easy transportation and reconstitution. Ironically, World War II could not have come at a better time as far as blood technology was concerned – an array of information about drawing, classifying, storing, and administering whole blood and plasma was settling into place by 1941 and was indispensable to the Allied war effort.

The central protagonist in this process of redefinition was the American Red Cross, the agency in charge of collecting, storing, delivering, and transfusing blood throughout World War II, first in its "Blood for Britain" campaign from 1940 to 1941, and then as part of the U.S. war effort after the bombing of Pearl Harbor. The Red Cross initiated two interrelated policies that threw into sharp focus the ways in which a deracialized discourse of blood could both undermine and undergird white supremacy. These two policies – promoting blood donation as the highest expression of citizenship and segregating "black" and "white" blood – both directly result from and are in dialogue with the technology that allowed blood to be stored outside the body.

"The heart's blood of the American public": the rhetoric of the American Red Cross Blood Donor Service

The American Red Cross (ARC) came to blood banking fairly late, establishing its first facility in 1941 under the aegis of the "Blood for Britain" program. Developing technology to dry plasma was a crucial part of the research on blood, particularly for Blood for Britain: whole blood was difficult to store and transport for the long transatlantic trip, and often clotted or became contaminated along the way. Moreover, whole blood would either have to be type O, or be matched directly to the recipient's type. Plasma is simply the fluid that supports blood cells: pure plasma, out of which all particles have been centrifuged, does not need to be typed and can move from any donor to any recipient. Dried plasma was easier to transport and preserve, and could be reconstituted with distilled water. Plasma prevented shock, a condition in which severe distress from injury or burns causes the capillaries to lose fluid, at which blood pressure plummets and circulation to the heart and brain effectively shuts down. Infusions of plasma "refill" the capillaries, restoring blood pressure and stabilizing the injured person for transportation and possible surgery.

The experience of World War I had shown that shock was a leading cause of death in combat; plasma became the focus of ARC research and its blood donation program. The ARC had established its Blood Donor Service (BDS) in February 1941 to supply blood and plasma to Britain and other Allied nations, and the Blood for Britain program accelerated work on plasma research, resulting in the development of an efficient method for drying and storing plasma. When Pearl Harbor was bombed on December 7, 1941, a network was in place to recruit blood donors and process blood into plasma, which by 1942 had grown to thirty-five fixed centers in major cities from Buffalo to San Antonio, Boston to Los Angeles, and sixty-three mobile units to service neighboring towns (Robinson, 1946: 28). But the need for plasma magnified the need for donors: a pint of whole blood yielded only a small amount of plasma. In July 1942, donation requirements were 20,000 pints of whole blood per week; by January 1943 the demand had grown to 50,000 pints a week, and the Army and Navy were projecting a need of 70,000 pints a week by the end of that year (*Teamwork from Publicity to Plasma*, 1943: 7). The ARC had to find more donors, and fast.

The ARC Blood Donor Service leadership, and in particular G. Canby Robinson, the Service's director, realized that the key to increasing blood donation was effective public relations. He appointed G. Stewart Brown to co-ordinate publicity nationally, and assigned his own assistant, Charles Coggin, to develop and disseminate publicity campaigns.[7] Two early in-house documents, *Publicity Kit for Chapters Participating in National Defense Blood Plasma Reservoir* (June 1941) and *Teamwork from Publicity to Plasma* (December 1941, revised March 1943) established the focus, method, and message of the ARC's ongoing blood drive.

The first priority of the Blood Donor Service was to flood the popular media, and hence a large portion of the American public, with positive images of blood donation. The *Publicity Kit for Chapters* covered every medium, from newspapers to radio to movies to posters. Enterprising publicity writers crafted whole editorials and "interviews" (already pre-scripted) for newspapers and radio, recommended that chapters approach newspapers about fashioning day-to-day stories about blood centers, and provided sample newspaper releases and "spontaneous" op-ed pieces, with blanks to be filled in for regional specificity. The booklet also gave explicit instructions on talking to radio program directors, how to drum up listeners with advance advertising, and included self-evaluation forms, on which chapter publicity teams could record responses to various approaches and rate the most effective. *Teamwork from Publicity to Plasma* instructed ARC chapters that "it should be the duty of some one in each [donor] center to see that news events or important happenings are given constantly to newspapers and radio stations, and brought to the attention of the public by any dignified means" (p. 15).

The BDS publicity campaign was wildly successful, and media attention on blood donation centers was constant. Donations rose to such an extent that at the program's height, between January and July 1944, weekly donations reached 110,923 pints nationwide (Robinson, 1946: 2). Movie studios and radio stations were eager to broadcast news items about the importance of donating blood, and "the centers averaged at least 30 newspaper stories and 90 radio announcements or programs a month per center, in addition to a tremendous volume of sponsored advertising of all kinds, the wholesale distribution of posters and leaflets, window and theater lobby displays ... and virtually every other type of publicity and promotion" (Robinson, 1946: 38). A 1943 letter from Coggin to local blood center publicity directors suggests the density of media involvement in the blood drive. Coggin lists the radio shows that would feature blood donation in some way between late October and early November of that year:

> Army Hour (half of program), NBC Oct. 24 ... That They Might Live (whole program), NBC, Oct. 30 ... The Johnston Family (plug), Mutual, Nov. 1 ... Sealtest Program (plug), NBC, Nov. 4 ... Stage Door Canteen (skit), CBS, Nov. 5 ... This Is Official (plug), BLUE, Nov. 7 ... We the People (interview with blind pianist, 16-time donor), CBS, Nov. 7 ... Bob Hope (plug), NBC, Nov. 7 or Nov. 9.

The image of blood as the medium for serving the nation while staying close to home was particularly resonant for the popular media of radio and motion pictures, which adopted the Red Cross's rhetoric in both commercial and government-sponsored productions. Studios inserted "frequent references to donating blood in feature motion pictures released by Hollywood" (Robinson, 1946: 43). As Robinson pointed out, blood donation was a "publicity 'natural' — personal, colorful, definite. If people gave blood, men lived; if they didn't, men died" (p. 33).

Movie trailers and short films were the domain of the War Activities Committee of the Motion Picture Industry, which was a professional organization midwifed into existence by the Office of War Information, a government agency that grew out of several attempts in the early 1940s to create a propaganda machine for the war effort (Winkler, 1978: 17). Along with the ARC, the OWI realized the power of the media: by 1942, 90 percent of Americans owned radios, "[a]pproximately eighty million Americans each week attended films, and the sixteen thousand theaters could accommodate eleven million at any given time" (Winkler, 1978: 57). The War Activities Committee, in partnership with major studios, produced a large number of short films, trailers, newsreels, and documentaries on a variety of war-related topics. One such film, now lost, was entitled *Brothers in Blood*, and followed blood donated by a man stateside, through the plasma extraction process, to transportation overseas, finally to its destination in the veins of a GI.

In the *Publicity Kit for Chapters* and *Teamwork from Publicity to Plasma*, the ARC laid the groundwork for the approach it would take in blood donation campaigns in the coming years. Giving blood was represented as not simply a way to aid the war-effort, although that was a large part of the campaign. Rather, donating blood was inscribed as a way to be fully an American, even if one could not sign up for active duty. The relationship between giving blood and joining the armed services was made explicit in several ways. The most effective was the use of "emblems" – really medals – awarded to donors: bronze for the first donation, and silver for the third, followed by a gold-colored "emblem" for members of the "Gallon Club" (*Teamwork from Publicity to Plasma*, 1943: 12). A vastly successful slogan for the BDS, later accompanied on Red Cross posters by a powerful *Saturday Evening Post* cover illustration by Mead Schaeffer, was "He gave *his* blood. Will *you* give yours?" In the poster, a uniformed, helmeted medic, wearing an armband that bears a red cross, leans over a wounded soldier as bombs explode in the background. In the foreground, at a dramatic angle, the soldier's rifle has been bayoneted into the ground and now serves as a makeshift IV pole for a bottle of reconstituted plasma. This image marries the rifle and the plasma, rendering them equivalent as weapons of war for the protection of "our boys," the popular/populist term for American fighting forces. In addition, the defiant phallicism of the rifle coupled with the medic's expertise and the soldier's physical vulnerability allows the poster's audience multiple identifications: to cathect with the masculine power of the U.S. military machine, experience the mastery over death of the medic administering the plasma, and feel the agony of the fallen soldier.

This image is particularly striking in comparison with another Red Cross illustration, which accompanies a newspaper ad used in the mid-1940s (see page 102). In the advertisement, "45 Minutes of Your Time Can Save a Wounded Soldier or Sailor," a Red Cross worker supervises a blood donation. However, in this picture both worker and donor are women, and fairly glamorous women at that. Whereas "He gave *his* blood" is intentionally gritty and explosive, set as it is in the midst of battle, the environment of "45 Minutes of Your Time" is the ARC Blood Donor Center, brightly lit and almost serene. The soldier lies on the ground, but the blood donor rests on a

He gave *his* blood. *Will you give yours?*

From Saturday
Evening Post cover
by Mead Schaeffer

From the Archives of the American Red Cross, National Archives and Records Administration.

hospital bed, supported by a pillow and covered with a blanket. Whereas the male medic's face is hidden as he leans over his patient, and his Red Cross armband is his most distinctive feature, the female nurse in "45 Minutes of Your Time" is also leaning over, but her focus is on the bottle receiving the blood, not the donor herself. Moreover, while her face is almost completely visible, her Red Cross patch (sewn on to the arm of a sharply ironed white uniform) is tiny and difficult to see. Both images invoke the miracles wrought by modern technology, but in very different contexts. In "He gave *his* blood," technology is in a struggle to the death with the permeability of the male body, with its susceptibility. The graphic is defined by ragged edges, the explosion in the background, by dirt, and the possibility of chaos. "45 Minutes

45 Minutes of Your Time Can Save a Wounded Soldier or Sailor

A pint of blood is a pitifully small thing to give for those who are giving their all overseas. The donation is painless. It has no harmful aftereffects. It takes only 45 minutes, including registering, rest, and refreshments. Yet the pint of blood you give, processed into life-saving plasma for transfusions, can save a wounded soldier or sailor fighting in Italy or in France or on the long, hard road to Japan. It is plasma that stays the pale hand of death. It is plasma that gives the wounded a fighting chance. It is plasma from the blood of volunteer donors back in the United States that is bringing thousands of wounded men home again . . . . Won't you give a pint of blood to save a soldier's life? Don't delay. Telephone the Red Cross for an appointment.

Donor Requirements

Anyone from 21 to 60 in good health, weighing 110 pounds or more, may donate. Those 18 to 21 may donate with the written consent of parent or guardian. Simply telephone for an appointment (and be sure to keep it). Eat a substantial meal 3 to 5 hours before donating and then snack if you wish—but eat no fatty foods for 3 hours before donating. Doing so makes the plasma unsuitable for use. Donations may be made every 8 to 10 weeks with not more than 5 a year.

Pharmacist's Mate Jim Cantrell, who was saved by five plasma and six whole blood transfusions. Will you give a pint of blood to save a life?

From the Archives of the American Red Cross, National Archives and Records Administration.

of Your Time" represents technology as incorporating the female body into a hygienic, unassailable environment, defined by the crisp lines of the bedsheets and of the nurse's uniform.

These two pictures, apparently so different – the male world of battle versus the female world of the home front; the grimy immediacy of the battlefield versus the shining hygiene of the Red Cross Blood Donor Center – have one striking similarity in the expressions on the faces of the soldier and the donor. Both lie in a near-trance, eyes closed, heads thrown back, mouths slightly open. The female donor, seemingly removed from the brutalities of war, looks remarkably like the soldier, "giving directly and literally of [her]self for our national defense" (*Give Your Blood to Save a Life*).

This imbrication of soldier and blood donor forged a seamless (if fantasmatic) conjunction between the phallic patriotism of military service and the home front (and therefore feminized) patriotism of blood donation that elevated the civilian to the status of honorary soldier. While government agencies also promoted the salvaging of crucial materials like scrap metal and rubber, dedication to industrial production, and growing one's own food to counter shortages and rationing, and repeatedly urged Americans to buy bonds to finance the war, the publicity campaigns around blood donation deployed a particularly effective rhetoric of military heroism and American exceptionalism (or, rather, the exceptional role that ordinary Americans could play in the war). Indeed, giving blood was sometimes represented as sending a part of one's self as a proxy into combat. In a memo that scripted possible articles to accompany corporate blood drives, Charles Coggin drafted "How Your Blood Goes To War," describing the donation process: "before he knows it, the donor has enlisted a pint of blood in the armed services" (House Organs memo).[8]

An early ARC newsreel, the first installment of *Red Cross News* (1942), pursues this connection between the heroic soldier and the average American. A segment entitled "Hero Sailor Repays Blood For Plasma" starts off as a typical appeal to its audience to donate blood. The variety of Americans and their common purpose is the focus: "Volunteers from all walks of life are eager to donate their blood. . . . Patriotic Americans, men and women, bare their arms to save the lives of our wounded fighting men." The end of the segment, however, explains its title. A young gunner's mate, still in uniform, has signed up at the blood center to replace the plasma he received at Pearl Harbor. "Here," intones the announcer, "is an American!"

This segment raises some interesting questions. Is the gunner's mate the exemplary American because he defended Pearl Harbor? In the context of the newsreel, no. Rather, he is "an American" for donating blood to replace the plasma he needed. How patriotic, then, are those Americans who give blood without the possibility of receiving its products: who give out of disinterested patriotism and the responsibilities of citizenship! In a deft reversal, the civilian's blood donation is participating in the defense of democracy *more* than the gunner's mate's donation, since there is no ulterior motive of reciprocation.

The BDS represented blood donation as a natural outgrowth of a diverse but single-minded American democracy, encapsulated in the phrase "from every walk of life." In his report on the Blood Donor Service, commissioned and published by the Red Cross in 1946, G. Canby Robinson emphasizes the democratic impulse central to the project: "the donors represented literally every occupation and every walk of life" (1946: 3). The ARC emphasized the symbolic mingling of civilians and soldiers in much of its publicity material: in March 1943, the Red Cross *Courier* reprinted a letter, intended for distribution nationwide, from a Colonel Hans Adamson, who had received plasma from thirteen different donors:

I have no way of knowing who these [donors] are. I don't know if they
are young, middle-aged, or old; neither do I know if they are men or
women from the North or South, East or West; nor do I know their
politics or religion. ... With their gifts of life-giving blood and plasma
from their veins into mine also went their patriotic ardor from their
hearts into mine.

The body of the serviceman now acts as the medium for the patriotic ardor
of unnamed Americans, just as plasma itself is the medium for blood solids, one
of which is "patriotic ardor." His survival gives them – typical but anonymous
Americans who are, of course, from "all walks of life" – an arena in which to
express their membership in the body politic itself through the transfer of their
"patriotic ardor" from their bodies to his.

The patriotism of giving blood was represented in a variety of ways, always
channeled through the ideal of democratic mutuality between donor and
recipient, and among donors. ARC blood donation promotional material often
focused on co-operation, either within communities or between donors and
recipients, as the ideal byproduct of the Blood Donor Service. In the fifth issue
of the ARC newsreel *Red Cross News* (1942), a daycare program that cares for
children as their mothers donate blood is deployed for a larger purpose. The
fact that the donation center constructs an environment in which women help
each other to achieve a larger war goal ends up as the focus of the segment,
entitled "Blood Donors Park Tots At Nursery Center." The camera focuses on
scenes of women giving blood as children are entertained in the nursery, and
exults, "Here's an excellent example of community co-operation!"

This mutuality of American identity extended to the Red Cross itself. A Red
Cross movie trailer, produced by the War Activities Committee, featured a
"Report From Humphrey Bogart At the Front" (1944). Bogie, an appealing
everyman himself, hammers home the importance of the BDS, calling plasma
"that gift of our blood to our men." More significantly, Bogart constructs a
sense of reciprocity between the armed forces, the Red Cross and the trailer's
viewers, since "the Red Cross is at their side, and the Red Cross is you." To
complete this connection, he makes a plea for cash donations, which can be
given to Red Cross workers at the cinema in which the trailer is being shown. [9]

As these examples illustrate, the Blood Donor Service constructed and
maintained a sophisticated public relations machine. With a single-mindedness
that would arouse jealousy in a political strategist of the 1990s, the BDS,
thanks in large part to the work of Charles Coggin, stayed "on message"
throughout the war. Although blood donation decreased dramatically in the
years after World War II, Coggin and Brown had achieved a triumph in public
relations: "by the alchemy of the Red Cross emblem [diverse Americans]

became one people. Nowhere, except in the matter of citizenship, can the fusion of such points of view be found" (*Know Your Red Cross*).

However, "the matter of citizenship" was no small thing. The connections that the Red Cross fused between donating blood and the donor's identity as an American citizen lay at the heart of the success of their public relations and recruitment plans. The mutuality that the BDS constructed among civilian Americans, "our boys" in the military, and the Red Cross itself was a building block in a larger edifice – a discourse of American citizenship that was at once deeply democratic and profoundly discriminatory (as the Red Cross itself was in its treatment of African Americans, the subject of a later section of this chapter). While the Red Cross may not have been the sole architect of this edifice, it was certainly happy to be sheltered by it and to shore it up from the inside.

"I Am An American": blood, democracy, citizenship, and the discourse of American ordinariness

Both the commercial and the government-sponsored media promoted what we might call a "discourse of American ordinariness" in their propaganda about blood donation. Just as the military forces fighting in Europe, Africa, and the Pacific were "our boys," and were represented in Red Cross publicity as heroic and yet average young men, blood donors were exceptional in their averageness.[10] Moreover, their averageness was the *source* of their magnificence. To be American meant to be both heroic and unmarked, to be extraordinary and neutral, to be an unambiguous member of a group and yet also an individual, to be "just American."

In the terms Ross Chambers has used about whiteness as a category of identity, the Red Cross represented "Americanness" as both "indivisible and singular" (1997: 192): on the one hand, the ARC characterized blood as a "gift of the American people" ('At His Side') – hence indivisible – but on the other hand, BDS publicity was full of stories of people from "all walks of life," individuals whose Americanness was both cause and effect of their donation. American identity could be both praiseworthy and exceptional, and unmarked and unexamined. Americanness was "aparadigmatic ... situated outside the paradigm that it define[d]. ... [Americanness was] not itself compared with anything, but other things [being "unAmerican," "Japs," not giving blood] were compared unfavorably with it" (Chambers, 1997: 189). It was not that Americans were a nation of superhumans; rather, to be an American was to be most fully human, so that American ordinariness was another form of human excellence.

Two pieces of promotional material best exemplify this discourse. A *March of Time* newsreel from November 1942 is a fitting launching-pad for a discussion of the heroic ordinariness of American citizenship that the Red Cross deployed as its most successful public relations strategy. The newsreel itself reaches for iconic value in its title alone: "Mr. and Mrs. America." An opening title sets the tone: "Serving their country more humbly but in the same measure as its fighting men are the American people, without whose support there could be neither Army nor Navy – nor Victory." The eponymous couple have a young America in the war, and the majority of the newsreel is taken up by a "typical" piece of V-mail from "Pa" to his son. "Pa" lists the various activities folks on the home front have been participating in, divided by age and gender. But the one activity that unites old and young, women and men, from (again) "all walks of life" is donating blood. "Since the Red Cross started its blood bank," Pa reports, "most of the people we know have gone up there to give some." The camera pans a long line of people, and then focuses on the clean, orderly blood bank, staffed by uniformed nurses.[11]

The second example comes from a very different source, but ends up promoting the same message. In February 1943, the ARC used "The Nation's Presswomen Speak," an ongoing radio discussion forum, to treat the issue of blood donation. The participants were high-powered newspaperwomen from the *Washington Post*, the Associated Press, and the International News Service. The host, International News reporter Lee Carson, introduces the evening's topic as "the kind [of story] that every reporter likes to write. It's a hero story. A story of real Americans" (p. 1). Mary Spargo of the *Washington Post* takes up the theme of exceptionalism and American identity: "To me the blood donor program is ... the greatest and most triumphant expression of the patriotism and will to victory of the American people" (p. 2). The participants do not dwell on the nobility of blood donation, however; rather, they shift to its democratic qualities. As Carson explains,

the privilege [of donation] isn't limited to any class or group of Americans. Brooklyn housewives, Hoosiers from Indiana, Hollywood glamor girls and Boston fishermen, bus boys and big shots, debutantes and dowagers, rich and poor ... all are marching to blood donor centers.

(p. 3)

Blood donation is for everyone and represents not simply a gift, but participation in the fight for democracy: when Jane Eads of the Associated Press asserts that "[a]ll of us in good health can well afford a pint of blood," Lee Carson responds, "That sort of makes it a democratic contribution" (p. 7).

Both of these PR materials are remarkable in their insouciant combination of understatedness and hyperbole. On the one hand, as Jane Eads points out, anyone can give blood as long as he or she is in good health. Red Cross materials emphasized the ease with which a person could donate blood: the briefness of the procedure ("45 Minutes of Your Time"), painlessness, and the readiness with which the body replenishes its supply. All Mr and Mrs America's neighbors participate in their town's blood drive, an activity shared by both sexes and adults of all ages. Even Lee Carson's affirmation of the democratic nature of blood donation comes close to diffidence: "That *sort of* makes it a democratic contribution" (my emphasis).

But this self-effacement is well matched by the crispness with which Mr and Mrs America and the presswomen assume American superiority. The definition of the BDS as "the greatest and most triumphant expression of the patriotism and will to victory of the American people" is not merely praise for the Red Cross (p. 2). It is also an unselfconscious declaration of the inevitability of U.S. victory in the war. Where there is an American will there is an American way. The story of blood donation is a "hero story" *because* it is a story of "real" — that is, ordinary — "Americans." Indeed, it is not the act of blood donation that makes them heroes, since anyone in good health can perform that service. Rather, it is the fact that "real Americans" are donating blood that makes it a "hero story": Americans bestow their heroism upon the Red Cross, not vice versa.

In the middle of 1944, Charles Coggin designed an inspired campaign around the discourse of American ordinariness: "Smith Week." He enlisted singer and hugely popular radio personality Kate Smith to call on all Smiths, members of America's most common name group, to make appointments for blood donation in the week of May 22 to May 27. Kate Smith was an ideal representative for the Blood Donor Service. Her public presence was enormous: she had a fifteen-minute daily spot on CBS radio called "Kate Smith Speaks," a mélange of "down-home philosophy, comments on current events and women's affairs" (Prial, 1998: 3), as well as a weekly variety show, "The Kate Smith Hour," on Friday nights. Moreover, she was not a figure of glamor. Her image was virtually asexual, and her body itself did not conform to standards of beauty, weighing in at over two hundred pounds. Rather, she appealed to audiences because her exceptional voice was contained by an image of homeyness and simple patriotism. According to legend, President Roosevelt introduced Smith to King George VI of England by saying, "This is Kate Smith. Miss Smith is America" (Prial, 1998: 1).The pamphlet the BDS put out, *"Calling All Smiths" Publicity Suggestions*, which was distributed to all thirty-five donor centers, maintained that "there is probably no radio personality who has become more a part of the American scene than Kate

Smith ... who introduced 'God Bless America' on the air and literally gave it the status of the country's unofficial national anthem" (p. 2).

"Smith Week" reconciled the apparently contradictory public messages of the Blood Donor Service: by donating blood you are (like) a hero (that is, a serviceman); by donating blood you are fulfilling your role as an American citizen, entering into "a modern kind of democratic citizenship" (Blakeslee, 1948: 31); by donating blood you are doing "a very simple service" (*Publicity Kit*, p. 4). Kate Smith was both exceptional and ordinary – a talented singer with a strong soprano voice and the bearer of the most American of names, singing the glories of the nation. The choice of the name Smith was brilliant not just because of Kate Smith's popularity (although that constituted a large part of the campaign's appeal). "Smithness" had achieved the status of iconic American ordinariness five years earlier in Frank Capra's *Mr. Smith Goes to Washington*, the quintessential narrative of the heroism of the regular guy. The eponymous hero's full name is Jefferson Smith, a gorgeous combination of the exceptional and the average, and he is, of course, played by James Stewart, the master of "inspired averageness" ("James Stewart, the Hesitant Hero, Dies at 89"). It would be hard to imagine a more populist movie than *Mr. Smith*, a picture in which a Boy Rangers leader is appointed Senator, and winds up exposing the corruption and double-dealing of career politicians. The fictional Jeff Smith is an ideal foil for the real-life Kate Smith: the people's voice raised in righteous indignation complements the people's voice raised in song.

It is hardly coincidental, too, that "Smith Week" coincided with the fourth annual "I Am An American" day. "I Am An American" day was instituted by Congress for the third Sunday in May, starting in 1941. In the words of Paramount News, the day was "set aside by the President for old and young, to rededicate the privilege of citizenship in this American democracy" (*Paramount News*, 1: 76). However, the celebration did not really capture the public imagination, or the concentrated attention of the media, until 1942, when it took on urgency due to America's involvement in World War II.[12] U.S. patriotism gathered about itself the mantle of anti-fascism and the struggle for democracy in explicit opposition to the imperialism of Japan, German Nazism, and Italian Fascism (see Zinn, 1980: 109).

"I Am An American" day was celebrated in a number of ways: parades in major cities and small towns, a special address by President Roosevelt or local officials, and an *en masse* recitation of the Pledge of Allegiance. The New York "I Am An American" day was probably the most lavish celebration, taking over Central Park for a huge rally, with estimated attendance of one and a quarter million people ("Vast Crowd," p. 8). The program of events, broadcast on NBC radio, WRUL and WNYC, was star-studded, featuring Lily Pons, Paul Muni, Marian Anderson, Supreme Court Justice Hugo L. Black, and Irving

Berlin singing his own composition (made famous, of course, by Kate Smith) "God Bless America." The *New York Times* observed the day with a lengthy lead editorial entitled "I Am An American."

"I Am An American" day exemplified the discourse of heroic American ordinariness. Like the Red Cross donors, "I Am An American" celebrants originated in "every walk of life," from every age group and every region. The Paramount News segment on the "I Am An American" day of 1942 highlighted celebrations throughout the nation, and the camera cast its eye over Chinese Americans in silk dresses, young black children, elderly white Veterans of Foreign Wars, as well as the column of citizens in parades. Citizenship was both a right and a privilege, something that could be assumed as ordinary and should be celebrated as something exceptional "in this American democracy."

"Smith Week" and "I Am An American" day performed similar cultural work: to construct new ideological identities for the average American citizen. In later sections of this chapter I will discuss the ways in which the changing meanings of blood and citizenship affected and were grappled with by two communities during the years of World War II: urban African Americans and West Coast Japanese Americans. First, however, I want to interrogate what the American Red Cross meant when they equated blood with citizenship: what new theories of citizenship were emerging in the war years from intellectuals and the popular media. The 1940s saw an efflorescence of writing about citizenship and its relationship to democracy in the context of American identity. Educational manuals such as *Education for Citizen Responsibility* (1942), *The American Citizen in Government* (1939), and *Democratic Citizenship in Today's World* (1944) were aimed at teachers in schools and colleges. Both texts included sources for further reading; *Education for Citizen Responsibilities* consisted of a series of essays, each of which addressed how a teacher could integrate questions of citizenship into different disciplines. *The American Citizen in Government* appended "Questions for Thought and Discussion" that were both factual and ideological – ranging from "What is a sales tax and what are the different kinds?" (p. 72) to "What would you suggest as a means of improving our courts and the administration of justice?" (p. 118) – to each of its chapters.

The history of citizenship as a concept has received considerably less attention from contemporary cultural and literary theorists than the idea of nation. [13] While there are strong connections between "nation" and "citizenry" as group nouns, it is crucial to pay attention to the differences. Like the nation, a community of citizens exists largely in its own imagination, since "all communities larger than primordial villages of face-to-face contact (and perhaps even these) are imagined" (Anderson, 1983: 15); despite the fantasmatic quality of this community, however, it is strongly felt as a "deep, horizontal comradeship" (1983: 16). Unlike the nation, which, as Benedict Anderson argues, is imagined in the language of parenthood – "motherland, *Vaterland, patria*"– or the vocabulary of terrain, "something to which one is naturally tied" (1983: 131), the citizen is an explicitly political construct predicated on *participation* in a political system (Klusmeyer, 1996: 3). Nationalism invokes ancient or even mythical ownership of the "fatherland" as its *raison d'être*, whereas citizenship represents a legal identity consisting of "an indefinite series of interactions between persons and things, which may be restated as rights" (Pocock, 1995: 45).[14] In Anderson's words, "[if] nation-states [that is, the structures that confer citizenship] are widely conceded to be 'new' and 'historical,' the nations to which they give political expression always loom out of an immemorial past" (1983: 19). In contrast to Margaret Mead's conception of the United States as a community "to which one tries to belong by effort" (Mead, 1942: 49), nation-ness is analogized to "skin-colour, gender, parentage, and birth-era – all those things one can not help" (Anderson, 1983: 131). The nation is mythologized as a genealogically pure entity, whereas the citizenry is connected through juridical structures. As J. G. A. Pocock argues, "the community of citizens is one in which speech takes the place of blood" (1995: 30).[15]

The *sine qua non* of citizenship is equality: "equal citizens are not discriminated against based on their identity. All citizens have the same political rights: to vote, to run for office, to speak freely, to assemble. ... Equal citizenship means that the government treats its citizens equally" (Spinner, 1994: 39). If the myth of nation is genealogical, the myth of citizenship is fraternal; if nationalism is powered by the trope of metaphor (the son takes the place of the mythic father/land), then citizenship is defined by the trope of metonymy (each sibling is linked to the other by association rather than substitution).

In the United States in the 1940s, citizenship was envisaged as a manifestation not simply of political superiority to other, less "free" countries, but as a sign of modernity and newness. Hence the invention of "I Am An American" day: a modern concept needed a new holiday. After all, one would imagine that July 4th, Independence Day, would be a perfect time to celebrate American citizenship, since it commemorates the issuing of the Declaration of Independence, a document that insists on independent citizenship for the soon-to-be-former colonies. July 4th, however, was too closely connected to the past, too strongly identified with "the founding fathers," genealogical and historical rather than fraternal and contemporary figures. "I Am An American" day had almost no historicized content: the only element of the past was the parade of war veterans, a group whose past necessarily coincided with the history that could be remembered by the living, not a past that lived only in records and history books. As Anton Lang wrote in *I Am An American: By Famous Naturalized Americans*: "Democracy is an experience ... it has to be renewed by every generation – by every citizen. It is growing, not fixed. You can't look at it as something that was won once and for all, a hundred and fifty years ago" (Benjamin, 1941: 18).

In his celebration of "I Am An American" day, Governor Lehman of New York expressed almost identical sentiments.

"To be an American ... means much more than to be born an American – it means much more than to be born on foreign soil and to have embraced American citizenship. To be a good American means that we must individually support the Constitution of the United States and ... take a personal inventory."

("Lehman Sets Sunday As Americanism Day")

The rhetoric of citizenship that emerged in the 1940s dovetailed with the changing meanings of blood to construct, in part, a discourse of populist, pro-American anti-fascism. In *On Native Grounds*, his examination of U.S. literary culture, Alfred Kazin ended with a plea that aligned American writing itself with the fight against fascism and Japanese imperialism: "Literature today lives on the narrow margins of security that the democratic West, fighting for its life, can afford. ... Never was it so imperative as it is now not to sacrifice any of the values that give our life meaning" (1942: 518). However conceptually close it may actually have been to U.S. white supremacy, Nazism was represented as unnaturally obsessed with blood purity and, as we shall see, much was made of the Japanese rule of *jus sanguinis* (the right of blood), which held that children of Japanese parents were Japanese nationals, no matter where they were born (Chuman, 1976: 167). In contrast to the claims of genealogy, citizenship was characterized in similar ways to the fraternity of transfusable blood: unarguably one's own, but – through the miracle of American modernity – able to link one to others who shared it (think of the newsreel *Brothers in Blood*, for example). This distinction resembles in some ways Werner Sollors' dichotomy "between *consent* and *descent* as the central drama in American culture" (1997: 6). In terms that resonate deeply for this discussion, Sollors poses the question "how can consent (and consensus) be achieved in a country whose citizens are of such heterogeneous descent? And how can dissent be articulated without falling back on myths of descent?" (p. 6).

A text that attempts to answer those questions through an interrogation of the intersections of blood, citizenship, modernity, and American identity, is *Wasteland* (1946), a now little-read novel by Jo Sinclair (the pseudonym for

Ruth Seid).[16] *Wasteland* is a fascinating and moving text that confronts the alienation of photo-journalist John Brown, né Jake Braunowitz, and his eventual recovery through the help of a psychiatrist, sessions with whom make up the frame of the novel. Jake hates himself and his family, particularly because they are Jews. He understands himself through racialized metaphors of blood and genealogy, both of which he attempts to escape through alcoholism, the separation of home and work lives, affairs with non-Jewish women, and emotional distancing from his family (a family he cannot physically distance himself from, however – at 35 he still lives with his parents, as do his older brother and younger sister). However, "[n]othing had done any good. Changing his name had not done it. Drinking had not, nor the things he did evenings" (*W* 22). He cannot flee his blood.

The novel's challenge is how to integrate the genealogical, blood identity of Judaism to the fraternal identity of American citizenship. *Wasteland* follows Jake's emotional recovery, a process that is facilitated by his younger sister Debby, who is a writer with the WPA, firmly opposed to their brother Sig's casual racism, a lesbian, and a heroic figure in the novel. Debby is secure enough in her American identity to speak Yiddish with her parents, but is not marked physically by Jewishness: she looks to Jake "like a gentile boy" (*W* 26) – Jake's link to fraternal Americanness.

At his first job, Jake gives an Anglicized name, John Brown, a name that "was beautiful. It was as American-looking, as anonymous, as any name he could think of" (*W* 78). For Sinclair, the choice of this anonymous American name is a way for Jake to radically disarticulate the "something inside ..., the blood" from the professional identity he constructs for himself, and both cause and effect of his alienation from himself and everything around him. The text itself insists on Jake's genealogy by using the name his family gave him – Jake – rather than the name he chooses for himself (John) or the diminutive that his sister Debby and his co-workers use (Jack). [17]

Jake's self-hatred bursts into his consciousness at a family Seder when he is 15. Previously, the Seder had been a high point of the year for him, an event full of spiritual and emotional connection. Particularly important to him was the recitation of the *Mah Nishtana*, the Four Questions, which he as the youngest son would chant. "Oh beautiful, Jake thought. ... Oh mysterious, of God and of life, that is handed down through the thousands of years. ... And my voice has to come now, the way it's written that the youngest son has to talk at this second. Me, Jake. I have a place in this story" (*W* 61). The shift from reverence and connection to scorn and disgust occurs when Jake completes the Four Questions and, looking around at the rest of his family, "[i]t struck him, with an appalling clarity, that they had not been listening. ... [T]he prayers were being uttered mechanically, a singsong reading of one word after another, one automatic phrase after another" (*W* 62). At that moment, Jake's family life is revealed to be a "damn lie!" (*W* 63). The illustrious history of patriarchs exposes the hollowness and cheapness of his own father, "a Jew. Was that the way it was to be a Jew? To be like his father in everyday life, then to sit at the Seder table like a patriarch of old – dignified, praying? It was a lie" (*W* 64).

Jake positions his father's stinginess and emotional emptiness in brutal contrast to the richness of the Jewish tradition. His religious and ethnic sense of self shifts from a mythic identification with "King David and his harp, Moses smiting the Egyptians" to the material realization that his Jewish blood connects him to a family whom he despises: "After all, he was a Jew, and it was something inside, in the blood and in the way one was born of Jews" (*W* 65). The knowledge that "his father was a dirty stranger and his mother a frightened, sad, incapable woman, that his older brother was a stranger with bored, cold eyes, that his sister was overly rouged and her flesh restless for he knew what" drives him to a knee-jerk anti-Semitism, the belief that "if his father was a Jew, then by God all Jews were like his father and he [Jake] would not be a Jew!" (*W* 66).

Set in diametrical opposition to Jewishness is Americanness. Whereas being Jewish is "dirty and rotten, stingy, illiterate," as his father is (*W* 70), being American is "strength and cleanliness," a transparent identity that does not have to explain itself (*W* 32). For Jake, Americanness is an alchemical compound of untrammeled identity and complete anonymity: being most yourself and at the same time being just like everyone else. He feels excluded from American identity by the conspicuous Jewishness of his name and, by association, of his parents. His life feels contingent, unsettled, because he cannot commit to his genealogy nor feel admitted to an effortless (quasi-Christian) American identity: "Nothing was regular with him, habit or custom, or breakfast at home, or even Christmas (wonderful thing celebrated by all the others at the office. ... He always received gifts, sure, but he knew all the time that it wasn't *his* holiday. See, there again he was different from everybody else!" (*W* 23).

Jake cannot find a way to reconcile his Jewishness with his desire for American ordinariness, a struggle that is embodied by the two constants in his life so far: "Friday nights and ... voting" (*W* 23). Voting represents the ideal American civic activity. It is the right of every citizen, both totally individual and totally anonymous. As Sinclair shows us, narrating Jake's consciousness through the second person:

> Voting was something that belonged to you. You wrote your name in
> the registration book, and you stood in line and marked the names of the
> guys you wanted in. You and all the rest of America. You were just like

all the others, all the voters. Your name was just as good as the next guy's. In the voting booth, nobody knew who was your mother, or your old man!

(W 23)

Jake envisions the right to vote (and hence American citizenship) as a way to erase his parents, or to excise them from his public identity. In contrast to the emotional slipperiness of his life, voting provides a level of stability. It intiates the citizen into an endless link of "all the others, all the voters," each vote carrying exactly the same weight as every other one. The candidates are even linguistically connected to the voters: both are undifferentiated "guys," and both make up "all the rest of America." The voter's choice is his or her own, "something that belonged to you," and cannot be decided by others. Thus the act of voting fully interpellates individuals, calling them both into their own identities and into "America" through their participation in civic activity.

The other "regular thing for him" – Friday night dinners with his family – stands in sharp contrast to this initiation into American identity.[18] The foods Jake's mother cooks are iconically Eastern European Jewish:

Ma's *cholah*, still a little warm. You started with *gefülte* fish, then chicken, then soup and noodles. They had always eaten soup last in their house; it was a Russian custom, he guessed. Sometimes there were dumplings instead of noodles. Then you ended with fruit compote, or stewed prunes.

(W 24)

Given Jake's antipathy, even hostility, towards all things Jewish, one would expect these Friday-night dinners to be a source of dread or at least discomfort. But they are a pleasure for him. The Jewish food "was food he loved. All week he ate ... American food. Roast beef, steak, apple pie, salad. But on Friday night there was the Jewish food, regularly, always the same. ... A custom, a landmark in the undirected week, a stable thing in a world that was insecure and perilous" (W 24). Yet Jake cannot fully identify with that fantasy of stability, and cannot reconcile it with the anonymous, neutral, transparent Americanism to which he aspires. In fact, rendered "weak and dizzy" by "what lay in his blood and his family," Jake imagines a way of life as different as possible from the world of *cholah* and *gefülte* fish. He is suffused by "the most intense longing of the anonymous kind of life he could live in the army. Everybody the same, no one squinting at you to see if you had a different way of eating or talking. ... Everybody the same, the same uniform, the same food and orders, the same reason for being there" (W 95).

The transition from neurosis to mental health, from self-hatred to self-esteem, from anti-Semitism to empathy for his family, culminates in two acts of volunteering: first to donate blood, and second to enlist in the Army. It is Debby who suggests that Jake accompany her to the Red Cross donor center. Like newspaper journalists all over the country in the mid-1940s, Jake has been to the donor center in a professional capacity, "to take pictures of people [giving blood]. It made swell art" (W 278), but he has not participated himself. Jake's description of the act of donating blood is deeply resonant of BDS publicity like *The Nation's Presswomen Speak* or Humphrey Bogart's dispatch from the front (not surprisingly, since Ruth Seid worked as an ARC publicist during the war). For Jake, giving blood constructs him as the ordinary American he has fantasized being: unique and anonymous, both "indivisible and singular" (Chambers, 1997: 192). As he says to his psychiatrist, "You give your blood. You couldn't give anything better. Why say, they couldn't take anything from you – that you give them on your own – that's more valuable. That's more you" (W 279). For Jake, giving blood is a way to "be like any guy in America," perhaps like the "real" John Browns (not so far from the Smiths of the "Smith Week" campaign) (W 281).

Debby has given blood three times before, but she has not forgotten "how I felt the first time. Awfully jittery. To give a pint of your blood to – Well, to the world! … I felt at one with everybody. Just *like* everybody" (W 281). For Debby, giving blood is a reciprocal process: from her to the world, and from "everybody" back to her. She is the complement to Col. Hans Adamson, whose veins contained the blood of thirteen donors: the gift of "patriotic ardor from their hearts into mine" is, in Sinclair's cosmology, both given and received by donors.

Debby is particularly inspired by the fact that "ten thousand people are doing the same thing, everywhere in America" (W 281), creating a community of mutual co-operation in a national project. She sees her donation gaining her admission, as the *Blood's Magic for All* pamphlet phrases it, to "a modern kind of democratic citizenship," a populism that can embrace Americans from "all walks of life":

"I feel as if I'm giving it for Jews too. Jews like Ma, who never had a break. And I'm giving a pint for the Negroes. … It's like giving your blood against any kind of segregation there is in the world. Anybody who is slapped in the face, laughed at. Pushed into a corner of – of society. They can have my blood."

(W 282)

Jake's feelings about giving blood are filtered through his psychiatrist's notes, the vehicle Sinclair uses to summarize and synthesize the changes Jake experiences throughout the novel. Jake sees his blood dissolved into a vat of Americanness. "In this offering of blood, [Jake] feels strengthened. ... Jewish blood, in his mind not too long ago a despised thing, has been accepted and now flows in the mixture of American blood. ... [Jake] has given his blood. ... He gave as a Jew and as a patriot, to some degree; but, most important, he gave as Everyman" (W 289). His difference is erased by his acceptance by the Red Cross, which his psychiatrist (as the ARC itself did) identifies with "the world, America at war" (W 288). Sitting in the blood center, he has "a strange feeling. His blood would merge anonymously with the city's, the country's, then with the world's blood" (W 282).

He has also given his name as "Jake Brown," the name he writes on his donor card. These two names, "Jewish" and "American," have merged to construct a new identity for him. After the bleeding is over, he asks Debby to call him Jake rather than Jack, a sign that his Jewishness has been robbed of its psychic power over him. Now Jews are simply one of the many "walks of life" from which blood donors come: far from being alien, they have, in Jake's imagination, been domesticated, subsumed under the larger, indivisible label of "America." Just as the ARC publicity promised hundreds of thousands of Americans, giving blood is for Jake "a hero story. A story of real Americans" (*The Nation's Presswomen Speak*, p. 1). Jake knows he is a meaningful human being — a "real American" — because he can give blood; when he was psychically incomplete he could not imagine doing so.

In fact, Jake takes that story one step further. Giving blood is not an end in itself, but a moment of transition that culminates in his enlistment in the Army. It is a short step from "enlist[ing] a pint of blood in the armed services" (Coggin, House Organs memo) to enlisting his whole body. Jake's choice to join the Signal Corps as a photographer represents his success in integrating all elements of his life: ethnic, civic, professional, patriotic.

By donating blood, Jake has become the representative American, indeed, the representative human, "Everyman." But the assimilability of his Jewish blood is an assimilability that Debby refuses. Despite her feeling of oneness, she sees this immersion in an undifferentiated Americanism as, in fact, undergirding a system of segregation she deplores, a system whose ramifications we will explore below. The same act that bestows modern citizenship upon white donors, enters their blood into the "mixture of American blood," is transformed in meaning by racialization. Debby reveals that "where we're going now [that is, the blood center], they keep Negro and white blood separate. Isn't it amazing? They make little ghettos for a thing like blood. When I give my pint, Jack, it's against that, too. Some day they'll know they can't do a thing like that. Part of my blood will show them that some day" (*W* 282). Just as eighteenth-century skeptics feared that lamb's blood would generate hooves and wool in transfusees, Debby imagines her blood effecting a kind of cultural transformation in the veins of the people who receive it. Her blood will "show" the nameless, faceless people whose lives it will save that segregation is wrong by successfully integrating into "them." Her difference, like the "one drop," will maintain its integrity even as it combines with the blood of any number of others.

Wasteland works through the thematics of blood donation that the publicists at the Red Cross Blood Donor Service devoted four years to establishing: blood as a sign of active and unambiguous American citizenship; blood donation as an act of community with both the rest of the American public and the armed forces; the Red Cross itself as a conduit for the union of donor and recipient. But as much as Sinclair wants to represent blood donation and its (to Jake) inevitable corollary, volunteering for active duty, as a heroic act of American ordinariness that can change the life of the donor as much as (or, psychologically, more than) the life of the recipient, her deep ambivalence about the racial politics of blood banking disrupts this utopian trajectory. Debby may have been instrumental to Jake's blood donation, but she also complicates its meaning, just as Sinclair introduces the symbolics of giving blood only to unsettle the metonymic economy of citizenship she herself proposes.

Indeed, the Red Cross's segregation of blood into "white" and "colored" both disturbs and affirms the new language of blood as citizenship, as American identity. In the next section, I will explore how the ARC's policy of segregation is very much like "mak[ing] little ghettos for a thing like blood": constructing a *civic* identity around inclusion and exclusion. In *Wasteland*, Jo Sinclair briefly shows her readers how a white ethnic fantasy of American citizenship through blood donation is compromised for a white, anti-racist (much is made in the novel of Debby's black friends – possibly lovers), leftist lesbian by racial segregation of blood. More important for our purposes, however, is how black urban communities in general, and leaders in particular, reacted to the ARC's policy, and how the issue of blood donation shaped black discourses of citizenship during World War II.

Segregating "Negro blood," erasing black citizenship

Debby Brown/Braunowitz's revelation that the Red Cross "keep Negro and white blood separate" opens a window on how the shift from blood-as-genealogy to blood-as-citizenship managed to reinstantiate Jim Crow racism in the 1940s rather than combating it. Although it gets only a brief (but impassioned) mention in *Wasteland*, the segregation of "Negro blood" was a live-wire issue particularly in urban African American communities in the 1940s.

Even before the ARC became the center of blood processing in the U.S. in the early 1940s, segregating blood by the race of the donor was not a new procedure. While it was not practiced uniformly, the fact that many of the breakthroughs in hematology came out of Johns Hopkins University Hospital in the segregated state of Maryland may have had a serious influence on blood-banking methods. In their discussion of the then groundbreaking blood storage and transfusion methods at Johns Hopkins in the 1930s, Robert Kilduffe and Michael De Bakey mention, almost in passing, the fact that blood was routinely labeled (and, one assumes, segregated) by race. For Kilduffe and De Bakey, this separation is part of "the many minutiae involved in the operation of a blood bank" and the importance of accurate record keeping.

> Obviously [they claim], it is essential that every flask or container of stored blood must have a *legible and permanently attached* label showing: (1) Name of donor; (2) race (white, colored); (3) date blood collected; (4) type ...; (5) results of serologic tests; (6) name of patient for whom intended (if known).
>
> (1942: 262; emphasis in original)

Kilduffe and De Bakey do not comment on the racial segregation of blood, and simply reproduce the form that Johns Hopkins used in 1940 to process and label blood. However, their silence on this issue implies that separation of blood by race was a procedure so standard that it did not require remarking upon.[19]

Moreover, as Keith Wailoo has shown, until the early 1940s, many U.S. hematologists believed that "black blood" was actually microbially different from "white blood," due to the discovery of sickle-cell anemia among black communities. Hematology was crystallized as a medical field just as James B. Herrick first observed the sickling of anemic cells in 1910 (Wailoo, 1997: 134). Herrick (mis)interpreted sickle-cell anemia as a dominant genetic trait unique to African Americans that could be "transmitted from one parent to his or her offspring, independent of the other parent's genetic endowment," which, for Herrick, exemplified the dangers of miscegenation (*ibid.*). Wailoo argues convincingly that because of the supposed threat of sickle-cell anemia and other blood-borne diseases assumed unique to or predominant in black people, "for many physicians in the early twentieth century, *Negro blood* was a term with clear technological origins and with biological, social, and public health meanings" (p. 136).

Strikingly, even before Linus Pauling and J.V. Neel published their findings in the early 1940s that sickle-cell anemia was a recessive trait that required both parents to carry the gene, the belief that "Negro blood" was defined by a tendency towards sickle-cell anemia was never raised by the Red Cross as a reason for segregating black blood from the general pool. Wailoo claims that sicklemia "provided rich biological material for defenses of segregation," and was used as an argument to prevent blacks from entering the military in World War II (1997: 147). However, not one of the extensive ARC documents that deal with blood segregation even attempts to identify a scientific or biological justification for the policy of labeling plasma according to the race of the donor. The decision to segregate plasma derived from the blood of African Americans does not seem to be a result of a *genealogical* belief in the substance of "black blood," either: the Red Cross kept careful records on all their policy decisions and nowhere in these records is a discussion of "black blood" in the sense Eva Saks has analyzed, "an intrinsic, natural and changeless entity" (1988: 48). Even extreme right-wing segregationists like John Rankin, Congressman from Mississippi, combined an old-fashioned anti-miscegenationist fear that cross-racial blood donation would cause racial difference to "crop out in [recipients'] children" with a political argument: even if segregating blood had no scientific backing, opposing the Red Cross was "communistic" and could only lead to the downfall of American democracy (*Congressional Record*, June 5, A2308). Scientists were routinely called upon by the liberal and African American press to deny that there was any scientific reason for labeling blood by the race of its donor: even the *New York Times* weighed in in mid-1942, in an editorial entitled "Blood and Prejudice" that attacked the ARC for "keeping alive ... the superstitions and mysticism associated with blood. Sometimes," the editorial concluded archly, "we wonder whether this is really an age of science" ("Blood and Prejudice," June 14, 1944).

Given the overwhelming weight of science, not least since Charles Drew, the director of the ARC's Blood for Britain campaign and developer of plasma product was an African American; given the armed forces' ambivalence over segregating blood at all; given the movement towards equal opportunity – although not desegregation – in the military and defense industry, it is reasonable to assume that the Red Cross's decision to segregate blood was not based on a belief in the substance of "black blood." Instead, it can be located in the Red Cross leadership's inability to imagine black people as part of the mutually constitutive polity that – according to their publicity – blood donation constructed and maintained. The edging together of the topoi of citizen, blood donor, and soldier into the fabric of "America" marginalized black identity through both policy-making and the formidable public relations network which the ARC built during the years of the war.

By 1941, as we have seen, blood donation was emerging from research hospitals and university laboratories into the public consciousness. The Blood for Britain campaign, directed by Charles Drew, had not segregated blood for processing into plasma, but by December 1941, Red Cross policy on racializing blood was confused and unclear. According to a *New York Star-News* article in January 1942, only white donors were being accepted for Blood for Britain. However, Rear Admiral Ross T. McIntire, the Navy Surgeon General, vociferously denied the claim that black donors were being turned away. This accusation was not made by the *Star-News* itself, however. Rather, the ARC's whites-only policy was publicized by Dr Earl S. Taylor, technical consultant to the Red Cross, in an article in the *Journal of the American Medical Association*, quoting directly from ARC directives.

Throughout January 1942, the Army and Navy on one side and the Red Cross on the other attempted to unload the blame for the Jim Crow policies on to each other. Rear Admiral McIntire wrote to the NAACP, insisting that the Navy had "never requested the American Red Cross to refuse to take blood from Negro Donors" (*Miscellaneous Information*, p. 1) even as ARC officials in New York, where this refusal "became a political issue," claimed that "we are acting upon the request of, and under instructions from, the Army and the Navy" ("Ho Hum," n.p.). By the end of January, the ARC had crafted a "Policy Regarding Negro Blood Donors" that apportioned blame equally between the Red Cross and the Armed Forces in enforcing a Jim Crow system of donation, while shifting responsibility for the policy onto individual servicemen whose supposed prejudices the ARC was duty bound to observe:

> The American Red Cross, in agreement with the Army and the Navy, is prepared hereafter to accept blood donations from colored as well as white persons.
> In deference to the wishes of those for whom the plasma is being provided, the blood will be processed separately, so that those receiving transfusions may be given plasma from the blood of their own race.

The Red Cross's press release achieved two objectives: first, to diffuse accountability for the policy among itself, the Army, and the Navy, and second, to represent the policy as the will of America's heroes, "those for whom the plasma is being provided," "our boys." The segregation of blood was not a decision but an act of deference to the defenders of democracy.

Although this policy statement seems fairly anodyne in the context of the discourse of the heroic American ordinariness of both soldiers and blood donors that was emerging from the ARC in the early years of the war, it represents a harsh (although indirect) denial of citizenship identity to black blood donors. The phrases "those for whom the plasma is being provided" and "blood of their own race" imply that black and white recipients would be equally disturbed by being transfused with blood from the other group. However, despite the passage of the 1940s Draft Act, which stated that "[i]n the selection and training of men ... there shall be no discrimination against any person on account of race or color," at the beginning of the war, the majority of blacks in the armed forces were assigned to service positions: of the 450,000 black troops in 1942, only 100,000 were in combat units, the rest being relegated to menial labor (Macdonald, 1943: 9). Black soldiers and sailors were trained in racially segregated camps located for the most part in the deep South. Reports began circulating in mid-1941 of black trainees being lynched by military police in Fort Benning, Georgia;[20] in Little Rock, Arkansas, Fayetteville, North Carolina, and Beaumont, Texas, black soldiers were shot dead by white police for not giving up their bus seats to white passengers; throughout the South, blacks were not appointed as military police or as officers (Macdonald, 1943: 2–3).[21] In the Little Rock case, in which a white police officer first knocked a black soldier to the ground and then shot him dead at point-blank range, the DA did not even attempt to prosecute, since "there was no prospect of conviction" by a white jury (Brandt, 1996: 130).

The Red Cross's policy statement renders the profound inequality between black and white soldiers invisible, and casts the desire for "raced" blood into the laps of both races equally. Moreover, its own representations of black soldiers reveal the ways in which the ARC implicitly delegitimated African American claims to citizenship through both blood donation and combat. Black donors, nurses, soldiers, and Red Cross workers were virtually invisible in ARC promotional material. Of the hundreds of photographs of plasma recipients that the BDS sent to chapters for distribution to newspapers, not one wounded man is black.[22] Almost none of the BDS publicity was sent to the black press, and none of it featured African American people.[23]

The erasure of black bodies from the scenes of participation in building American identity at home and abroad seems to stand in direct contrast to the visibility of blood labeling. In fact, the suppression of images of black blood donors and recipients is simply the other side of the same coin. As Richard Dyer has argued, "black is always marked as a colour (as the term 'coloured' egregiously acknowledges) and is always particularizing; whereas white is not anything really, not an identity, not a particularizing quality, because it is everything" (1988: 45). The disappearance of black people is a sign of their inability to be part of the visible obviousness, the "everything" of white American identity; the labeling of their blood is a sign of their inevitable particularity and difference from that "everything." For the purposes of the Red Cross Blood Donor Service, there was blood and then there was blood donated by Negroes. This is particularly important given that blood was not actually labeled "Negro" and "white" according to the race of all donors (although public opinion assumed that this was the practice). Blood donated by whites (and, one assumes, Asian Americans, Latinos, and Native Americans) was unlabeled, unmarked. Only the blood given by blacks was labeled as such. Whiteness is both visible, in that it is continually and solely represented as the norm, and invisible, since it is completely unremarkable.[24]

The policy of marking only donations from African Americans was codified nationally in late 1944 with the inauguration of the "Dedication Label Plan." Prior to this new plan, the ARC affixed to all plasma and blood a label identifying it as the product of the BDS and the gift of "volunteer donors." Red Cross workers were instructed to indicate on the same label that the donor was black, although there was not a policy on how this information should be conveyed. With the introduction of the Dedication Label plan, the BDS issued specific instructions on how to identify blood by the race of the donor.

The plan itself was designed to connect donors more viscerally with the abstract idea of the recipients of their blood, and more effectively equate the gift of blood with membership in the armed forces. Donors were encouraged to give their blood on behalf of friends or relatives in the military, and to fill out a label dedicating their blood in the names of their loved ones at the front. While they could not direct the plasma from their blood to the dedicatees, donors could participate in the metonymic power of citizenship: since all citizen-soldiers are equal, they are also interchangeable. Hence, blood donated in one soldier's name could, in good faith, go to save another of the communally owned "our boys."

Ironically, the Red Cross recognized and publicly acknowledged that the plan could be no more than a metaphor, given the mechanics of plasma derivation. In a press release announcing the plan, "Donors to Label Red Cross Blood with Own Names," the ARC admits that "labels on the plasma must necessarily be symbolic, since the individual's blood loses its identity in the laboratory processing." The label itself confessed the symbolic nature of label dedication, describing its contents as "symboliz[ing] in part the blood gratefully donated" by the dedicator. Under the Dedication Label plan, blood donation was rendered even more personal: donors could be identified by name by plasma recipients, as individuals and not just anonymous Americans.

This personalization of the donation process was complicated by the codification of racial labeling that accompanied the plan. Although ARC publicity never mentioned segregation as a part of the plan, the instructions issued to chapters, *How to Set up and Operate the New Red Cross Blood Donor Dedication Label Plan* (1944), gave detailed guidelines on how to keep the blood of black donors separate:

Labels inscribed by Negro donors will be marked "AA" on the back. Other inscribed labels will be unmarked. ... In accepting a label from a Negro donor [the volunteer] is to mark "AA" on the back or blank side so that such labels may be affixed to cartons of "AA" plasma at the laboratories. This should be done inobtrusively, preferably after the donor has gone.

The blood need not be labeled explicitly by the race of the donor: simply labeling it at all is enough. The act of marking, of separating the black donor from other "unexamined" Americans, is enough to establish the unmarked, indivisible identity from which blackness must be separated. Most ironic is the Red Cross's apparent desire to shield black donors from the pain of seeing a racial classification attached to their blood. Marking "should be done inobtrusively," or in the donor's absence, as if to shield donors from the knowledge of the racism the ARC perpetuates. The implicit message to this veiled marking is "don't let them know they're not like us," even as the policy of marking creates a difference out of no difference. It is not clear in whom the shame of marking inheres: the volunteer or the donor. I would speculate, however, that the guidelines suggest this delicacy as a way to spare black donors the embarrassment that must accompany open acknowledgment of their compromised citizen status.

A highly public campaign around citizenship as the center of American identity had to wrestle with the structural inequities in the democratic process that subordinate African Americans. However, such self-examination was almost impossible in the populist (but official) discourses of Americanism disseminated by the Red Cross or through such events as "I Am An American" day. The closest official organizations came to an admission of inequality was the Office of War Information's pamphlet *Negroes and the War*, which placed racism squarely in the past. Under the title "We've Come A Long Way," the pamphlet trumpeted "advances" that now read as embarrassments. In terms of work opportunities, the pamphlet side-steps the fact that many blacks were limited to manual and service labor by transforming Jim Crow into a virtue: "We are not ashamed of working with our hands, of an honest day's work, honestly done" (n.p.). This clumsy sleight of hand becomes insulting when the pamphlet turns to the education of black children. "We stay longer in school. Ten years ago only 26.6 percent of children went beyond the fourth grade. Now that figure has been raised to 37.5 percent" (n.p.). [25] By claiming share-cropping and unskilled labor as examples of the ennobling potential of "honest ... work," and citing the appalling statistic that almost two-thirds of black children had no more than an elementary school education as an achievement, *Negroes and the War* shows that African Americans cannot aspire to the status of full citizens with complete educations and managerial jobs. Their place in the war economy is as loyal and infantilized subordinates, subcitizens.

In *Wasteland*, white ethnic Jake Brown/Braunowitz can claim a universal citizenship through donating blood and joining the armed services. His blood does not require a *"legible and permanently attached* label" that is constructed not simply at the same time as but, I would argue, for the implicit *purpose* of, denying black donors the same identity. Ralph Ellison crystallizes this point in *Shadow and Act* in his observation that the "unwillingness to resolve the conflict in keeping with his democratic ideals has compelled the white American, figuratively, to force the Negro down into the deeper level of his consciousness" (Ellison, 1995: 100). The corollary to this argument, that in fact the construction of a seemingly fraternal citizenship depends upon the designation of an Other as subcitizen, has been made by several critics and historians, including Toni Morrison, David Roediger, Ruth Frankenberg, and Michelle Fine: *"whites needed blacks in order to become privileged. . . .* Whiteness [or in this case, white citizenship] is produced *through* the exclusion of and denial of opportunity to people of color" (Fine, 1997: 60; emphasis in original). As Freud has pointed out, "it is always possible to bind together a considerable number of people in love, so long as there are other people left over to receive the manifestations of their aggressiveness."[26]

How, though, did black Americans negotiate these changes in racial, biological, and social discourse? A newly urbanized and, particularly in New York, radicalized black community had access to a new set of organizing and rhetorical tools in the early 1940s. A new generation of black leaders like A. Philip Randolph, Adam Clayton Powell, Jr., and Roy Wilkins were unafraid to point out the disparities and hypocrisies of the new discourse of citizenship, and they appropriated the language of blood, loyalty, and American ordinariness for their own purposes.

In some ways, African Americans had a clear and unambiguous argument that went to the heart of white America's claims of democracy and fraternal citizenship. Wilkins wryly observed that "it sounded pretty foolish to be against park benches marked JUDE in Berlin, but to be *for* park benches marked COLORED in Tallahassee, Florida. It was grim, not foolish, to have a young black man in uniform get an orientation in the morning on wiping out Nazi bigotry and that same evening be told he could buy a soft drink only in the 'colored' post exchange" (quoted in Brandt, 1996: 93).

But black intellectuals had to counter the invisibility that accompanied the markedness of difference. They had to devise strategies that both laid claim to the unmarked heroism of American citizenship and neutralized the "particularization" of blackness. The greatest challenge was to take on the mantle of effortless Americanism, to be invisible through unremarkable representation; and, as 1940s black activists realized, one of the keys was to appropriate the language of blood, citizenship, and ordinariness that the Red Cross had so successfully constructed.

"We Are Americans, Too!": black action and reaction

Blood and citizenship were certainly on the minds of black intellectuals, political activists, and journalists. In the keystone essay in his landmark collection *What the Negro Wants*, Rayford Logan laid out his answer in the title: "The Negro Wants First-Class Citizenship" (1944: 1).[27] Moreover, Logan recognized the enormous symbolic blow which the Red Cross's segregation of blood dealt to African American citizenship, citing the "extreme bitterness" caused by the ARC's policy: "when our nation goes to war to assure the victory of 'democracies' over the 'fascist' nations, we naturally become more insistent that democracy, like charity, should begin at home" (1944: 7).

One of the major black intellectuals engaged in the project of defining black identity through citizenship in the 1940s was A. Philip Randolph. Randolph, previously the organizer of the Brotherhood of Sleeping Car Porters, founded and headed the March On Washington Movement (MOWM) in the early 1940s. The MOWM was initially conceived as a way to pressure President Roosevelt to desegregate the armed forces and, even more importantly, the defense industry, which was heavily black due to the ongoing migration of rural black workers searching for jobs in urban areas.

Randolph advocated mass action: a 1941 demonstration by 10,000 black workers who would "march down Pennsylvania Avenue asking for jobs in defense plants and the integration of the armed forces. It would shake up Washington" (quoted in Pfeffer, 1990: 47). In a brilliant show of intimidation dressed up as deference, Randolph wrote to Roosevelt and other political figures, asking them to address the projected crowd. The march was planned as an all-black event, and the estimated number rose to 100,000 which frightened white powerbrokers even more, particularly since Washington restaurants, hotels, and other public accommodations were completely segregated (Pfeffer, 1990: 49).

While Roosevelt did not desegregate the military, he did offer one concession in exchange for Randolph's calling the March off: Executive Order 8802, signed in June 1941, which created the Fair Employment Practices Committee, whose mandate was to rid wartime industry of racial discrimination. Rather than being thrown off-course by Roosevelt's concessions, Randolph reconceived the March on Washington as an ongoing project, the March on Washington Movement.

I wish to discuss two of the projects that came out of the MOWM: the "I Am An American, Too!" campaign, and a pamphlet put out by the MOWM, *The War's Greatest Scandal! The Story of Jim Crow in Uniform*, which appeared in 1943. Both projects proposed a radically new way of thinking of black identity, taking up the discourse of blood as citizenship that threatened to further marginalize African Americans, and recentering it around black demands for civil rights. Moreover, unlike the NAACP, the MOWM focused on black urban life and economic issues, particularly in the North and Midwest, and worked out of a model of all-black mass political action, rather than lobbying seats of power or pursuing legislative change.

As its name suggests, "I Am An American, Too!" was a direct response to "I Am An American" day. Randolph envisaged it as a week-long program of nonviolent demonstrations against Jim Crow in federal and state government, in schools and on railroads, and scheduled the week to coincide with "I Am An American" day. Although the projected co-ordinated action did not materialize, and was transformed into a series of extremely successful local actions and a large rally in Chicago, "I Am An American, Too!" is fascinating in the ways it appropriates and reshapes definitions of American citizenship that white Americans took for granted. [28]

Randolph saw black political action as a way to redefine the goals of the U.S. war. In a broadside entitled "March on Washington Movement Presents a Program for the Negro" (n.d.), he warned his constituents not to be deceived by the rhetoric of democracy that undergirded official propaganda about Allied goals. "This is not a war for freedom. It is not a war for democracy. . . . It is a war to maintain the old imperialisms. It is a war to continue white supremacy and the subjugation, domination, and exploitation of the peoples of color" (Randolph, quoted in Pfeffer, 1990: 3). Negroes could be America's and democracy's salvation, however. In fact, supporting black civil rights "may save the day for the cause of the Democratic way of Life" (*ibid.*: 4).

As Spencie Love has argued, the motif of African American sacrifice as an agent for the redemption of the nation was a familiar one, and a rhetoric to which images of blood were intrinsic: "the theme of black people's blood – their suffering and sacrifice – as the price for full citizenship, and the related theme of redemption and justice for the whole community, white as well as black" have been powerful elements of African American historiography, both formal and folk (1996: 69–70). Love identifies within black prophetic leadership a topos of black Americans "as a people destined to spill their blood so that America can become what it professes to be," a historical tradition that reaches from Crispus Attucks to the soldiers of World War II (*ibid.*: 70). Randolph adds a new twist to this rhetoric by reconstructing the metaphorization of blood as citizenship as a palimpsest through which his black listeners could read the older prophetic tradition lying just beneath a newer discourse of modernity and democratic rights.

Randolph achieves this interleaving of different discursive formations by recasting the African American sacrificial role as a vanguardist position.[29] Randolph's genius was to activate his audience not only by attacking the manifest inequalities of citizenship, but by showing how segregation of blood, of the armed forces, and of the defense industry robbed African Americans of their sacred role in the national drama: as agents whose self-sacrifice "may save the day for the cause of the Democratic way of Life" (quoted in Pfeffer, 1990: 4). In a reconfigured version of "March on Washington Movement Presents Program for the Negro" that appeared in *What the Negro Wants*, Randolph represented black demands for citizenship status as part of a larger program of fraternity and democracy, beyond merely self-interested desires for improvement.

> The oppressed darker races want something more.
> They want much more.
> They want the cause of true democracy to march forward.
> They want the Brotherhood of man to triumph.
>
> (Logan, 1944: 159)

Randolph's packaging of the March on Washington movement as a mass movement among the black rank-and-file intimidated white politicians, even as the MOWM's rhetoric echoed the language of "I Am An American" day and Roosevelt's pronouncements on anti-fascism. The change of the title of "I Am An American, Too!" to "We Are Americans, Too!" for a massive rally in Chicago resonated with white America's self-image as a collectivity of individuals. And while Randolph's March on Washington and "I Am An American" seem to be direct antecedents to Martin Luther King, Jr.'s 1964 March for Civil Rights and the slogan "I Am A Man," the rhetoric was markedly different. Certainly, Randolph's use of "Goodwill Nonviolent Direct Action" prefigured the strategy deployed by King a decade later, and picked out similar targets: segregated restaurants, public transportation, cinemas, and so on. But King's power base was the Southern black church, and his rhetoric, which grew out of the tradition of African American Christianity, focused on the common humanity of all people. Randolph, by contrast, used the secular (although sacred) language of *citizenship* and invoked the long history of black self-sacrifice for the nation's health, even as he assailed the United States for cutting off African Americans from the democratic promise of U.S. citizenship. "Fellow citizens," he demanded, "ARE NEGRO AMERICANS NOT CITIZENS?" (Logan, 1941: 159).

Questions of citizenship, fraternity, the redemptive power of blood, and the perversion of that power, provide much of the force of the MOWM pamphlet written by Dwight Macdonald, *The War's Greatest Scandal! The Story of Jim Crow in Uniform.*[30] The pamphlet details the indignities and brutality, occasionally to the point of murder, visited on black soldiers in Southern training camps and overseas, and the irony embodied in the willingness to allow black soldiers to spill their blood, but not to share it with white comrades. As with "I Am An American, Too!" *The War's Greatest Scandal* claims as its primary goal the desire for the United States to achieve its goals of democracy, "to realize freedom, truth and justice in the national life. Our struggle for complete equality for all men regardless of race, religion, or national origin is the basic struggle to preserve and extend democracy in these United States" (Macdonald, 1943: 2).[31]

In *The War's Greatest Scandal*, Macdonald draws a thumb-nail sketch of African Americans who have given their lives for the United States, from Crispus Attucks to the black regiments of World War I. He calls particular attention to the unusually heavy casualty rates of black troops, who were often used as advance guards and shock troops: another way in which blacks led the way to American freedom with their blood. The pamphlet repeatedly draws analogies between Jim Crow, Father Coughlin's anti-Semitism, and the Fascist Silver Shirts on the one hand, and Nazi racism on the other.[32] Moreover, just as black heroism benefits the whole nation, military segregation is represented as an injustice not simply to Negroes, but to "every real friend of democracy" (Macdonald, 1943: 15).

The War's Greatest Scandal linked the "jimcrowing" of the military with the segregation of blood from black donors in a section entitled "Red Cross, Double Cross" (Macdonald, 1943: 11). The policy of separate labeling is represented as the final sign that American democracy is teetering on the edge of disaster. By separating blood, the leadership of the armed forces and the Red Cross have ideologically miscegenated with Hitler, since

> the difference [between blood of different races] exists only in the imagination of a Hitler — or of the directors of the Red Cross, the Surgeon Generals of the U.S. Army and Navy, and the Secretaries of War and Navy. ... This episode shows us how far those in command of our armed forces have come to accept the racial mythology of the enemy.
> (Macdonald, 1943: 12)

At the end of the "Red Cross, Double Cross" section, Macdonald summarizes the issues at stake in black subordination. Explicitly connecting the segregation of blood by black donors with the shortcomings of white

American democracy, Macdonald directly addressed a challenge to his white readers: "Either you advance towards real democracy, and the Negro with you; or you go backward to racialism and fascism" (1943: 12). *The War's Greatest Scandal* positioned African Americans as the pivotal force between democracy and fascism.

A striking element of *The War's Greatest Scandal* is that Macdonald does not discuss the racial attitudes of common soldiers and sailors themselves. Racism and segregation are identified with military police, military officials, government leaders, and Red Cross leadership. In fact, according to Macdonald, white servicepeople are also victims of racism, since it renders absurd *their* blood sacrifice. The racism of the rank-and-file is interpreted as a result of misinformation from the leadership, not as an autochthonous expression of race hatred. Jim Crow "spreads the most vicious of Hitler's doctrines among the very soldiers and sailors who are dying in battle with Hitler's armies" (Macdonald, 1943: 15). The pamphlet implicitly promulgates an anti-racist populism that sets in opposition anti-democratic authorities and citizen-soldiers (which was certainly not the case, as Nat Brandt and other historians of black involvement in World War II have amply shown).

These interrelated themes – the spilling of black blood for the nation's salvation, the conflict between the needs of rank-and-file soldiers and the racism of the military brass, the centrality of democratic citizenship to American success in the war – are neatly encapsulated in an editorial cartoon by *New York Amsterdam News* artist and editor Mel Tapley.[33] Rather than focusing on the racism endemic to the military, from enlisted men up to the Chiefs of Staff, Tapley romanticizes the "little guy," whether black or white. Entitled "An American Tragedy," Tapley's cartoon opposes "our boys'" democratic disregard for racial difference to the Red Cross's unAmerican and militarily dangerous policy of blood segregation. In four panels he represents the ramifications of the policy for white wounded soldiers, black enlistees, the doctors who must enforce the policy, and the success of America's participation in World War II.

The first and third panels illustrate the dangers of blood segregation to individual soldiers and, by extension, to the armed services as a whole. In the first panel an emaciated, heavily wounded, and bleeding white GI crawls up to a Red Cross van, staffed by a rotund medic. The feet of another soldier, wounded or dead, protrude in the bottom left foreground of the panel. In an ironic reversal of the Red Cross poster "He gave *his* blood," the ARC worker does not care for the wounded soldier but shrugs his shoulders at the supplicant. "You might as well wait here, bud," the ARC man tells him, "we ain't got nothin' but Negro blood left." The two feet sticking out into the bottom of the frame suggest the results of having to wait for white blood.

From the *New York Amsterdam News.*

The third panel is even harsher. The setting is outside a hospital, crudely labeled "Red Cross Transfusion Center" (inaccurately, since no such institutions existed: transfusion was only one of several procedures at field hospitals). The "Transfusion Center" has two visible front doors, which resemble the segregated facilities that were part of both military and civilian life, and one invisible back door. White soldiers stream into one door on stretchers and crutches as black GIs saunter out of the other door. In the rear of the building is a steaming mound of bodies labeled "White Stiffs" to which another corpse is about to be added. In the foreground of the panel, a white soldier in a head bandage and sling remarks to his buddy, "Geez, looks like the colored lads is the only ones 'ats got round-trip tickets at the 'horspital' today!!" His friend replies, "' Guess they only got Negro blood! We gotta wait — *if* we kin last!!"

Tapley makes it clear that the white GI's target here is not black soldiers, but the ARC policy of segregating blood. Moreover, in the second panel he implicitly argues that white soldiers are as opposed to the policy as their black counterparts.[34] In the foreground, a doctor (who looks suspiciously like Hitler, with a little brush mustache) wails "What a dilemma!! The labels have come off! ... Now how can we tell the white from the Negro plasma?" In the background a skeletal white patient sits up in bed and replies "H—, Doc! So what!? I ain't rankin'!" Unlike the doctor, the patient has his priorities straight: his chart hanging at the foot of the bed shows a downward slope that only the transfusion of plasma can arrest.

The final panel invokes the imagery of innumerable Red Cross posters: the soldier in a makeshift hospital bed with a doctor leaning over him. In the cartoon, however, this soldier is black, a phenomenon represented in none of the ARC literature that I found. The soldier grabs the doctor's sleeve and implores, "Lissen, Doc! − If I need a transfusion, gimme *anybody's* blood so long as I get back to the front!!" Here Tapley explicitly includes the black soldier in the ranks of "our boys" while differentiating him from the white medical establishment that has condemned to death soldiers of all races. The black and white soldiers' use of nonstandard English − a sign of their American ordinariness − acts as a kind of cross-racial, class-based solidarity that contrasts with the elevated diction of the (possibly fascist) doctor in the second panel ("What a dilemma!!").

In many ways, Tapley has appropriated the language and imagery of the Red Cross. His strip shares much of the ARC's iconography: the cross itself, the supine soldier tended to by a doctor, the battlefield crisis. Blood is still the sign of participation in the democratic project of America, but as much in being withheld as in being administered. Most importantly, the Red Cross, rather than embodying the nexus of citizen-donor and citizen-soldier, is the obstacle to that communion. The ARC's claims to saving soldiers are exposed as a lie by the pile of corpses outside the "Transfusion Center." Moreover, by attempting to maintain the racial order by segregating blood, the Red Cross has in fact reversed it with tragic results: white soldiers must wait for transfusions of "white" plasma.

Opposition to the Red Cross's policy poured out of the black press in the form of cartoons, articles, poems, editorials, photographs, and "exposés" of deaths that could have been avoided by a nonracial policy.[35] However, the policy itself was not rescinded until 1950, when the ARC insisted that there had been a "misunderstanding and misconception" about the purpose of racial labeling. Marking blood by race was "for the purpose of medical research" not for "racial discrimination" ("Red Cross to Omit"). The article in the *New York Times* that reports on this decision mentions nowhere the controversy over labeling and segregation during the war, and simply rebuts any possibility that blood could have a race. Just as the Red Cross rendered African American donors and soldiers invisible, the policy of separating out and labeling blood by black donors has disappeared, and along with it the black activists who challenged the ARC and the U.S. government.

"Citizens of Japanese blood": citizenship, loyalty, and Japanese internment

While discourses of blood and citizenship were crucial to changes in European and African American identities in the 1940s, and to the reinstantiation of (and resistance to) Jim Crow during the war years, no discussion of the relationship between race, blood, and citizenship during this period can go without an analysis of the "evacuation" and internment of Japanese Americans on the west coast between 1942 and 1945. The U.S. government, through the agency of the Western Command under General John DeWitt, ordered 110,000 American citizens of Japanese descent from their homes in California, western Washington and Oregon, and northern Arizona, imprisoned them in "Assembly Centers" and then remanded them to "Relocation Centers" (a euphemism for concentration camps) often in barren, windswept areas.[36]

As historians of Japanese settlement in the U.S. have shown, the story of internment is in many ways simply an intensification of the anti-Japanese racism that plagued Japanese American communities throughout the west coast. From the first arrival of Japanese in San Francisco in 1869, followed by major immigration from the mid-1880s to the 1920s, Japanese immigrants faced enormous disadvantages. As Ian F. Haney López (1996) points out, "in its first words on the subject of citizenship, Congress in 1790 restricted naturalization to 'white people,'" which barred the Japanese who came to the U.S. a hundred years later from the rights of citizenship. The 1913 Alien Land Act prevented aliens not eligible for citizenship from owning land, effectively excluding Japanese immigrants. In 1922, the Supreme Court formally affirmed the Congressional restriction on naturalization in *Ozawa v. US*, and by 1924, Congress had passed the Japanese Exclusion Act, which severely limited Japanese immigration.

Given the restrictions on American citizenship for Issei (immigrants born in Japan), second-generation Japanese (Nisei) were in a peculiar position. Born in the United States, they immediately acquired the rights of U.S. citizenship. At the same time, the Japanese rule of *jus sanguinis* accorded them Japanese nationality. A small but significant number of Nisei were sent back to Japan for their education as children or young adolescents, creating a group (known as Kibei) who were politically American but in many ways as culturally Japanese as their non-citizen parents. Most Nisei stayed in the U.S., however, and fiercely identified with American culture, both popular and civic.

White observers of Nisei culture remarked on their "pathetic eagerness to be Americans" (Weglyn, 1996: 34; see also Chuman, 1976; Hosokawa, 1982; McClain, 1994). The self-appointed Nisei leadership rejected the language of blood through which *jus sanguinis* gave them Japanese nationality, and embraced the American citizenship that was denied their parents. The first Japanese American organization, the Loyalty League, was formed in 1919. Unlike analogous white ethnic immigrant groups such as the Knights of Columbus (Italian), the Ancient Order of Hibernians (Irish), or the Workers' Circle (Jewish), the Loyalty League was not formed for financial self-help, to celebrate ethnic heritage, or to advance a political platform. Indeed, the group decided not to use the word "Japanese" in its name so as to downplay their origins. It was not until the 1930s that a variety of west coast Nisei groups coalesced into the Japanese American Citizens League (JACL), the first Nisei organization to include the word "Japanese" in its name.[37]

As the names of these groups demonstrate, second-generation Japanese Americans were well aware of the stakes of citizenship, not least because their parents were so limited by the prohibition on their naturalization.[38] The JACL's strategy was ostentatious patriotism and polite lobbying of legislators. Unlike the March On Washington movement, the JACL could not articulate blood and citizenship to form a rhetoric of heroic American identity: by law, Japan had a claim on their "blood." More importantly, a mass Japanese American culture was less than sixty years old, even in 1940, and there was no tradition of Nisei as the conscience of the country that A. Philip Randolph could borrow from African American oral culture.

The bombing of Pearl Harbor exacerbated this tension between the Issei's exclusion from citizenship and the Nisei's embracing of it. On December 7 and 8, Roosevelt issued Executive Orders 2525 and 2526, which restrained German, Italian, or Japanese nationals from communicating with or aiding the enemy, and confiscated firearms and cameras, restricted travel, and limited membership in nationalist organizations. However, attention soon shifted away from German and Italian aliens, and onto the Japanese alone. On February 19, 1942, the President promulgated Executive Order 9066, which declared that since

the successful prosecution of the war requires every possible protection against espionage and against sabotage to national defense, [Roosevelt would] authorize and direct the Secretary of War, and the Military Commanders whom he may from time to time designate ... to prescribe military areas in such places and of such extent as he or the appropriate Military Commander may determine, from which any or all persons may be excluded, and with respect to which, the right of any person to enter, remain in, or leave shall be subject to whatever restrictions the Secretary of War or the appropriate Military Commander may impose in his discretion.

(*Hirabayashi v. United States*, 1943: 86)

The next day, Secretary of War Henry Stimson handed over control of the Western Defense Command, which encompassed the Pacific coast, to Lieutenant General John L. DeWitt, and within two weeks DeWitt had proclaimed the entire west coast (all of California, western Washington, western Oregon, and southern Arizona) to be a "military area." On March 24, DeWitt imposed a curfew on Italian and German nationals and all west coast residents of Japanese descent, of whom about two-thirds were Nisei, and between March and November began issuing proclamations to "evacuate" all Japanese Americans from western military areas to "assembly centers," and finally to "relocation centers" further into the country's interior.

DeWitt is a fascinating, though odious character. In the official documents in which we hear his voice, his contempt and disgust for people from a Japanese background are broadcast clearly. According to DeWitt, at stake in the evacuation was the impossibility of determining Japanese "loyalty": "American citizenship does not necessarily determine loyalty," he claimed.[39] In his pronunciamentos, DeWitt tangles up race, citizenship, nationality, loyalty, and identity, contradicting himself, but always returning to the same conclusion: the Japanese cannot be trusted. On the one hand, he is forced to admit that the majority of Japanese evacuees were "American-born, had been through American schools, had not developed Oriental thought patterns or been subjected to so-called Japanese culture."[40] On the other hand, DeWitt needed to believe in the total unassimilability of even U.S.-born Japanese Americans, that they could not function as real American citizens. In the same report he claimed that the "Japanese race is an enemy race and while many second and third generation Japanese born of the United States soil, possessed of United States citizenship, have become 'Americanized,' the racial strains are undiluted" (DeWitt, 1943: 34).

What exactly is it that DeWitt believes is conducted through the "racial strains"? Clearly not citizenship identity, since that is assigned to every person born on U.S. soil; nor "Oriental thought patterns," whatever they might be, since Japanese Americans brought up in the U.S. could be schooled out of them. Certainly, whatever they represented, DeWitt believed they needed to be destroyed, either through education, or some other more brutal method. These "racial strains" were not a risk for white ethnic enemy aliens: "You needn't worry about the Italians at all except in certain cases. Also, the same for the Germans, except in individual cases. But we must worry about the Japanese all the time until he is wiped off the map" (*Hearings*, 1943: 740).

For DeWitt, there is something that the Japanese, however Americanized they might be, whether citizens or not, cannot achieve, and that lack makes them a threat. The name he gives this quality is "loyalty." By shifting the argument for internment away from citizenship, which would otherwise raise the issue of habeas corpus, to loyalty, DeWitt creates a kind of conditional citizenship, one that cannot speak for itself. Nisei are "citizens of Japanese blood" – a working contradiction, given the technologies of citizenship functioning in the 1940s – whose status *as* citizens is compromised and hence must be undergirded by more than just the fact of having a U.S. passport.

The argument for Nisei removal and internment depended upon the assumption that their citizenship had less integrity than that of other Americans. By dint of being Japanese they were condemned to an economy of genealogy, closed off from the juridical identity of citizenship. The transformation of blood from a sign of genealogy (vertically inheritable within a closed group of parents and children) into a sign of citizenship (horizontally transferable through modern scientific advances from any one citizen to any other) could not be extended to Japanese Americans.[41]

The Nisei could not reliably prove their "loyalty" because their Japaneseness embroiled them in an identity, whether they liked it or not, that rendered their citizenship suspect. As Supreme Court Justice Stone maintained in his unanimous decision in *Hirabayashi v. United States* (1943), a case in which a Nisei from Washington State challenged the constitutionality of the curfew from 8 p.m. to 6 a.m. imposed on all Japanese Americans in military areas:

> Whatever views we may entertain regarding the loyalty to this country of the citizens of Japanese ancestry, we cannot reject as unfounded the judgement of the military authorities and of Congress that there were disloyal members of that population, whose number and strength could not be precisely and quickly ascertained.
>
> (1943: 99)[42]

In fact, it was not that Japanese Americans were necessarily disloyal. After all, "loyalty is a matter of mind and of heart not of race" (Douglas, concurring, *Hirabayashi v. United States*, 1943: 107). Rather, it was impossible to tell, since "no ready means existed for determining the loyal and the disloyal with any degree of safety" (DeWitt, 1943: 9).[43]

The JACL's response to the evacuation and internment was to make a show of loyalty that would prove their worth as citizens and, they hoped, overcome the arguments from race and blood that were being promulgated by DeWitt.

Statements were issued from the group and by its leadership. The JACL's president Sabura Kido announced, on behalf of the League, "We are going into exile as our duty to our country. ... We have pledged our full support to President Roosevelt and to the nation. This is a sacred promise which we shall keep as good patriotic citizens" (Chuman, 1976: 170). The League did protest the evacuation but in muted tones, and they emphasized loyalty over outrage. In a press release sent out soon after the issuing of Executive Order 9066, the JACL announced their "complete agreement" with "any policy of evacuation definitely arising from reasons of military necessity." Moreover, as "American citizens, we cannot and should not take any other stand. But, also, as American citizens believing in the integrity of our citizenship, we feel that any evacuation enforced on grounds violating that integrity should be opposed" (Hosokawa, 1982: 148).

But for the federal government, Japanese American citizenship did not have integrity, in large part because of the belief that Japanese Americans were not capable of intellectual independence from their father/land(s). Intrinsic to what Michael Ignatieff calls the "myth of citizenship" is the belief that "political choice requires independence of mind; independence of mind presupposes material and social independence; citizenship therefore inheres only in those capable of material, social, and intellectual independence" (Ignatieff, 1995: 57). General DeWitt, the Supreme Court of the United States, and the U.S. Congress did not believe that Japanese Americans *were* capable of that independence, or, if individual Japanese Americans were, the group itself was potentially too disloyal to be trusted. [44] Under the terms of removal and internment, Nisei were no longer citizens but "non-aliens": they were both separable from the citizenry as a group, and unrecognizable as individuals within that group – the opposite of the ideal (that is, typical) American citizen.

The JACL believed that the best response to DeWitt's argument that "racial strains" incapacitated "loyalty" was simply more affirmations of how loyal Japanese Americans were. They requested tests that could measure loyalty, the separation of the loyal from the disloyal, the admission of the loyal into the armed services. However, when each of these requests was honored, the form they took worked to intensify the symbolic distance between the structural impossibility of true Japanese American citizenship and the effortless, heroic citizenship of white Americans.

Japanese Americans' opportunity to prove their loyalty came in 1943, when the Selective Service Administration opened up the draft for Nisei. On the lengthy form were two questions:

27. Are you willing to serve in the Armed Forces of the United States on combat duty wherever ordered?

28. Will you swear unqualified allegiance to the United States of America and faithfully defend the United States from any or all attack by foreign and domestic forces, and forswear any form of allegiance or obedience to the Japanese emperor, or to any other foreign government, power or organization?

(Quoted in Weglyn, 1996: 154)

Ichiro Yamada, the protagonist of John Okada's novel *No-No Boy*, answered "no" to both questions, a decision that sent him to a federal penitentiary for two years. *No-No Boy* is a striking complement and contrast to *Wasteland*, and it is with this novel that I want to end this chapter. Both Jake Brown/ Braunowitz and Ichiro experience intense conflict over the authenticity of their American identities. Both doubt the meaning of their citizenship and both are plagued by the disjuncture between the genealogical ethnic traditions from which they come and the fraternal American identity they desire. Both characters, by the end of the texts, have achieved a level of acceptance from and integration into "Americanness," but from radically different events. While Jake's story ends with his blood donation and enlistment in the Signal Corps, Ichiro's ends with three deaths and an unknown future.

Stephen H. Sumida movingly summarizes the conflicted loyalties that Nisei had to negotiate when faced with questions 27 and 28 in relocation camps:

How can I be drafted into the U.S. Army when my citizenship has been revoked? Can the U.S. government unilaterally revoke the citizenship which is mine by birth? If my citizenship has not been revoked or has been restored, why am I imprisoned in this camp without ever having been charged with a crime or given a fair trial? How can the issei be asked to renounce their Japanese citizenship when the U.S. denies them any other? And how can I "forswear," that is, "give up," allegiance to the Japanese emperor unless I have such allegiance in the first place, and what if I never had it?

(Sumida, 1989: 225)

Many Nisei responded "yes" to both questions. Mike Masaoka, the JACL lobbyist in Washington, DC, insisted that to the federal government in general and the military in particular, "Nisei protestation of loyalty was so much hogwash. ... We had to have a demonstration of blood" (Weglyn, 1996: 140). Ironically, blood and citizenship were finally merged in the language which Japanese Americans used to describe the need to sign up for active duty. Members of the Fair Play Committee, formed at the Heart Mountain concentration camp to protest the enforced draft and segregation of "no-no boys," declared that "the first duty as loyal American citizens is to protect and uphold the Constitution of the United States. ... [I]f we know of a cause and a country worth our blood, then we need never feel ashamed to look the enemy in the eye" (Emi, 1989: 51). The FPC's statement imbricates the multiple pressures on Nisei men in the camps: the claim to loyalty, the willingness to shed blood as proof of that loyalty, the understanding that the enemy whom the Nisei looks in the eye may reflect his own face more than his white colleagues. But this statement is also a challenge. After all, the FPC supported no-no boys, and denied that saying no was a form of disloyalty: "We are not being disloyal. We are not evading the draft. We are all loyal Americans fighting for JUSTICE AND DEMOCRACY RIGHT HERE AT HOME" (quoted in *ibid.*: 52).[45]

Ichiro Yamada is far less certain about his right to say "no." Much like Jake Brown/Braunowitz, he feels torn between his Japanese genealogy and his American political identity. Returning home to Seattle from two years in prison, he finds his father has become an alcoholic, his mother maintaining the delusion that Japan has won the war and waiting for a ship to take them back to Japan, and his brother Taro so ashamed of him that he is about to join the army. Ichiro feels exiled from his American self, but unable to regain any sense of being Japanese: like Jake, he is disgusted by the example of his heritage that he sees in his parents, and is nostalgic for a time when he felt embraced by his origins:

There was a time that I no longer remember when you used to smile a mother's smile and tell me stories about gallant and fierce warriors who protected their lords with blades of shining steel and about the old woman who found a peach in the stream and took it home and, when her husband split it in half, a husky little boy tumbled out to fill their hearts with boundless joy. I was that boy in the peach and you were the old woman and we were Japanese with Japanese feelings and Japanese pride and Japanese thoughts because it was all right then to be Japanese ... even if we lived in America. (*No-No Boy*, p. 15)

In this meditation, Ichiro invokes the Japanese folk-tale of Momotaro, the little boy who emerges from a split open peach to bring joy to an elderly childless couple and eventually save their village from ogres.[46] At the same time this fantasy erases the child's actual Japanese origins. Momotaro has no ancestry, he has no past, he has no genealogy. He emerges fully formed from the center of the peach, and takes on a human (that is, Japanese) identity. Even though the story is one of perfect filiality, there is no biological relationship between Momotaro and his elderly "parents."

The myth of Momotaro is the reverse of Ichiro's actual experience. Born to Japanese parents, he is a citizen in a country to which they have no claim. All they have to connect with each other is genealogy – they do not share the same political or cultural identity. Ichiro imagines himself as the bisected peach pit, physically split between Japanese and American halves, one genealogical, the other juridical. The Japanese half has been erased by his time in prison, but that has compromised his "American half" so that "I am only half of me and the half that remains is American by law because the government was wise and strong enough to know why it was that I could not fight for America. . . . But it is not enough to be American only in the eyes of the law and it is not enough to be only half an American and know that it is an empty half. I am not your son and I am not Japanese and I am not American" (p. 16). Ichiro's lover Emi recognizes the compromised citizenship of Japanese Americans in her analysis of how their lives began to disintegrate: "It's because we're American and because we're Japanese and sometimes the two don't mix. It's all right to be German and American or Italian and American or Russian and American, but as things turned out, it wasn't all right to be Japanese and American" (p. 91).

Ichiro's complement is Kenji, his contemporary, whose leg was destroyed in the war. The wound has turned gangrenous despite multiple amputations, and over the course of the novel we see him dying. Kenji and Ichiro's relationship is chiasmatic, "one already dead but still alive and contemplating fifty or sixty years more of dead aliveness, and the other, living and dying slowly" (p. 73). Kenji is "more American than most Americans because he had crept to the brink of death for America" (*ibid.*), and his family is Americanized, eating roast chicken and lemon meringue pie and watching baseball. Kenji fantasizes about the possibility of running away from being Japanese: he exhorts Ichiro to "go someplace where there isn't another Jap within a thousand miles. Marry a white girl or a Negro or an Italian or even a Chinese. Anything but a Japanese. After a few generations of that, you've got the thing beat" (p. 164).

Rather than feeling embraced and absorbed by America, as Jake Brown/ Braunowitz imagines happening as he donates blood, or as he believes will happen after he enlists in the army, Kenji envisions an ideal America that will swallow him whole, into an open space that is empty of Japanese. The only way to fully participate in America is to dissolve the "racial strain" with white or black or Chinese "blood": for all his baseball-watching and pie-eating, Kenji cannot imagine an American citizenship that is compatible with a Japanese genealogy.

By the end of the novel, Kenji has died from his wounds, Ichiro's mother has committed suicide, and Freddie, another no-no boy, has been killed in a car accident. Ichiro has turned down two jobs offered by well-meaning white employers, and is wandering the streets of Seattle late at night. "He walked along, thinking, searching, thinking and probing, and, in the darkness of the alley of the community that was a tiny bit of America, he chased that faint and elusive insinuation of promise as it continued to take shape in mind and in heart" (p. 251). Ichiro's new birth into Americanness is hesitant, partial, "faint and elusive" – quite different from Jake's triumphant entrance into the pulsing bloodstream of America.

As Iris Marion Young has ruefully argued, "many among the excluded and disadvantaged [have] thought that winning full citizenship status, that is, equal political and civil rights, would lead to their freedom and equality" (1995: 176). At a moment in which Americans were thinking explicitly about citizenship as a mutuality of bodies, and blood was a symbol of the interconnectedness of citizens, structures were forming that would fashion barriers around that mutuality. Where African Americans could be rendered invisible as citizens, Japanese Americans had to be ejected from the body politic. Their citizenship could not exist on the same terms as the citizenship of white ethnic "enemy aliens" like Germans or Italians: they could not represent one of the "walks of life." In the final moments of *No-No Boy* Ichiro *is* walking, chasing an "insinuation of promise" so faint it is almost invisible. The promise, we might imagine, is the one we started with, the promise of "a modern kind of democratic citizenship." However, those words take on a different meaning when they are more than a sales pitch for blood donations. For Ichiro, and for thousands of Nisei like him, for A. Philip Randolph and the thousands of March on Washington activists, that promise was "faint and elusive" indeed.

5

Reading the "Book of Life"

DNA and the meanings of identity

We used to think our fate was in the stars. Now we know, in large measure, our fate is in our genes.

(Watson, 1980)

What Is Life? DNA as ontology

As rhetorics of blood, citizenship, and racial identity were shifting ground in the mid-1940s, a new way of looking at genealogy was forming in laboratories around the United States and Europe. Appalled by the results of the research on atomic structure that had been so compelling in the first half of the twentieth century, Western scientists shifted their focus from physics to biochemistry — a field that unpacked the mysteries of life rather than providing the tools for dealing with death. Just as physics had been devoted to discovering the smallest possible entity in the physical world, the biologists created a new field of molecular biology that searched for the most basic constituent element of life.[1]

Erwin Schrödinger's *What Is Life?*, published in 1944, was the bible of the new microbiology (not coincidentally, Schrödinger was already a well-known physicist). Depending on the research of Max Delbrück, Schrödinger speculated that genes were information-carriers that moved hereditary information from parents to children. The existence of something like genes, that is, some system by which visible characteristics could be handed down generationally, had already been theorized by Gregor Mendel in his famous pea-plant experiments in the mid-nineteenth century. Or rather, Mendel's experiments became famous well after he published them in 1865: not until 1900 were they taken up by the scientific community as meaningful. By the beginning of the twentieth century, though, biology had become a field dominated by the microscope and the desire to see previously invisible elements – microbes, viruses, bacteria – that teemed within living things.

Mendel's study suggested that there was something inside the body that caused inherited traits to be transmitted in a schematic way, and biologists started looking for whatever that thing was. Over the next forty years they discovered chromosomes, the thread-like bodies within the cell on which genes are arranged in a linear order, that were made up of nucleic acid, which was made up of individual nucleotides. Each new discovery led to the finding of a smaller, more basic element: from chromosomes to genes, from the cell nucleus to nucleic acid to nucleotides to the nitrogen, sugar, and phosphorus that formed them (Stent, 1980: xiii–xiv). Schrödinger's suggestion that genes were essentially vehicles for information, telling organisms how to look, grow, and function, inspired the postwar generation of scientists to merge biochemistry and genetics into the new field of molecular biology to find out "what life is" (Watson, 1980: 12).

The molecular biologists of the 1950s created a discourse around genetics whose powerful effects we are still feeling almost half a century later, a discourse that saw genes as the answer to the most basic of ontological questions: "What are we?" and "What does it mean to be human?" At the core of the language of contemporary genetics is the figure of DNA (deoxyribonucleic acid), the material out of which genes are made. In his bestselling account of his and his colleagues' discovery of the structure of DNA, *The Double Helix* (1968/1980), James D. Watson imagined the chemical as "the secret of life," the key to the mysteries of human (and in fact all organic) existence (p. 24). Watson and his colleagues responded to Schrödinger's question, "What is life?" with the answer "DNA."

That such a profound philosophical question can have such a mechanistic answer says a great deal about the ways in which molecular biology has shaped our understanding of the relationships between the interiors of our bodies and how we function in the world. The combined force of DNA testing in judicial contexts and the launch of the Human Genome Project, both established in the late 1980s (and about which I will have more to say below) has transformed the place of genetics in the cultural imaginary of the U.S. in the last two decades of the twentieth century. While the details of molecular biology are out of the reach of most Americans, there is a sense that we know what DNA is, what it can tell us about ourselves, and how central it is to every part of our lives as organisms. Indeed, DNA seems to occupy the space of what Evelyn Fox Keller has called "master molecules": entities that, if we can only correctly isolate them, will provide us with a map of the etiology of human disorders ranging from alcoholism and schizophrenia to reading disabilities and PMS. As Fox Keller argues, "[o]nly partly can this expansion of the category of genetic disease be attributed to the development of scientific know-how. In part it is a result of the ideological and institutional expansion of molecular genetics; in part it is simply a result of the cultural triumph of genetic reductionism" (1994: 89).

At the same time, I do not want to capitulate to the fatalism implicit in Fox Keller's argument. The languages of genetics have osmosed to the very edges of the ways in which we talk about ourselves, from television programs to criminal proceedings to educational theory to medical research, but the "genetic reductionism" that Fox Keller deplores has more than one manifestation. Certainly, some of the discourses of DNA have made room for a genetic determinism that is not so far removed from the eugenics of the beginning of the century, and has forged an even stronger fantasmatic link between the workings of embodied heritability and abstract qualities like intelligence, compassion, and social belonging. But for others, DNA has a utopic quality, bringing people together on the basis of the vast majority of genetic material which all human beings share and looking backward to shared prehistoric ancestors, the originators of the genes we all carry around inside us.

In this chapter I will explore some of the topoi that DNA occupies: the "genetic fingerprint" in criminal prosecutions, the key to disease, the sign of our essential difference from each other, and the symbol of our interconnectedness. I read three texts intended for nonscientist audiences for which DNA and genetic heritability are crucial concerns: Harlan Levy's *And the Blood Cried Out* (1996), a popular account of the use of DNA evidence in criminal trials from the first use of genetic fingerprinting in 1987 to the O.J. Simpson double murder trial that brought DNA testing to the forefront of public discussion in 1994; Shirlee Taylor Haizlip's memoir/family history *The Sweeter the Juice* (1994), which traces the racial mixings of her black-identified family and chronicles her search for her mother's "lost" siblings, all of whom passed into the white world in the 1920s and 1930s; and the revelation in 1998 that DNA testing had genetically linked descendants of the enslaved Sally Hemings to her owner Thomas Jefferson, affirming centuries-long Hemings family claims that Jefferson had fathered some if not all of Hemings' five children.

Through all of these topoi, DNA is imagined as the bearer of *true* information. That is, while there is considerable debate about what genetic information can be interpreted to mean and how it links to nonmolecular reality, no one argues that DNA does not show with indubitable accuracy the workings of the human (or any other) body on the molecular level. To all intents and purposes, DNA *is* the truth, incontrovertible. Moreover, the discourse of DNA imagines the body's most basic truth as existing in a realm invisible to the majority of Americans. I want to think, then, about not just how we imagine DNA manifesting itself in everyday life, but also how we fill the immense gap between the strangeness of molecular biology, with its wire models, complex formulae, and geometic diagrams, and the "commonsense" assumptions about genetics that are commonplace in U.S. cultural life.

Finally, I hope to untangle the constructions of DNA as meaning. DNA is envisaged as answering a welter of knotted questions about ontology (Who are we?), etiology (Where did we come from?), taxonomy (Where in nature do we fit?), epistemology (How can we know the world?), teleology (What is our purpose?) and, broadly speaking, eschatology (What will happen to us?). These are heavy burdens for a set of molecules so tiny. While I want to clarify what it is DNA *can* tell us, I also want to examine what it is about the place genes occupy in our cultural (and even personal) imaginations that leads us to believe not simply that DNA research could give meaningful answers, but that these answers are to be found most reliably on the molecular level.[2]

Nowhere has this confidence in DNA as the source of answers been more clearly played out than in reactions to the Human Genome Project (HGP), a $3 billion federally funded, multi-year initiative, among whose goals is to map all the genes within the forty-six human chromosomes (that is, the human genome), working out causal links between genes and organismic processes. Launched by Congress in 1988, the HGP is co-sponsored by the Department of Energy and the National Institutes of Health, an alliance that indicates the broad sweep of the project's goals. This is no easy task: the human genome contains about one hundred thousand genes, many of which serve minimal purpose, and some of which serve several purposes (Deaven, 1994: 13). Through technologies like polymerase chain reproduction, technicians can take segments of DNA and reproduce them in identical copies, making it easier to read and compare genetic material from several different people, working out which genetic structures are specific to individuals, and which are characteristic of human beings overall.

The HGP's goal is to construct two kinds of maps of the genome: genetic and physical. A genetic map would determine where on each chromosome specific genes are located, and in which order. Genes exist in what are called base pairs, linked couplings of complementary nucleotides that connect to sugar phosphate backbones in the shape of a spiral staircase (the phosphates are the skeleton of the staircase, the nucleotides are the steps). The order of the nucleotides determines the function of the genes they comprise. A physical map would represent the distances between the genes in the form of a whole chromosome from end to end.

The HGP's larger goal is to read the human body on the molecular level, and to link genes to traits. A central motivation behind this is the desire to root out the causes of heritable terminal diseases such as Huntington's chorea and cystic fibrosis, as well as to locate which specific genetic mutations cause diseases like breast cancer and Alzheimer's, with a view towards more effective cures and even prevention for such diseases. However, there is hardly a one-to-one relationship between gene and trait. Many genes are "uninformative" — they seem to be just fillers on the chromosome. Moreover, mapping and sequencing genes is not a transparent process; its value depends in large part on "the questions one wants the genome map or sequence to answer" (Primrose, 1998: 9).

Genes do not announce themselves by trait: they don't wear labels that say "breast cancer" or "Parkinson's disease" or "schizophrenia." In fact one doesn't look for a specific gene, but for easily identified marker genes that are linked to the gene for the trait being examined (that is, a gene that reproduces along with the trait-specific gene and is found at the same location within a chromosome as that gene). In addition, the genetic patterns that molecular biologists read look nothing like DNA as it exists within the body. Through a complex process of microfuging, hemolyzation, dissolution, chemical separation, lysation, precipitation, and electrophoresis, scientists extract DNA from blood and render it legible as strips of black, white, and grey squares.[3]

The rhetoric of the HGP is complex, particularly since it has embarked on several projects at once: mapping and sequencing the genome, constructing DNA libraries of cloned genetic material that can be internationally available, linking genes to manifested traits, and (although this goal ranks near the bottom of the list) exploring the ethical, legal, and social implications (ELSI) of genetic research and engineering. A bevy of metaphors surround the human genome as it is: the genome is the "book of life," an "ancient hard disk" (an oddly anachronistic presentism), and a "computer operating system" (Doyle, 1994: 52). Whereas the most common technological metaphor for the body at the turn of the century was the machine or the factory (see Seltzer, 1992), DNA is imagined as part of an enormous computer network that combines both database and operating system.

In part so as to nip in the bud futuristic fears of genetic engineering à la *Brave New World*, or more recently *Gattaca*, the HGP has worked hard to present a positive, even heroic image of its work. The Project sells itself as being about pure science on the one hand and helping people on the other, about the noble quest for knowledge and the selfless desire to prevent and heal disease. Implicitly, the HGP also broadcasts its work as a kind of "ontological research — investigating the mysteries of human life itself," not surprisingly, given that the initial Project Director was James D. Watson (Doyle, 1994: 66).

This revelatory claim dovetails with the belief in DNA as the material of truth: if we can get deep enough inside the body to unlock DNA's codes, we will know without a doubt what it means to be human and what materially differentiates human beings from other organisms and from each other.[4] Being able to sketch the shape and configuration of standard genetic structures, such a belief implies, will lead categorically to an understanding of normality and mutation, of health and disease in body and mind and, by association, the health of society. DNA research offers the promise of reconciling the visible outside and occulted inside of the body. It goes beyond medical care, which in comparison seems at best primitive and at worst barbaric, bypassing the vagaries of treatment and going directly to the origin.

I have traced the dream of corporeal transparency throughout this book, and in the discourses of DNA this fantasy approaches its apotheosis. Moreover, DNA materializes the sense that one element of the body can synecdochally speak for and even supplant the whole organism. A sample of DNA from any source within a single body – blood, semen, hair, skin – is the same as any other sample from any other source. Hence we can imagine the body as a collation of millions of copies of the same chunk of information (albeit very complex information) gathered together in the shape of a person. The most basic truth of the human body – what we are – becomes a dizzying prospect in the face of DNA discourse, since the DNA fantasm constructs us as both full of an immense number of meanings (genes full of information), and without a significant, knowing center. Unlike the phrenologists of the nineteenth century, or the hematologists of the mid-twentieth, geneticists posit no anatomical hierarchy. DNA from the brain is no different from DNA from toe-nails, no less packed with genetic information but no more significant as a text to be read.

This fantasy of knowability, however, is less self-evident than it seems. Perhaps the most troubling element of the HGP is the effortlessness with which it constructs categories of "normal" and "diseased" or "mutated" genes. The pathologizing of difference is certainly not a new phenomenon, but it is particularly disturbing to see within a technology whose extravagant truth claims have been so fully digested by both professional and lay audiences. How, after all, do we define normality? How do we determine the standard by which mutation is measured? What is genetic mutation evidence of? How do we distinguish between mutation and disease? As Elisabeth Lloyd poses the question, how do we judge the social as opposed to organismic ill-effects of a putatively genetic difference between people (1994: 106).

Without culturally defined judgments of normal or ab/subnormal outcomes, "genes cannot be labeled as normal or abnormal in any but the most trivial respect – that is, insofar as they differ from the paradigmatic unidimensional causal pathway currently accepted for that gene" (Lloyd, 1994: 107). For example, we see differences in stature within specific parameters as part of the

normal variation of height within and between families: the fact that I am 5'3''
and my brother is 6'1'' does not cause our family concern about possible
genetic mutation. However, the fact that I am a lesbian and my brother is
straight might lead to quite a different result in some circumstances, given the
attempts of research into a "gay gene." The concept of "proper functioning" is
enormously elastic. Is a benign tumor a sign of disease as obviously as it is a
sign of genetic mutation? As Lloyd asks, what values do we have to attach to
genetic mutation in order to classify it as disease? Physical disability of some
kind? Or social behaviors that fall outside the cultural norm? Moreover, these
questions do not even approach the possibility of "abnormal" phenomena as
not genetically caused.

It is not, then, that genes do not tell us what we are on the most basic level
– the stuff we are made of, and the multiple possibilities housed within our
bodies. Clearly, DNA analysis can do just that. A deeper issue is the desire for
DNA to tell us *who* we are, our place in the world, our relationships to others,
which is beyond the power of nucleotides to communicate. Nonetheless, DNA
seems to offer a profound revelation of identity in many of the same ways that
fingerprinting offered in *Pudd'nhead Wilson*, and beyond the limits of
fingerprinting. Not only can DNA identify, it can link, forging the connection
between past and present through heritable genetic arrangements that take on
the shape of a narrative of succession. Just as Tom Driscoll's fingerprints prove
him to be his uncle's murderer and not his uncle's biological nephew, DNA
analysis can be both synchronic (he was at a certain place at a certain time), and
diachronic (his genetic material stretches back in time to his mother and father
and beyond), evidence of who he is and what he has done. It is to these two
uses of DNA as ontological evidence that I will now turn.

Traces and matches: ontology on trial

While the Human Genome Project is so immense, technical, and complex that
most Americans would have trouble imagining what kind of direct impact it
might have on their lives, the deployment of DNA evidence for criminal trials
and identification more generally seems as familiar to contemporary U.S.
culture as fingerprint technology. From its first U.S. use in 1987, DNA
matching of criminal defendants has become if not routine certainly matter-of-
fact. The high profile of DNA evidence during the double murder trial of O.J.
Simpson in 1994 may have complicated public perception of the impermeability of a case built around genetic matches, but it certainly cemented the
role of DNA in criminal investigations, which led to the unquestioned
invocation of DNA testing in the impeachment trial of Bill Clinton in 1998.

Developments in the technology of DNA testing have been swift-moving and had enormous impact. The innovation of variable number tandem repeat technology, in which a short nucleotide sequence can be repeated tandemly up to a hundred times, and polymerase chain reaction (PCR) procedures, by which small sections of DNA can be reproduced *ad infinitum* with little to no degradation in genetic material, has had a major effect on the industry of DNA analysis, making available larger volumes of testable genes.[5] Given how recent DNA evidence is – it has been in common usage in courts for little more than a decade – the scientific power it wields is remarkable.

DNA evidence is used in criminal trials for identification purposes, to link an accused person to the scene of a crime, either because the supposed perpetrator left some genetic material at the crime scene (some hair, semen, blood, skin) or because the victim's DNA traveled with the perpetrator (for example, traces of blood on shoes or clothes or hair on clothing). Genetic evidence is not used often, mainly because of the price of laboratory analysis, but it has become at the very least the technology of last resort, implicitly exotic but putatively foolproof. It is what Bruno Latour has called a "quasi-object"; DNA evidence mediates between the human and the nonhuman, between the real, the social, and the narrated elements of culture. That is, while we imagine DNA to be an object of fact, we experience it through the story we believe it can tell, and the social meanings it bears. DNA is as much signifier as signified.

Indeed, for Harlan Levy, who champions genetic evidence in his popular book *And the Blood Cried Out: A Prosecutor's Spellbinding Account of the Power of DNA* (1996), DNA is *the* transcendental signifier. In chapter after chapter, which deal with early uses of DNA evidence in the late 1980s as well as high-publicity cases such as the Central Park Jogger assault and rape and the O. J. Simpson trial, Levy imbues forensic DNA testing with Solomonic power that allows courts "to go beyond balancing the rights of the accused and the rights of the state, and to aim straight at determination of the truth" (Levy, 1996: 21). This truth is wholly objective, favoring neither accuser nor defendant; it is purely indexical, pointing out the guilty and the innocent by lining up their genetic markers.

The ontological claims of DNA form a crucial part of Levy's analysis of DNA evidence. Marrying a futuristic vision of science as omnipotent agent of knowledge to the familiar language of imperialist expansionism, Levy rewrites science fiction's exploration of the unknown reaches of the galaxy as a voyage into the recesses of the body in search of the truth of the self:

The producers of *Star Trek* got it wrong. Space is not the final frontier. Within each of the cells of the human body, there is a vastness comparable to that of outer space. The exploration of this inner frontier is already beginning to produce answers to some of humankind's most profound questions – about where we came from, how we are all alike, how each of us is an individual.

(1996: 22)

Scientific research is a form of exploration into the wilderness of the body. Borrowing the rhetoric of the Human Genome Project, Levy imagines cells as occupying limitless space. But unlike the immensity of outer space this inner space *is* knowable, if only in some as yet unseen future. As Levy speculates, "[s]omeday in the not too distant future, we will learn just how much of our destiny lies in our DNA and how much in our own hands" (1996: 22–3). This concept of DNA sounds rather like Evelyn Fox Keller's "master molecules," and yet for Levy, the possibility that DNA can *really* tell us about ourselves is utopian not fatalistic.

Levy's vision of a criminal justice system organized around DNA evidence is peculiarly optimistic. He lauds DNA's "great potential as a new tool for doing good ...; [genetic forensics] can promote a more just society, both by making punishment of the guilty more likely and by assuming exoneration of the innocent" (1996: 18). On the one hand, Levy acknowledges that not all criminal trials are created equal, since "most of the defendants have themselves been brutalized by society," and are too often represented by a vastly overworked cadre of publicly (under)funded defenders (*ibid.*: 19). Nonetheless, he sees the District Attorney's work as "profoundly idealistic and socially redeeming ... to sort out the innocent from the guilty, and to press for appropriate punishment for the guilty" (*ibid.*).[6]

Despite this self-proclaimed idealism, Levy's presentation of DNA as the righter of wrongs and dispenser of flawless justice has a markedly conservative slant. Perhaps most troubling is his assumption that "justice" and "criminal justice" are synonymous; that is, that justice is about crime and punishment rather than social equity and equal access to resources.[7] Levy places the development of forensic DNA technology in the context of the "explosion of violent crime" in the 1980s, as well as a growing "fear of crime ... often focused on murder and rape, the most fearsome of crimes" (*ibid.*: 20). Ironically, Levy does not link the increase in violent crime and the *perception* of unruly criminality in urban areas to his own experience of the "go-go '80s" (he began his legal career in a large corporate law firm until he moved to the DA's office), nor does he compare that perception with actual numbers of violent crimes committed during the decade (*ibid.*: 18). Instead, the truth-value of DNA evidence speaks metonymically for the fact of criminality.[8]

And the Blood Cried Out makes an explicit link between the new signifier of DNA and the old signifier of blood as the carrier of identity. The forensics of

DNA effect a neat twist on the 1940s construction of blood as citizenship: for Levy, DNA is the sign of anti-citizenship, of criminality *as* identity. As the book's title suggests, Levy grounds his discussion of genetics in the biblical story of Cain's murder of his brother Abel, in which Abel's blood cried out from the ground to accuse his murderer. Assuming a prophetic tone, Levy looks back to the biblical source and forward to the power of science:

> Thousands of years would go by before blood would cry out again and positively identify a murderer. ... In 1987, it would be a man, not God, who would divine the identity of a murderer through blood. But the blood calling out the murderer's name would not be the victim's but the murderer's own.
>
> (Levy, 1996: 17)

The omniscience of God is replaced by a comprehensive genetic database of sex offenders that can be disseminated both nationally and internationally; as Constance Penley and Andrew Ross put it, people's bodies "become a particular kind of text which can be reduced to code fragments banked in transnational data storage systems" (1991: 6).[9] The substance of blood becomes molecular genetic material, both tiny and "vast." At the same time, Levy acknowledges the narratability of DNA that both interweaves with but can potentially disrupt the real of genes. Rather than being "cold, hard things," the facts of genetics are "extracted, developed, and argued, they become the plot twists of a real-life thriller. The skill and artistry with which facts are developed and argued often determines success or failure" (1996: 80). It is this narrative component to genetic evidence that opens up a hole in Levy's network of body:DNA:truth.

Narrative is unpredictable, logy, unquantifiable. And it is in this realm of narration that DNA as incontrovertible evidence (and Levy's absolute faith in it) faces its most difficult obstacles. The two main forms narration takes in terms of DNA forensics is the translation of human body parts into legible genetic information, and the correspondence between genetic patterns and the frequency with which they occur, particularly in specific ethnic and racial groups. These narrative stumbling-blocks have been the source of much debate both among geneticists and for judicial applications of genetic evidence. Strikingly, Levy downplays the intensity of the debate, holding fast to his argument that the body speaks for itself.[10] However, even he is forced to acknowledge the effects of the interpretive aporias that are part and parcel of genetic forensics (although he attributes these crises of interpretation to insufficient scientific understanding of the human genome, not the nature of DNA evidence itself).

The most passionate debate over "genetic fingerprinting" in criminal trials erupted over an issue that DNA evidence was supposed to have erased through its objective display of truth: racial and ethnic difference. Given how similar human beings are to each other in genetic make-up, loci at which genes differ from person to person are crucial for establishing a link between two separate pieces of DNA. But, even with the ability to manufacture long chains of repeating DNA, labs cannot reconstruct the entire genome of each person. They examine several stretches of genes and attempt to match them. The question arises, then: How can one prove that the genetic patterns revealed are uniquely those of the person whom they match?

More complicating was the practice by law enforcement and genetic scientists to compile racially and ethnically specific match likelihoods, defining the chances that another person could have the same genetic arrangement at the same site on the chromosome as a given probability within a certain group, such as one in a million among African Americans or one in 475,000 among whites, or a similar formula. It is this practice of estimating probabilities within racial groups that generated a bitter debate among geneticists in the early 1990s, and that illustrates the problems of the confusions of identity of DNA: as simply a real object and as a real, social, and narrated quasi-object.

In an issue of *Science* (1991) Richard C. Lewontin and Daniel L. Hartl published an article that pointed directly to the ambiguities of the narratibility of DNA as an indicator of sample matching.[11] As Lewontin and Hartl argue, DNA match probability within populations can depend a great deal upon what story one tells about those populations. Imagining, for example, that "Hispanic" is an undifferentiated group creates a very different sense of genetic intermixing from acknowledging the differences (and often continental distances) between Puerto Rican, Chicano, Salvadoran, Ecuadorean, Dominican, and Brazilian (to name a few) populations. Moreover, some Latin American countries like Argentina and Peru experienced major infusions of immigrants from Italy, Eastern Europe, North Africa, and East Asia. The genetic patterns of Guatemalans, many of whom have exclusively or mostly American Indian heritage, can hardly be imagined as lining up with the DNA of Cubans, a large number of whom have predominantly African backgrounds.

Similarly, one story about the ethnic constitution of whites in the United States limns a heterogenous, ethnically intermixed group: the proverbial melting-pot. But, as Lewontin and Hartl argue, most of what might be called white ethnic populations are fairly homogenous in the U.S. Moreover, even if Jews do not exclusively choose other Jews as partners, or Irish other Irish, or Norwegians other Norwegians, exogamous partnerships are fairly new – often no more than one generation old. In addition, regional shifts within a population group (Lewontin and Hartl give the example of Moorish settlement in southern Spain, and other examples are plentiful, such as the concentration of African-descent people in the Bahia region of Brazil, or the ethnic combinations of any borderland area) mean that there can be major genetic dissimilarities within a single country, let alone a region or race. Finally, Lewontin and Hartl found "one-third more genetic variation among Irish, Spanish, Italians, Slavs, Swedes, and other [so-called 'white'] subpopulations than ... on the average, between Europeans, Asians, Africans, Amerinds, and Oceanians" (1991: 1747).

Given these differences and similarities, as well as the tendency towards endogamy that was the rule until only a generation or two ago, Lewontin and Hartl argue that a story which constructs meaningful racial categories and then assigns to them genetic probabilities is at best mistaken and at worst "terribly misleading" (1991: 1749). What can "white" or "black" mean, let alone the hugely various categories of "Hispanic" or "Asian" (Korean? Pakistani? Uzbeki? Non-Han Chinese?)?

Interestingly, the response to these objections does not take a narrative but a "scientific," that is, statistical form. Levy, and Ranajit Chakraborty and Kenneth K. Kidd, two geneticists who responded to Lewontin and Hartl's article in the same issue of *Science*, skate over the fact that the shape of genetic material is in large part the result of human decisions about reproduction (let alone the social pressures inherent in the decisions about partnering and childbearing that people make all the time). As Chakraborty and Kidd affirm, "no assumptions regarding 'random mating' or 'population substructure' are needed" to compute genetic matching within broadly defined racial and ethnic groups, since what is at stake is the accuracy of the sample and the comprehensiveness of the database against which the sample is compared (1991: 1736).

Scientific evidence itself cannot tell its own story in the courts. Up until 1993, it had to conform to standards of professional acceptability that were established in the 1920s, commonly called the *"Frye* standard," after the case in which the standard was articulated (Levy, 1996: 110). Given that most laypeople do not feel confident enough to judge scientific evidence, the court in *Frye* ruled that any scientific method used in evidence must have "general acceptance" by the professional community of researchers. Given the debate that emerged in the early 1990s over the issue of probability in DNA testing within ethnic and racial groups, *Frye* was a tough standard to achieve. Although in 1993 the Supreme Court found that the *Frye* standard was too "austere" (*Daubert v. Merrell Dow Pharmaceuticals*, quoted in Levy, 1996: 122), the Court insisted that scientific evidence be "not only relevant but reliable"; that is, having been tested, published in a peer reviewed journal and, ideally but not necessarily, generally accepted.

For Levy, the disagreements between Lewontin and Hartl on one side and

Chakraborty and Kidd on the other were not theoretical. He represents Lewontin and Hartl as loose cannons, emotionally unstable and scientifically unreliable (Lewontin "hit the roof" in one conversation; both Hartl and Lewontin imagined that their opponents were conspiring with the FBI to delegitimate them). More importantly, Lewontin and Hartl argued that until better ethnic and racial population data could be gathered, probability matches were at best unreliable and at worst inaccurate. At the very least, they recommended that the hypertrophic probability matches cited by forensic geneticists – one in seven billion or one in fifty million – be slimmed down. To Levy this is appalling: here is a technology that speaks the truth being sidelined by minutiae and the squabbles of ivory tower specialists.

Levy's book attempts to link complex scientific discoveries with the suspense of a crime novel, and on the whole he is successful. *And the Blood Cried Out* is a hybrid text: part police procedural, part scientific primer, part sensationalist true-crime account, part policy brief. Most striking about Levy's approach, though, is the absence of actual people from his case studies. Certainly, he acknowledges that each case involves people: they are the victims of crime, the accused, the police, the lawyers on both sides, the laboratory technicians, the judges, and the juries (as well as news reporters, the "general public," geneticists, and other marginal cast members). But, given the gruesome nature of many of the crimes Levy analyzes, the physical bodies of victims and perpetrators are transformed into mere carapaces for the genetic material teeming in inner space.

This disembodiment of the carriers of genetic material carries over into Levy's defense of the constitutionality of taking genetic material from a suspect. Blood, he argues, is not covered by constitutional guarantees, and taking blood "does not violate a suspect's privilege against self-incrimination because the privilege applies only to oral testimony. Blood is evidence, not testimony; it can be seized pursuant to a search warrant" (Levy, 1996: 100). Thus blood can testify against the body from which it was extracted; transformed into evidence, genetic material speaks as a discrete object, totally divorced from the organism that gave it life and whose most basic physical structures those genes shape. Not only is blood read as evidence, it is imagined as no longer corporeal, estranged from embodiedness.

The promise of DNA, like that of fingerprints, is dehumanization, "moving all emotional issues ... off center stage. DNA would provide 'objective' scientific proof of identity or innocence" (Levy, 1996: 106). The further we can get into the body, the greater the level of molecular particularity that can be derived, the more removed we are from *personal* specificity. Ontology turns inside out: the more we can know about identity on a cellular level, the further we seem from a conception of human beings as eccentric collections of characteristics. In fact, the language of genetics uses the rhetoric of "traits" rather than "characteristics": something pulled or drawn from the self instead of something engraved upon it.

Levy's dream of a vast data bank of convicted violent criminals, particularly sex offenders, is an extension of this disarticulation between a material body and its genetic components. A person would not even have to be in the same country when a DNA match was made, or even alive: preserved materials could be matched to a database entry years after a crime was committed. He imagines DNA as both a "truth machine" and a "time machine," ranging across time and space to identify rapists and murderers as such: even the victims themselves are displaced by swabs of vaginal discharge, swatches of blood or saliva, a single hair.

Nowhere has this recently been clearer than in a case in Wisconsin late in 1999. A prosecutor in Milwaukee, lacking an actual person to attach rape charges to, indicted the DNA of a suspected repeat rapist. "John Doe" was identifiable only by his processed DNA, which had been derived from semen samples taken from the three unnamed survivors of rape. These attacks ranged over the course of almost six years, but "John Doe" had never been apprehended. Fearing that the six-year statute of limitations on rape would expire, the district attorney for Milwaukee County indicted "him." "We know that one person raped these three women," DA Norman Gahn was quoted as saying. "We just don't know who he is" (Dedman, 1999: 1). In this case, the body and its identifiers are now completely divorced from each other – DNA becomes the self in the absence of the body. "John Doe" exists both as a genetic reality and as a legal fiction – his DNA is waiting for his body to catch up with him.

I am not arguing here that DNA evidence cannot serve an important function in discovering and prosecuting the perpetrators of violent crime, or in exonerating those falsely accused, both of which uses of genetics Levy discusses at length and in depth. Rather, I am struck by how closely Levy's rhetoric of DNA resembles Francis Galton's language about fingerprints (although without the explicitly eugenicist and racist intentions that Galton brought to his work). Genetic fingerprints, like actual ones, are useful because they remove investigation of a crime away from the bodies of the perpetrator and the victim; they bypass acquaintance or familiarity and move directly into identification. The difference between Galton and Levy, though, is the difference between other meanings which fingerprints and DNA carry. Given the ontological freight that DNA bears, the sign of criminal activity – the match – is also, implicitly, a sign of selfhood. Fingerprints reveal where a person has been and what she has done; DNA reveals who she is.

The fantasmatic link between the Human Genome Project and forensic DNA identification lies not on the surface of police investigation but deeper down, in the uneasy connections between identification and identity. The debates over racial grouping for DNA evidence strike at the very heart of how Americans imagine identity, and at the fragility of genetic explanations of the category we call "race." For Levy, the issue is one of sufficient proof: genes speak for people clearly enough that the people need not speak for themselves, and genetic matching trumps human motivation (it is no coincidence that Levy generally focuses on unambiguously brutal and bloody crimes in which the perpetrators are easily defined as monsters: multiple violent rapes, slashing murders of women and children, and the like).

Levy conflates identification and identity into the (for him) eternal but oddly anonymous dyad of perpetrator and victim through the process of shrinking the self down into the minuteness of clustered genes. Lewontin and Hartl offer one challenge to this way of looking at how actual people create new genetic combinations or maintain the same pool of chromosomal material, but even this challenge is moored (or even mired) in the anonymity of the "sample population." In the remainder of this chapter I will examine how two sets of circumstances splice the seeming discorporeality of genetic identification with deeply felt patterns of identity that both echo the shifts and hybridities of the genetic map of the United States, and attempt after more than a century to effect a *rapprochement* between identity, heredity, and self.

Family ties and genetic links

Shirlee Taylor Haizlip's family memoir *The Sweeter the Juice* is also a hybrid text: part autobiography, part family history, part meditation on racial identity in the U.S., part detective story. Haizlip traces her mother's and her father's families over the course of several hundred years from before slavery to the birth of her children. Her larger goal is to show the ways in which racial identity, particularly African American identity but also whiteness, is the result of (or, perhaps, has calcified despite or even because of) multiple intermixings of different kinds of people – those of European descent with Africans/African Americans, black people with Native Americans, Indians with whites, and so on. In using her own (admittedly unusually well-placed and highly educated) black family as a case in point for the racial variety of the United States, Haizlip searches through her family tree to find predecessors of the African, Irish, German, English, and Native American branches. Most gripping is her account of her mother Margaret Morris' father and siblings, all of whom passed as white, and who cut off all contact with Margaret until Haizlip herself tracked down one of her aunts and other relatives decades later.

What is unusual about Haizlip's story is her sense of her own racial identity.

As David Chioni Moore has noted, the African American heritage narrative –
of which Alex Haley's *Roots*, which Moore analyzes in depth, is the prototype
– typically traces its origin exclusively back to Africa as *the* ontological source:
"*Roots* argues that in tracing his ancestry to a single indisputable source in
Gambia circa 1700, Alex Haley has found out ... indisputably *who he is*"
(Moore, 1994: 11). Despite his multiple ancestries as recent as two post-slavery
Irish immigrant great-grandfathers on his father's side, Haley implicitly applies
the one-drop rule to his own genealogy, identifying Kunta Kinte (who
represents only 1/256th of his genetic self) as the founding figure of his family
rather than his Cherokee or Irish ancestors. Certainly this is not surprising,
given the legacies of slavery and segregation that formed contemporary beliefs
in what constitutes racial identity.

Indeed, as Moore points out, "[o]ne would have been stunned ... to have
found Haley's ancestral discursus [at the beginning of *Roots*] beginning with a
fully genealogically defensible sentence: 'Early in the spring of 1750, in the
village of Ballyshannon on the upper end of Donegal Bay, a man child was
born to Paddy and Mary O'Reilly,'" instead of the now iconic birth of Kunta
Kinte in the village of Juffure in Gambia (Moore, 1994: 15). But this is exactly
what Haizlip does. Her history of her mother's family echoes Haley's epic
introduction to his own family chronicle, but she transposes the events from
Africa to Ireland:

> My mother's family story begins as many American stories begin, with a
> transatlantic journey. The year was 1860, and the family travelers were
> Irish, from County Tipperary: William Maher, my mother's great-
> grandfather, his wife, Mary Katherine, and his daughter Margaret.
>
> (Haizlip, 1994: 35)

Rather than tracing her primary predecessors back to the ancestral village,
Haizlip represents them in transit, already on their far less traumatic middle
passage between Ireland and Washington, DC. Like racial identity itself, her
mother's family is in motion when we first see them. Haizlip resists a sense of
racial fixedness, a decision that gains resonance through the process of her
search for her mother's "white" siblings:

> I began my search for my mother's family believing that I was looking
> for black people "passing for white". ... But what I ultimately found, I
> realized, were black people who had become white. After all, if you look
> white, act white, live white, vacation white, go to school white, marry
> white and die white, are you not "white"?
>
> (*ibid.*: 266)

Moreover, by the end of the book, considering the substantial numbers of her white ancestors, she even questions her own classification as black, theorizing that "I would probably now describe myself as a person of mixed race rather than as black, although I know I will never lose my black feelings," that is, her acculturation to a black community (*ibid.*: 267).

That is not to say that Haizlip does not invoke as incontrovertible a connection to her ancestors as Haley does to his. While race may not be an ontological essence for Haizlip, genes are. Indeed, I would argue that DNA replaces race as the ruling metaphor for human identity in *The Sweeter the Juice*. Just as Alex Haley feels like he finds himself listening to a Gambian griot tell centuries-old stories of the Kinte clan, Haizlip recognizes herself looking into the faces of her long-lost relatives. Her rationale for the search she embarked on for her "white" family members is telling. While recognizing that "the division in my family has caused so much pain," she explains that "my children and I need to know the rest of what has shaped me" (Haizlip, 1994: 39). By this, Haizlip does not mean shared environment, family customs and traditions, or values — after all, the Morrises who passed had to reject explicitly all of those bonds in their new lives in the white world. "The rest," for Haizlip, is chromosomal: "Simply put, part of their genetic codes belongs to us as well" (*ibid.*: 34).[12]

In *The Sweeter the Juice*, the most significant evidence of genetic relationship between people is visible on the body itself, in facial features and physical attributes or indirectly through heritable conditions like the neurological disorder that stretched down through the generations from her slave-owning white great-great-grandfather to her own cousins. At the beginning of her research, Haizlip traces her mother's line back through Edward Everett Morris, Margaret's grandfather and a former slave. Edward had been the son of his owner, James D. Halyburton, whose maternal great-aunt was Martha Washington. Despite the distance in family relation and in time, Haizlip connects her own family's features to Washington's, imagining an unbroken genetic link: "From pictures, Nelly Custis, Martha Washington's granddaughter, could be my sister, or my mother's sister. Are these pure coincidences or are they nature's advisories that blood will tell?" (Haizlip, 1994: 47).

Haizlip's inclination throughout her book is towards the latter conclusion. Meeting a cousin and her daughter for the first time, Haizlip imagines them as reproductions of previously unknown genetic material, the missing link between herself and their shared ancestors. Like Haley hearing the griot in Gambia, Haizlip sees in the faces of her family the genetic story of her own heritage. Her cousins "did not realize how much they had fulfilled my dream of seeing another great-grandparent's image ... the woman their chromosomes had copied gene by gene" (Haizlip, 1994: 105–6).

In fact, there is little that Haizlip does not attribute to genetic inheritance, from emotional stamina to a connection to the supernatural – the result of "the genes of fantasy, tale-telling from our mingled roots" (1994: 138). Analyzing her mother's childhood trauma of parental abandonment followed by "rejecting relatives, the numerous guardians, the moves, the madness [of her eventual long-term caregiver], the cruelty, the death and dying ... I wonder how she stayed sane, how she survived, how she became loving and able to give. Then I think there must be a gene for resiliency" (*ibid*.: 97). Likewise, she imagines that "the independent thinking, leadership and political advocacy are the results of tendencies passed down from those oppressive times [of slavery and segregation] through more than six generations," like the prominent nose or thin lips that were another heritage from her Morris ancestors, or the strong chin of the Taylor family (*ibid*.: 108).

The truth of DNA is, for Haizlip, not just the truth of personal history. It is also evidenced on a national level. Genetic material is what connects Americans to each other, from the most august to the most lowly, from Martha Washington to the working-class, mixed-race Morrises, and to Americanness as an identity. The mixed-race body is the meeting place for the diversity of generic heritage that Haizlip sees as defining the United States, and that she herself embodies. In her own poem that she uses as an epigraph, Haizlip reconstructs U.S. history through the multiple claims to the American soil by Native Americans, Africans, and immigrants, all of whom, in her words, "loved the land" (*ibid*.: 8). By the end of the poem, however, America is not defined by terrain, and Haizlip's own connection to the land has been internalized: "This then is my claim: I am in all America / All America is in me" (*ibid*.).

This interpenetration of self and nation occurs on the genetic level rather than the material or political planes. Despite her invocation of land – profoundly resonant in a country in which white immigrants were ceded homesteading rights over ground that had been taken from Indians and vainly promised to freed slaves, hence in which one segment of Haizlip's ancestors benefited at the expense of the others – Haizlip sees herself as the culmination of the literal mixing of blood in which "[g]enes and chromosomes from Africa, Europe and a pristine America commingled and created me" (*ibid*.: 15).

The persistence of history is parallel to and explained by the persistence of genetic material. We cannot forget slavery and its miscegenated past because it perseveres within the body itself, playing itself out generation after generation. How long might it take to move beyond the mixed-race history of the U.S.? Certainly as long as it takes for a gene to be swallowed up. In a discussion of the connections between her own immediate family and its past, Haizlip shifts into a meditation on the gene as immortal marker of genealogical linkage:

How far down does a gene travel before it mutates and becomes kinky hair instead of straight, gray eyes instead of blue, pale skin instead of tan, thick lips instead of thin? When do the chromosomes break and recombine to create genetic changes? As fragments of genetic material move among the chromosomes, how many generations can a family 'look' sustain itself? How long do the transposable elements of DNA move from place to place, controlling the expression of genes? When does the genetic information wear itself out completely?

(*ibid.*: 46)

Given that Haizlip speculates about family resemblances between her siblings and children on the one hand and distant ancestors Martha Washington and Sir Walter Scott on the other, a possible answer to her final question might be "never." Moreover, even those genes that lurk, recessive, within the folds of the body, are not necessarily hidden for ever. They can always make their appearance unexpectedly, like the regrowth of previously nappy hair that Haizlip's father experienced in his seventies, "straight, like an Indian's. It was as if some recessed Native American hair gene had escaped and overpowered its African-American brothers and sisters" (*ibid.*: 31).

An image like this of competition and struggle between genetic components is unusual in this text, however. The trajectory of genetic identity in *The Sweeter the Juice* moves from separation and atomization towards reconciliation and connection on the personal and national level, and Haizlip imagines her own body as the ground for that reunion. As a child she thought of her mixed racial and ethnic heritage as a series of separately articulated identities, each with its own place in her body but not connected to each other. She was, in her own mind, a kind of miscegenated Frankenstein's monster, with "English ears, Irish eyes and black hair" (*ibid.*: 101). This childhood sense of separation between the different elements is similar to Twain's invocation of the one-thirty-second of black "blood" that circulates through Roxana's body in *Pudd'nhead Wilson* that "outvotes" the thirty-one parts of white ancestry. Haizlip envisaged each part of her heritage as self-contained, a self-image that led to an examination of "my hands, arms, legs and feet" in the desire to find out "which held my Indian blood, my colored blood, and my white blood" (*ibid.*): a *reductio ad absurdum* of the segregation of the national body that was an instrinsic part of Haizlip's youth even in the comparatively integrated world of southern Connecticut of the 1940s and 1950s.

But this segregation is, of course, only fantasmatic. Haizlip tells this story of her childhood speculation that each part of her racial make-up might occupy its own corporeal space in order to point out its impossibility. Just as the segregation of the body politic was an artificial structure that attempted to erase the long histories of racial intermixture within the United States, Haizlip's youthful desire to identify and label the different strands of "blood" in her veins is superseded by the recognition that genetic heritage manifests itself through the visibility of hybridity. On the one hand, the "blood will tell" – Martha Washington's mouth or Edward Everett Morris' nose or Julian Taylor's "Indian" hair – but the manifestation of those features is evidence of a chromosomal interrelation between people defined as racially different from each other. Whereas the judicial use of DNA evidence assumes a body unmoored from human relationship, and even a person set outside the pale of membership in a common humanity, Haizlip's search for her genetic material in both her white, black, and Native American ancestors and her (passing for) white contemporaries insists on commonality between individuals who might otherwise seem totally unrelated. Genetic research proves not the intrinsic differences between Americans but their intimate links. While statistics about the percentage of white ancestry for black people and vice versa are "subject to interpretation and reinterpretation ... the fact that anthropologists and biologists continue to glean these truths from their study of genetic data gives weight to the claims that there are no 'real white Americans'" (Haizlip, 1994: 15). DNA is truth for Haizlip, there is no question about that, but the truth it represents is one of racial unknowability and human relationship on the most basic level.

   Whereas for Levy, DNA's utopian promise is as a divider – the bad guys from the good, the guilty from the innocent – the idealized topos which genetic evidence occupies for Haizlip is located in unification and reconciliation. Where race, as a social construct, divides (and unequally), DNA unites through the bodily signs of facial features and the psychic connections of family traits across race and class. Moreover, these links are not simply familial, at least not directly. They are arrayed across the human species. "It is a consoling idea," Haizlip muses in the last paragraph of *The Sweeter the Juice* (1994: 268),

   that everyone on this earth is a shade of the protein called melanin; that black and white alike, we are all a gradation of a color called brown. I know that in the blueprint for every human being there are some three billion units of DNA, arranged over twenty-three pairs of chromosomes. Spread throughout that mix are about a hundred thousand genes. No one has counted the human couplings that resulted in genetic mixings and crossovers. And Lucy, that ancient group of fossil bones found in Africa, is the mother of us all.

Haizlip's first "consoling idea" rests on the outside of the body, in the skin – not surprisingly, given the ravages that minute differences in complexion wrought on her mother's family. But the commonalities of skin do not do the imaginative work she needs to envision the most basic bond between human beings. Skin is too changeable either with tanning or make-up (she comments on the heavy white powder with which her "white" aunt Grace Cramer covers her face); it can vary across the body, a variable which the judge's instruction for Alice Jones Rhinelander to strip to the waist tried to circumvent. Haizlip believes in a bodily link more basic, more immutable.

For Haizlip, the lesson of the racial boundaries that have divided on the surface what is incontrovertibly affiliated beneath is a literalization of the liberal saw, "we're all alike under the skin." Both literally and metaphorically she moves beyond the evidence of integument and the way that skin contains and defines individuals, breaking the body down into its "three billion units of DNA," in effect dehumanizing bodies into their constitutive molecules. We are, she says, our genes. But this molecularization is for Haizlip a distillation of what is most essentially human. Our genetic material separates us from other animals, and solders us to each other.

This vision of DNA verges on science fiction/fantasy along the lines of *Fantastic Voyage*: the further we get into the body the huger it becomes until it encompasses us, not the other way around. DNA is not inside us; we are inside it, or rather, inside the network of genetic combinations that make up both the North American continent and the whole world. Moreover, our DNA is immortal, extending from the beginnings of human life down to today, present in both the fossilized bones of an unknown prehistoric female corpse and the blood of herself and her readers. We are only a few degrees of separation from each other within this immense web of chromosomes. Whereas Harlan Levy constructs DNA within a rhetoric of limitation and minutiae, Shirlee Taylor Haizlip incorporates DNA into a *weltanschauung* of amplitude and sorority (this is in large part a story about mothers, daughters, and sisters). Sisterhood is indeed global, and transhistorical; sisterhood is chromosomal.

The mother of us all: Sally Hemings and the disappearing black Jeffersons

Haizlip's invocation of the universality of DNA and its power to link all human beings to a common African ancestor is not just utopian; it is also wry. Try though they might to deny any racially mixed ancestry, Haizlip implies, white people are descended from Africans, from the *Ur* African Lucy. If Lucy is "the mother of us all," and the one-drop rule still obtains in the American imagination, then *all* humanity is black, following the condition of the original progenitrix.

The image of a black woman as a founding mother is as foreign to mainstream U.S. culture as a picture of an African Jesus, or the popular post-Black Power scene of Leonardo's *Last Supper* rendered with black figures, both of which can be found in Afrocentric emporia around the United States. Given the marginalization of women generally and women of African descent in particular throughout the history of European hegemony in the Americas, the narrative of racial identity which Haizlip suggests has a crisply subversive edge. It is not too far from a version of the founding of the United States that long had *sub rosa* currency and in the past few years has been substantiated by genetic research: the story of a child or children fathered by Thomas Jefferson and borne by his slave Sally Hemings.

Jefferson's biographers have long denied the possibility of a sexual relationship between the President and Hemings, a slave who was decades his junior and was brought into the Jefferson household through Thomas' wife Martha Wayles Jefferson. In fact, Hemings was Martha's half-sister: both shared a father, John Wayles. Hemings accompanied her half-niece Maria Jefferson to join Thomas in Paris in 1786 and remained in France until the Jeffersons returned in 1789, during which time historian Fawn Brodie speculates the relationship between Jefferson and Hemings began (Lander and Ellis, 1998: 13).[13] Although it is not clear when Hemings first became pregnant, since her son Madison claimed she first conceived in Paris but there is no extant record of a child, she definitely conceived and gave birth to a daughter, Harriet, at Monticello in 1795; the baby died in 1796. She bore a son, Beverly, in 1798, and a daughter in 1799, who died in infancy. Over the next nine years, Hemings gave birth to three more children: a second Harriet in 1801, Madison in 1805, and another son, Eston, in 1808. All the children were conceived when Jefferson was at Monticello (Gordon-Reed, 1997: 195–6).

In the two centuries between the birth of Hemings' children and the discovery of probable genetic connections between Jefferson's and Hemings' descendants, a bitter dispute raged over whether Jefferson and Hemings were sexually involved, and whether that involvement produced children. Muddying the controversy was the fact that the first suggestion that such a relationship had existed came from James Callender, a previous Jefferson supporter, who in 1802 spread the story about Jefferson's "nigger children" with his slave "Dusky Sally" in an attempt to smear the then President (Gordon-Reed, 1997: 59). The issue was framed in terms of attacks on Jefferson and defenses of him, in terms of scandal and reputation. Jefferson's "defenders" set the pattern for subsequent biographers, claiming that such a relationship would have been "impossible."[14]

The fragility of arguments against a Hemings–Jefferson relationship rested in large part on the paucity of evidence on either side, but particularly within the anti-Hemings camp. As Annette Gordon-Reed has argued, "the historical battleground in the dispute over the alleged Jefferson–Hemings liaison has not been over what amounts to absolute proof. The battle has been over controlling public impressions of the amount and the nature of the evidence" (1997: xv). Given that Gordon-Reed is both an attorney and a historian it is hardly surprising that she uses the terminology of "evidence" and "proof" in explicitly legal contexts: in her investigation of the controversy, she insists that the testimonies of both sides carry equal weight, and to be equally subject to the same burden of proof.

The Jefferson–Hemings debate remained largely ideological, with the Jeffersonians maintaining the upper hand both in the historical record and as guardians of the Jefferson legacy (no small consideration, since Jefferson descendants have access to free tuition at the University of Virginia and burial in the Jefferson family graveyard at Monticello, among other perks). However, in late 1998, Eugene A. Foster and his colleagues revealed in *Nature* that the Y-chromosome DNA haplotypes (that is, specific sets of genetic arrangements) from male-line descendants of Thomas Jefferson's paternal uncle matched those of descendants of Hemings' youngest son, Eston Hemings Jefferson. Foster and his team took samples from five male-line descendants of Field Jefferson, Thomas Jefferson's uncle, five male-line descendants of the two sons of Thomas Woodson, who was identified as the child Sally Hemings conceived in France, and one male-line descendant of Eston Hemings Jefferson, as well as samples from three male-line descendants of the three sons of John Carr, the grandfather of Jefferson's nephews Samuel and Peter who were also rumored to be the father(s) of Hemings' children. Because a substantial amount of the Y-chromosome is passed relatively unchanged through generations from father to son, it is a reliable indicator of male-line relationship (Foster *et al.*, 1998: 27).

Foster and his colleagues found no haplotype correspondence between the Jeffersons and the Woodson or Carr descendants, but did find significant correspondence between the Jefferson and Hemings descendants. These findings led them to the conclusion that "the simplest and most probable explanations ... are that Thomas Jefferson, rather than one of the Carr brothers, was the father of Eston Hemings Jefferson" (*ibid.*). Although Foster *et al.* suggested other genetic possibilities for this correspondence, they dismissed such theories as "unlikely" (*ibid.*: 28).

These revelations garnered front-page attention in the U.S. and international press, as well as a fair amount of soul-searching. What is most interesting to me, however, is the ways in which the news generated a series of evaluations from a variety of Americans about the relationship between the biological body, the racial body, and the body politic. Certainly, Foster's research produced evidence for the biological connection between Thomas

Jefferson and at the very least one of Sally Hemings' children. But it also highlighted the ironies of the genetic apartheid that had so long been the official policy of the white mainstream, and which had been so early and so often transgressed and denied simultaneously.

Most immediately affected by this news were members of the Monticello Association, an élite organization of the descendants of Jefferson's two daughters. The Association had long excluded the Hemings family, citing the absence of material evidence that they were Jeffersons. However, the Association was hardly extreme; its president Robert Gillespie aligned himself with "the mainstream historians [in their belief] that Jefferson wouldn't have fathered Sally Hemings' children" (Smith and Wade, 1998: 24). The DNA evidence, however, "chang[ed] my attitude" (*ibid.*).

Indeed, the DNA evidence seemed to render established Jefferson experts disoriented to the point of being tongue-tied, so difficult it was for them to integrate this new information into their image of their subject. Joseph J. Ellis, who had recently published a landmark biography of Jefferson, *American Sphinx: The Character of Thomas Jefferson*, in which he had dismissed the stories about Jefferson and Hemings, focused on the DNA research as evidence, using explicitly legal language to couch his volte-face:

> It's not so much a change of heart, but this is really new evidence. And it
> – prior to this evidence, I think it was a very difficult case to know. ...
> [B]ecause I got it wrong, I think I want to step forward and say this new
> evidence constitutes, well, evidence beyond any reasonable doubt that
> Jefferson had a longstanding sexual relationship with Sally Hemings.
>
> (Alexander, 1998: 7)

What is striking about these comments is that they are considered *news*. That is to say, the intermixing of black and white was a reality from the first arrival of Africans in North America in the early seventeenth century. Miscegenation was a common trope of slave narratives and abolitionist tracts, noticed by foreign observers and Americans alike. Indeed, the rumors about Jefferson and Hemings were translated by William Wells Brown into one of the many versions of his novel *Clotelle*, variously subtitled "The Senator's Daughter" and "The President's Daughter." Nonetheless, white Jefferson descendants, and many white observers, "had to be dragged kicking and screaming by the production of DNA evidence into admitting the possibility" that the claims of Eston Hemings Jefferson's progeny were legitimate (Truscott, 1998: 10).

The Jefferson–Hemings story reveals a deep vein of denial within the U.S. imagination about slavery. On the one hand, the impregnation of slave women by their owners and overseers has become a near-cliché of slavery narratives, with Alex Haley's representation of his ancestor Kizzy's rape by the venal Tom Lea in the book and television versions of *Roots* as an archetype of the genre. On the other hand, the rhetoric of distance disembodies this scenario: with the dissolution of desegregation policies and the widespread belief that racism has been banished to the lunatic fringe, the crime of slavery has been rendered "unimaginable," and hence exempt from actual consideration.[15]

Mainstream press interviews with African Americans about the Jefferson–Hemings relationship reveal a significantly different set of beliefs about the constitution of the United States, and the material effects of the racial mixing that was at the very least a major economic element in the gross domestic product of the U.S. until emancipation. For many black Americans, the evidence of the sexual politics of slavery has lain on the surface of their bodies for centuries. As Fareed Thomas, a high school student in Los Angeles, asked in the days after the Jefferson–Hemings story hit, "[w]hy did 'white society' need DNA evidence to accept what 'ordinary people with common sense like me' had recognized as a fact long ago?" (Terry, 1998: A18).

Thomas' language resituates the rhetoric of common sense and American ordinariness from the white mainstream to the black margins. Black invisibility is recast as white blindness, and white scientific expertise is displaced by black knowingness and clear-sightedness. "Look at the black people in this class," Don Terry quotes history teacher Fahamisha Butler as saying; "we are the color of the rainbow. Our ancestors didn't come over from Africa this way" (Terry, 1998: A18). In the same article titled "DNA Results Confirmed Old News About Jefferson, Blacks Say," African Americans of all classes, from the publisher of the *Chicago Reporter* to a high school teacher to a blue-collar worker invoked the common sense of the visible as preceding and superseding the élite evidence of DNA (not to mention the lower position Jefferson occupied among blacks than whites, given his slave-holding).[16]

Perhaps one of the sharpest ironies of this story is that by the middle of his life Eston Hemings Jefferson was passing for white, at least part of the time. In the 1830 Census, Sally Hemings and her two sons Madison and Eston (all freed after Thomas Jefferson's death in 1826) were listed as white, although from the memoirs of Madison Jefferson it seems clear that both sons' neighbors had heard that they were the children of Jefferson and a slave (Gordon-Reed, 1997: 2). Madison and Eston lived as black in Ohio in the 1860s and 1870s but by 1873 all of Madison's siblings "had left the world of blacks and become part of the white world" (Gordon-Reed, 1997: 18).

Eston Hemings Jefferson's children had been born into whiteness, and their current descendants – at least by Shirlee Taylor Haizlip's definition – *are* white. As one of them, Julia Jefferson Westerinen, described in a letter to the *New York Times* just after Foster and his team published their *Nature* article, the contemporary Hemings descendants were in the odd position of claiming a black heritage which their ancestors had been only to happy to give up. Westerinen was well aware of the chasm between her family and others of similar mixed descent who did not pass:

> We cannot know what it is like to be a modern African American or what it must have been like for Sally Hemings when Jefferson stepped over what should have been a boundary of decency in the master–slave relationship. Our branch of the family passed into white society, and we've never experienced the life that might have been ours had circumstances been different.
>
> (Westerinen, 1998)

Rather than dwelling on racial difference, however, Westerinen used the historical fact of her ancestor's passing to unite the body politic into one family. All Americans, she claimed, "come from a long line of ancestors and cannot say we are from 'unmixed' backgrounds. Our common heritage cannot be denied." Annette Gordon-Reed echoed these sentiments on the public television program *Newshour with Jim Lehrer* in November 1998, citing as "the moral of this story ... that we're not two separate people, black and white; we are a people who share a common culture, a common land, and it turns out a common blood line" (Alexander, 1998: 7).

The rhetoric of the "American family" as an intertwined racial fiber can fray easily, however. As Drew G. Faust pointed out in a letter to the *New York Times* shortly after Westerinen's letter, the claim that "we're all one American family" is dangerously close to the white male slave-owners' self-image as paterfamilias, talking of their "families white and black." Faust focuses on the disjuncture between biology and mutuality, since "in the context of American slavery, sexual liaisons between masters and slaves were almost certainly not romances [and] were in many cases rapes. ... Proclaiming ourselves family means little if we use the language of our slave-owning forebears to obscure persisting realities of inequality" (Faust, 1998: A24). Or, in the words of high school student Fareed Thomas, "[w]hat kind of society are we living in when we had a President that even owned slaves?"

Thomas' blending of past and present tenses gets at the root of the question here. For black (and a few white) commentators, the United States is still living with the unexorcized ghost of slavery. That is visible on the skin of the majority of people of African descent living in the U.S. – evidence enough for those people who see variations in color among their own family members, as well as those who experience the legacy of slavery through white racism and unequal access. But the desire by the white mainstream to "leave slavery behind" has served to erase the easily visible as a legitimate discourse and resituate what qualifies as meaningful evidence back into the blood, where it cannot be seen without the imprimatur of expertise. Or rather, where it *could* not be seen: the mechanism of denial has, in the Hemings–Jefferson case, been undone by its own logic.

This is the paradox of DNA: it divides us, it connects us. Our DNA makes us human, but to focus on genetics is to dehumanize the bodies that are its source and its making. It is minuscule and, some believe, omnipotent. The utopian (and paranoid) promise of the Human Genome Project is that we will be revealed to be the sum of our parts; the message of Shirlee Taylor Haizlip and Sally Hemings is that those parts are more various than we had ever imagined (or wanted to imagine). Perhaps the greatest irony of DNA research is that a tool that has placed unprecedented numbers of African Americans behind bars over the decade since its development is now invoked as the proof that those incarcerated bodies are barely differentiated from the bodies of those who turn the key. Indeed, they could very well be related.

Epilogue

Future bodies, present selves

We must find another relationship to nature besides reification and possession.
(Donna Haraway)

It is hard to imagine that things have not always been the way they are now, or that they might one day be so different that cultural investigators of the mid-twenty-first century will find us as mysterious and intriguing as we do the denizens of U.S. culture of a hundred, fifty, or even thirty years ago. But it is also inevitable that the world shifts, meanings change, language reshapes itself to speak to us differently. The twentieth century has been the enduring site of a desire to burrow into the body to find something true and enduring about "human nature" or "race" or "identity," as well as the dramatically different answers that emerged from such an investigation at different moments from the end of the nineteenth to the end of the twentieth century.

The particularly utopian tenor to corporeal exploration that characterizes the past ten years is both comforting and alarming. It is comforting at least because it constructs the body as a site of truth that can effect justice and reconciliation, that can recognize difference while looking towards a commonality on the basic level: DNA. But the rhetoric of genetics also bears the legacy of scientific quantification and eugenics. However paranoid the vision of a genetically "purified" world, we are right to fear it when every news bulletin brings breaking research on how fetuses can be altered in the womb and genes in plants, animals, and perhaps human beings can be manipulated, whether for profit or prophylaxis. Disability rights activists alert us to something real when they insist that we suffer an immeasurable loss when we value life only in terms of its functionality and flawlessness.

Moreover, the emergence of genetically based medical science reinforces the immense gaps in access to medical resources between socioeconomic groups in the U.S. and between the United States and poorer countries to the south and east. For example, costly developments in reproductive technology – *in vitro* fertilization and other fertility treatments, new technologies that allow parents to determine chromosomally the likelihood of a fetus's sex, *in utero* surgery on first- and second-term fetuses – have ballooned in proportion to the increased condemnation of and governmental controls over poor women's fertility.

We are a substantial distance from phrenology and palm-reading, both medically and fantasmatically. The surface of the body is no longer imagined to hold the secrets of the self (even as surgery becomes less and less invasive, using lasers rather than scalpels and television screens rather than the bare eye). Thanks to recent television programs like *ER* and *Chicago Hope*, lay viewers can gain an intimate knowledge of medical practice, and even gaze inside bodies along with the fictional doctors.[1] Bodies become evidence of *themselves* – of their fragility, power, organicity.

Our Bodies, Ourselves is the title of the bible of the women's health movement, a book whose goal has been to empower women to make informed and self-caring medical choices. But the body/self continuum has been, as women have long realized, a rocky and risky path. For have we not been too long defined by our bodies, locked within the trap of corporeality? And yet have we not been forbidden a real connection with our bodies, and instead been the objects of a quantifying gaze?

Writing this book has been exhilarating, but also heart-breaking. How easy it is to fall into the pattern of looking at bodies and believing we know something – all – about the people who live their lives within them. How easy to distance ourselves from the embodiedness that dehumanizes. How hard, too, not to feel judged.

Writing a book like this requires distance even as it calls for empathy. The discourses of science encourage the initiated to stand behind the shield of quantification, to imagine the trait not the personality. But the stories I found make quite different demands. Look at the palms of your hands. Press your fingers on a piece of glass. Feel the curve and weight of your skull. Take off your shirt, stand in front of the mirror as Alice Jones stood in front of the jury. Watch your blood move from vein to glass tube. Imagine your blood peopled with the thousands of ancestors you bring with you.

I began this study with the words of Adrienne Rich exhorting her readers to recognize the corporeality of our bodies rather than abstracting and quantifying them into "the body," a body no one lives or breathes within. I end with Donna Haraway, a very different kind of feminist activist, who constructs a very different kind of corporeal ontology. How, Haraway asks, can we have bodies that resist being shaped into things to be measured and compared? How can we not make the natural world into the opposite of the human, a thing to be owned, a realm into which the marginalized can be swept and appropriated for the "needs" of science?

In her now classic essay "A manifesto for cyborgs," Haraway offers two strategies for the subordinated to

> tak[e] global vengeance ...: 1) the production of universal, totalizing theory is a major mistake that misses most of reality, probably always, but certainly now; 2) taking responsibility for the social relations means refusing an anti-science metaphysics ... and so embracing the skillful task of reconstructing the boundaries of daily life, in partial connection with others, in communication with all of our parts.
>
> (1989: 275)

This is a massive task. How, after all, do we reconstruct boundaries that are changing so quickly in geopolitical, medical, legal, and personal realms? And yet I can imagine no other scheme. Our bodies are always already inscribed within the languages of science, gender, race (and haven't these been languages so often spoken at the same time through the same mouths?) that we cannot simply have recourse to a romantic dream of the oneness of humanity and the harmony of the "American family," a family that too frequently has been the locus of betrayal and coercion.

Instead we must look back as well as forward for clues: back to the moments in which an apparent hegemony was countered by refusal to be spoken of or spoken for. The March on Washington Movement was one of these moments; so, too (although wholly different in so many other ways) was Wallace Thurman's skewering of the "color consciousness" of his peers, and Sally Hemings' refusal to disappear from the list of items history has been forced to keep alive by having to deny.

Sally Hemings: a woman of whom no material image remains; a woman who was for much of her life a legal chattel, and yet who engineered her own freedom and those of her children through the work of her sexualized body. Hemings' story resists the easy comfort of the family romance: if all Americans are part of a common family, then Hemings shows us that it is a family constructed through abduction, appropriation, subordination, and enslavement as well as love and interconnection. Perhaps Hemings was the original cyborg — existing only in language, visible only through microscopic technology, a hybrid of slave and free, black and white, the disfranchised mother of a different kind of American dynasty whose identity is legitimated by legal illegitimacy.[2]

In Toni Morrison's *Beloved*, the newly freed Baby Suggs stares at herself, looks at her own body, and feels disoriented and alarmed.

But suddenly she saw her hands as though with a clarity as simple as it was dazzling, "These hands belong to me. These *my* hands." Next she felt a knocking in her chest and discovered something new: her own heartbeat.

(Morrison, 1988: 141)

It is that moment of disorientation, pleasure, simplicity, bedazzlement that attends the untotalizable merging of blood, skin, and self, even when the stakes are significantly lower than they are for Baby Suggs. We recognize ourselves as our own and as strange. "These *my* hands": this can be a radical stance when divorced from systems of domination – as Baby Suggs tells her congregation gathered in the Clearing, it is an act of rebellion to claim one's own body when it has already been delineated, defined, assigned.

It has been a long journey from Tom Driscoll's fingerprints to Baby Suggs' hands. *Pudd'nhead Wilson* and *Beloved* are set within a few decades of each other, but they were written a century apart. This historical irony only serves to remind us – *again* – that the American talent for transforming bodies into things (information, statistics, evidence, databases) is part of the legacy of slavery. As our bodies become increasingly complex, we must resist the genocidal language of the frontier and embrace Baby Suggs' sophisticated vision. "These *my* hands": two hands, the skin, the bone, the flesh, the blood, the labor, the skills, the touch, the twin possibilities of connection and violence. The continual (e)merging and reshaping of blood, skin, and self.

Notes

Notes to Chapter 1

1. I make a distinction here between capital-C "Census" and small-c "census": the "Census" is an official government document, linked to a specific year; the "census" is the process more generally – what censuses usually do, as opposed to what *this* census actually does.
2. In mid-1999, the Supreme Court ruled statistical sampling unconstitutional.
3. The *New York Times* article that reported on the beginnings of this debate did not comment on the interconnections between Woods' multiracialism and U.S. imperialism. Woods' father had been a GI in Vietnam during the war, had met his mother during that time, and brought her back with him to the U.S.
4. Prior to early July, this issue had been relegated to the back pages of the *New York Times*, and awarded one or two columns. On July 9, an article on the "multiracial" classification appeared on the first page of the "National Report" section, and took up three columns and a kick-quote.
5. We might read this as the final nail in the coffin of the "melting-pot" ideology of American identity that predominated thinking about ethnicity for so much of the twentieth century. Multiracial people are prevented from melting: they must classify themselves officially as a combination of discrete parts. Or perhaps it is not completely dead. In response to a *New York Times* editorial on the Census issue by Orlando Patterson, in which Patterson suggested replacing race with national and ethnic background, Gareth John constructed a slippery-slope argument in order to recenter the category "American":

    > On the last census form we had no choice but to describe ourselves as "white, not Hispanic." If current trends continue, our children will presumably be required to classify themselves as "Anglo Saxon-Jute-Brythonic-Gael-Americans." Surely it would be simpler and more apposite if they just called themselves "Americans."
    >
    > (John, 1997: A18)

Despite these wranglings and the reactionary rhetoric they invoked, we might imagine the 2000 enumeration as the first truly postmodern census. For, as Benedict Anderson has argued, the census of modernity is about unitariness, since "the fiction of the census is that everyone is in it, and everyone has one – and only one – extremely clear place. No fractions [nor, one assumes, multiples]" (1983: 66).

6. Foucault's argument is crucial to the theories of visibility that I will be exploring below, but it is not directly translatable from Western Europe, particularly France from which he takes most of his archival material, to the United States. The greatest difference is the institution of domestic slavery, followed (after the brief hiatus of Reconstruction) by the establishment of legalized racial segregation throughout the country, and concentrated in the southeast. In the context of slavery, black bodies were brutally rendered anonymous, forced not into docility but raw subordination. African Americans were not "body" but "flesh" – barely, if at all, distinguishable from livestock (Spillers, 1994: 457).

7. This analogy goes only so far. Foucault makes an important distinction between the "birth of the clinic" (that is, the contemporary practice of medicine) and the scene of the experiment. The medical gaze is by definition diagnostic: it is observing, not intervening. An experiment implies some interaction between the instigator and the object of scientific inquiry. However, much of the scientific work I examine here consists largely of looking at bodies and *not* interacting with them. As I discuss below, I focus on questions of measurement, quantification, judging-by-looking, and policy-making from the visible: phenomena that constitute the bulk of the practices around reading the body as evidence.

8. For an in-depth discussion of the mid-nineteenth-century U.S. bourgeois insistence on emotional and moral transparency, see Karen Halttunen, *Confidence Men and Painted Women: A Study of Middle-Class Culture in America 1830–1870* (New Haven: Yale University Press, 1982). Of course, as Kathy Peiss points out, many white women achieved their complexions with some kind of face powder, "wash" (that is, whitening formula), and even skin bleach. See Peiss, *Hope in A Jar: The Making of America's Beauty Culture* (New York: Henry Holt & Company, 1998).

9. I'm aware, too, of how close this legalistic language is to the language of the Congregationalist Church from which, as Ann Douglas showed in *The Feminization of American Culture*, so many theorists of the sentimental fled in the mid-nineteenth century. Testifying, witnessing, being examined and cross-examined, presenting evidence of salvation, were all crucial parts of the conversion experience from the days of the Massachusetts Bay Colony in the 1630s. See Patricia Caldwell, *The Puritan Conversion Narrative: The Beginnings of American Expression* (New York: Cambridge University Press, 1983).

10. Thomas Laqueur makes an analogous argument in *Making Sex: Body and Gender from the Greeks to Freud* (Cambridge, MA: Harvard University Press, 1990). In his fascinating exploration of changes in conceptions of sexual difference, particularly from the "one-sex" model of before the late eighteenth century to the "two-sex"

model of the nineteenth century and beyond, Laqueur shows that medical knowledge in fact had to catch up with popular understandings of sex. As he richly illustrates, "the reevaluation of pleasure [that is, from the assumption that women like men needed orgasm in order to conceive to the belief that women did not and should not feel pleasure during sex] occurred more than a century before reproductive physiology could come to its support with any kind of deserved authority" (p. 9).

11. A striking example of mapping as ideological is laid out in Janet Abu-Lughod's "On the remaking of history: how to reinvent the past," in Barbara Kruger and Phil Mariani (eds), *Remaking History* (Seattle: Bay Press, 1989, pp. 111–30), which is illustrated by global maps. These maps represent land masses proportional to their size, a proposition that seems, on the surface, perfectly reasonable. What the maps do, however, is reveal the ideological imbalances of commonly accepted world maps (much like the one imprinted on shower curtains around the United States), in which certain land masses, like the U.S., are represented as disproportionately large compared to actual surface area, and others, such as Africa, are shockingly small. Traditional world maps represent not size but power: how else would it be possible that in a map from the late 1980s the entire African continent of 11.6 million square miles could tidily fit twice over in the space allotted to the (now former) Soviet Union, with an actual land mass of only 8.7 million square miles?

12. For a detailed discussion and spirited critique of craniometry and other anthropometric and eugenicist sciences, see Stephen Jay Gould, *The Mismeasure of Man* (New York: Norton, 1996).

13. In the sociology of knowledge and the "strong program," the paradigmatic text is David Bloor, *Knowledge and Social Imagery* (Chicago: University of Chicago Press, 1991); the work of Bruno Latour, such as *The Pasteurization of France* (New York: Oxford University Press, 1988), and *Science in Action* (Cambridge, MA: Harvard University Press, 1987), and Donna Haraway in *Simians, Cyborgs, and Women: The Reinvention of Nature* (New York: Routledge, 1991), is an excellent introduction to two different kinds of science studies. For a detailed overview of the debates within the history and sociology of science that comes out strongly in favour of Latour's "actor-network" theory, see Steven C. Ward, *Reconfiguring Truth: Postmodernism, Science Studies, and the Search for a New Model of Knowledge* (Lanham, MD: Rowman and Littlefield Publishers, Inc., 1996). Joan Wallach Scott's article "The Evidence of Experience" (first published in *Critical Inquiry* and later anthologized in James Chandler *et al.* (eds), *Questions of Evidence: Proof Practices, and Persuasion across the Disciplines* (Chicago: University of Chicago Press, 1994) articulates and anticipates many of the concerns of a post-foundationalist history. Two recent anthologies – Richard Delgado (ed.), *Critical Race Theory: The Cutting Edge* (Philadelphia: Temple University Press, 1999), and Kimberlé Crenshaw *et al.* (eds), *Critical Race Theory: The Key Writings That Formed the Movement* (New York: New Press, 1996) – collect much of the important scholarship in critical race studies, explaining the field's connections to and distances from critical legal studies.

14. This is the central argument in Bruno Latour's *We Have Never Been Modern*, trans. Catherine Porter (Cambridge, MA: Harvard University Press, 1993). In a passionate argument for the cross-pollinating of inquiry, Latour creates the category of the "quasi-object," a phenomenon like the ozone layer or abortion or racial identity that is "simultaneously real, discursive, and social. [Quasi-objects] belong to nature, to the collective and to discourse. If one autonomizes discourse by turning nature over to the epistemologists and giving up society to the sociologists, one makes it impossible to stitch these resources back together" (p. 64).

15. The desire to reach into previously inaccessible parts of the body still motivates new surgical techniques. One of the most recent developments has been open-uterus fetal surgery to repair damage caused by spina bifida (a condition in which the skin over part of the spinal column is not fully formed, causing anything from club feet to lower-body paralysis to serious brain damage), a technique still in the experimental phase. Surgeons in Nashville slice open the uterus of a pregnant woman, pump out the amniotic fluid, and remove the 4-month-old fetus, small enough to lie in the palm of the hand. They then sew up the skin on the back to seal in the spinal column, replace the fetus in the amniotic sac, restore the fluid, and sew up the uterus. This surgery renders fully visible a process – the growth of an embryo inside the womb – that was previously accessible only through mediating technology such as ultrasound, and allows the hands and eyes of surgeons into a part of pregnant women's bodies that has heretofore been sealed off, at least prior to delivery.

16. Wills was careful, as were his predecessors, to draw a distinction between what was known as "intuitive evidence" and "moral evidence," terminology that in effect had been in legal procedure for several centuries. Intuitive evidence, which constituted "demonstration," was "perceived instantaneously, and without any conscious intermediate process of reasoning"; it "concern[ed] only necessary and immutable truth; and its first principles are definitions, which exclude all ambiguities of language, and lead to infallibly certain conclusions" (Wills, 1872: 3). Wills acknowledged, though, that intuitive evidence was hard to come by. Much of the time we must rely upon "our own observation and experience, or the testimony of our fellow-men," that is, moral evidence. Demonstration and moral evidence had a very different status in the nineteenth-century legal world: in the former, "ABSOLUTE CERTITUDE is the result; to which MORAL CERTAINTY, the highest degree of assurance of which truths of the latter class admit, is necessarily inferior" (*ibid.*: 5).

17. Wills quotes a number of sources from the eighteenth century, including Burke and Paley, that insist on the superiority of circumstantial over positive (that is, eyewitness) evidence, and then expresses amazement that such wise heads could believe in such "sophisms" (1872: 29). He states in the strongest terms that such beliefs are "fallacies," and that the writers he cites stacked the deck by selecting "extreme cases, the strongest ones of circumstantial, and the weakest of positive evidence" to support their arguments (*ibid.*: 31).

18. For an analysis of Field's impact on legal codification and some mid-twentieth-century analyses of how and why codification has been resisted in both civil and criminal legal arenas, see Alison Reppy (ed.), *David Dudley Field: Centenary Essays, Celebrating One Hundred Years of Legal Reform* (New York: New York University School of Law, 1949).

19. The equivalence works only one way. An "exciting event" can be used as proof for the veracity of *res gestae*, but the utterance of a "spontaneous exclamation" (as *res gestae* is also known) doesn't prove that there was an exciting event (Binder, 1975: 43).

20. In this sense, *res gestae* exceptions are very close to "present sense impression" exceptions, that treat statements "describing or explaining an event or condition made while the declarant was perceiving the event or condition, or immediately thereafter" (*Federal Rules*, 1990: 128).

21. Dying declarations are generally admissible only in criminal homicide cases in which the victim is categorically unavailable, or in attempted homicide in which the victim is incapable of testifying. However, they have been taken into consideration in some states in civil cases (see Binder, 1975: 172–4). Usually, nonhomicide dying declarations are classified as excited utterances (not surprisingly – being close to death would excite anyone), and are admissible as such.

22. Many thanks to Bob McRuer for making me aware of Cintron's work.

23. One example of the effects of discourses of measurement that Cintron provides is the weather. Prior to the development of meteorological technology, people told the weather through perception: "it's hot," or "it's humid," or "it's snowing," or, with more sophistication, "it looks like it's going to rain." Meteorology brought with it barometers, thermometers, rain gauges, and a never-ending array of weather-predicting equipment (which now gets its own billing by brand name along with the human weather forecaster on local news broadcasts). Next to the exact measurement of 45 degrees, "it's chilly" seems so imprecise as to be almost useless: it's relegated to the realm of the primitive. Now "weather reports ... are one of the modern ways by which nature becomes known" (Cintron, 1997: 213).

24. One effect of this professionalization was, of course, the formation of professional associations such as the American Medical Association, the American Sociological Society (later the American Sociological Association), the American Social Science Association, and so on. For a detailed discussion of professionalization in the social sciences, see Thomas L. Haskell, *The Emergence of Professional Social Science: The American Social Science Association and the Nineteenth-Century Crisis of Authority* (Urbana: University of Illinois Press, 1977).

25. I discuss Morton in more detail in Chapter 2.

26. See Mary Poovey, "Figures of arithmetic, figures of speech: the discourse of statistics," in James Chandler *et al.* (eds), *Questions of Evidence: Proof Practices, and Persuasion Across the Disciplines* (Chicago: University of Chicago Press, 1994, pp. 401–21). Poovey observes that at the beginning of the discipline in the 1820s and 1830s, statistics were not methodologically uniform: "statistics about trade were

gathered and used in very different ways from statistics about crime; statistics about geography were demonstrable in a manner very different from statistics about suicide" (p. 404).

27. A glance at a typical issue of *The Eugenics Review*, founded in 1908, bears this out. The third volume of the journal (1911–12) contains an obituary for Galton, citing his father's "enormous appetite for mensuration" (a not insignificant detail among eugenicists!). The majority of articles in the journal contain statistical information, and some kind of graph or chart to represent that information (an article on the "Heredity of Feeblemindedness" is a Mendelian carnival of genetic charting).

28. I wrote this introduction over a summer surrounded by students studying for medical examinations. Their textbooks, replete with four-color illustrations of bits of bodies (gaping mouths, lengths of intestine, infected eyes) in various stages of disintegration and disease, reinforced my sense of the medicalized body as always already cut up and measured. Several illustrations of organs in these books had superimposed upon them rulers, indicating the real-life size of the thing in centimeters. This kind of education goes hand-in-hand with the dissection of cadavers: the body of the patient is learned as inert, segmented, both hypercorporeal as flesh and decorporealized as "example."

29. For a marvelous Lacanian analysis of Holmes' use of evidence, see Slavoj Žižek, "Two Ways to Avoid the Real of Desire," in *Looking Awry: An Introduction to Jacques Lacan's Thought through Popular Culture* (Cambridge, MA: MIT Press, 1990).

30. The interaction of enumeration and serialization creates the contemporary phenomenon of the "serial number" – an individual item or person identifiable by its own code, but imagined as one in an endless sequence of minutely different but analogous numbers.

31. See also Lauren Berlant's stunning essay "America, 'fat,' the fetus", in *The Queen of America Goes to Washington City: Essays on Sex and Citizenship* (Durham: Duke University Press, 1997, pp. 83–144). Berlant extends Petchesky's argument into an analysis of how contemporary reproductive rhetoric "turn[s] women into children and babies into persons" (p. 84). She shows how in "fetal motherhood . . . the pregnant woman becomes child to the fetus, becoming more minor and less politically represented than the fetus, which is in turn made more *national*" (p. 85).

32. This distinction is Antonio Gramsci's. "Direct domination" is the raw, external power exercised by the State. "Hegemony" is more complex: it is a combination of the "consent given by the great masses of the population to the general direction imposed on social life by the dominant fundamental group," and the "apparatus of state coercive power" funneled through the structures of civil society and private life (p. 12). The following discussion owes a great deal to Gramsci, particularly the "Study of Philosophy" section of the *Prison Notebooks*.

33. This does not mean that the theorizing about the connections between body and culture have always conformed to a single argument. For a critique of the mind/body split (although, I would argue, a reinstantiation of it that reverses the terms), see Jane Tompkins, "Me and My Shadow," *New Literary History: A Journal of Theory and Interpretation* (19.1 (Autumn 1987), pp. 169–78); for a rigorous

exploration of the ways in which the materiality and intelligibility of the body are constructed through discourse rather than pre-existing it, see Judith Butler, *Bodies That Matter: On the Discursive Limits of "Sex"* (New York: Routledge, 1993a); for a meditation on the body as creative space, see Audre Lorde, "Uses of the erotic," in *Sister/Outsider* (Freedom, CA: The Crossing Press, 1984, pp. 53–9), and Gloria Anzaldúa, *Borderlands/La Frontera* (San Francisco: Aunt Lute, 1987); for a discussion of the interfaces between bodies and machines, see Mark Seltzer, *Bodies and Machines* (New York: Routledge, 1992).

34. See, for example, Michael Moon and Eve Kosofsky Sedgwick, "Divinity: a dossier, a performance piece, a little-understood emotion" and other essays in Sedgwick's collection, *Tendencies* (Durham: Duke University Press, 1993, pp. 215–51); Rosemarie Garland Thomson, *Extraordinary Bodies: Figuring Physical Disability in American Literature and Culture* (New York: Columbia University Press, 1996); Kate Bornstein, *Gender Outlaw: On Men, Women, and the Rest of Us* (New York: Vintage, 1995); Elizabeth Grosz and Elspeth Probyn (eds), *Sexy Bodies: The Strange Carnalities of Feminism* (New York: Routledge, 1995); John Hockenberry, *Moving Violations: War Zones, Wheelchairs and Declarations of Independence* (New York: Hyperion, 1995); Sally R. Munt, *Heroic Desire: Lesbian Identity and Cultural Space* (New York: NYU Press, 1998).

35. I'm thinking, too, of Gloria Anzaldúa's description in *Borderlands/La Frontera* of her writing as a process in which she works loose a cactus needle from under her skin. When the needle is dislodged and the wound healed, the process starts all over again. Writing for her is being in a state of continual disequilibrium, even discomfort.

36. Toni Morrison, too, has used scars as a sign of the intimacy and distances between black people's lives in slavery and freedom, most explicitly in *Beloved*. The chokecherry tree of scars on Sethe's back is a sign of the brutality and generosity of white and black people, the reminder of her own murderous violence and unquestioning love, dead flesh that resembles a living organism.

Notes to Chapter 2

1. Briefly: on his first day in Dawson's Landing, Wilson is standing in town with a few townspeople "when an invisible dog began to yelp and snarl and howl." Wilson comments, "I wish I owned half that dog. ... Because I would kill my half" (*PW* 24). But, as Twain points out later in the novel, "irony was not for those people" (*PW* 71), and they brand Wilson a "pudd'nhead" in short order. For a discussion of this episode as "a highly condensed text that ... critiques the power of categories as essences" see George E. Marcus, "'What did he reckon would become of the other half if he killed his half?': Doubled, Divided and Crossed Selves in *Pudd'nhead Wilson*; or, Mark Twain as Cultural Critic in His Own Times and Ours," in Gillman and Robinson (eds), *Mark Twain's* Pudd'nhead Wilson: *Race, Conflict and Culture* (pp. 190–210).

2. In *Flawed Texts and Verbal Icons: Literary Authority in American Fiction* (1984), Hershel Parker argues that given the discontinuous way in which *Pudd'nhead Wilson* and its companion text *Those Extraordinary Twins* were written, the reader needs to be particularly careful in reading intentionality into any of the characters' actions. For example, in *Those Extraordinary Twins*, Twain originally portrayed Tom Driscoll as "ruther harum-scarum," and irresponsible, but not as Roxana's son (1996: 365). Likewise, when the palm-reading scene was first written, it was intended to be part of *Those Extraordinary Twins*, a text into which the baby-switching plot was introduced after the fact. Thus Tom's hesitation over having his palm read was, Parker claims, totally unrelated to fear of being exposed as "really" black, but instead was connected to his burglary raids on Dawson's Landing to pay his gambling debts.

   Parker's argument, although at times tendentious ("don't believe anything that anybody has said [about the composition of *Pudd'nhead Wilson*]" he warns his readers (p. 118)), is diligently researched and convincingly maintained: that "when [Twain] put *Pudd'nhead* together, he hoped in a general way that Tom would seem black in the passages written when he was all white, but he did not make any attempts to *make* him black in these passages" (p. 9, emphasis in original). While Parker is right that Twain did minimal rewriting on several sections of the novel, including the palm-reading scene, it is not self-evident what Twain *could* have done to "*make* [Tom] black" at that moment (or at all). The point of the novel is that Tom is, to all intents and purposes, white, and that he believes himself to be white until he learns otherwise.

   Moreover, Chapter 11 of *Pudd'nhead Wilson* is more effective than its *Extraordinary Twins* counterpart, since the reader assumes Tom's knowledge of his parentage, even if it was not initially written with that in mind. Ultimately, Twain was better off leaving the chapter the way it was and allowing his readers to fill in the gaps. I shall discuss the ramifications of the revelation of his "real" identity below; however, even taking into account Parker's argument, I am confident in discussing the palm-reading scene the way the narrative chronology implies: that Tom does know he is Roxana's son, and that his snatching his palm away from Wilson is a result of that knowledge.

3. In talking about palm-reading, phrenology, and the like, I use the term "knowledge systems" rather than "sciences" or "pseudosciences." On the one hand, I do not believe that they are valid scientific methods, or that the ways they taxonomize bodies stand up to serious interrogation. Moreover, as Sander Gilman and Nancy Leys Stepan, among others, have shown, nineteenth-century knowledge systems based on the body were almost invariably deployed to reinstantiate ethnic, racial, gendered, and class inequities through the "evidence" they provided of marginalized people's inferiority: smaller skulls, inadequately shaped brains, misproportioned limbs that were somehow found to proliferate among the working classes, people of color, Southern and Eastern Europeans, Jews, and women of all groups (see, for example, Sander Gilman's *The Jew's Body* (New York: Routledge, 1991), and *Difference and Pathology: Stereotypes of Sexuality,*

Race, and Madness (Ithaca: Cornell University Press, 1985); also Nancy Leys Stepan, *"The Hour of Eugenics": Race, Gender, and Nation in Latin America* (Ithaca: Cornell University Press, 1991). However, these methodologies were, on the whole, supported by what was believed to be irrefutable scientific evidence — scientists like Francis Galton, Joseph Simms, and Herbert Spencer spent years building up data to prove their theories.

Given that *Pudd'nhead Wilson* itself accepts a whole range of sciences and pseudosciences on relatively equal footing (although with differing degrees of irony), and that I am less interested in whether these modes of reading and knowing the body are accurate than in the ways in which they were used in the novel and in Twain's world to create and maintain certain hierarchies, I am unwilling to distinguish between "real" science and what we would consider "fake." As this scene shows, *Pudd'nhead Wilson* assumes that palm-reading can provide a whole range of information about Luigi and Angelo, and about Tom himself, and that palm-reading is a systematized field of knowledge that can be mastered and applied.

4. There has been a rich and detailed body of critical work on what novels can tell us about constructions of identity, the technologies by which identity can be "exposed," and what the bodies that bear those identities mean. One must start with Michel Foucault's work, particularly his *History of Sexuality: An Introduction*, trans. Robert Hurley (New York : Vintage, 1980), and *The Birth of the Clinic*, trans. A. M. Sheridan Smith (New York: Vintage, 1978), both of which limn the ways in which bodies became coherent to the post-Enlightenment West through the discursive structurations of science. This work has been rigorously taken up by Judith Butler, particularly in *Bodies that Matter: On the Discursive Limits of "Sex"* (New York: Routledge, 1993a). Combining a psychoanalytic and cultural studies approach, Sander Gilman's *The Jew's Body*, as well as his other work on embodiment and identity, links the racialism and anti-Semitism of German anatomists with the representations of Jews in German literature and culture.

In the study of U.S. literature, as early as 1963 Thomas F. Gossett was analyzing the links between racialist notions of identity, and the ways in which literary texts naturalize those notions, in *Race: The History of an Idea in America* (New York: Oxford University Press, 1997). In his chapter "Literary naturalism and race" Gossett points to the Anglo-Saxonism of turn-of-the-century novelists such as Frank Norris, Owen Wister, and Jack London, as well as the racist phrenology of much early naturalism, as exemplifying the belief that character is borne out on the surface of the body. Seven years later, Joel Kovel's ambitious study, *White Racism: A Psychohistory* (New York: Pantheon Books, 1970), posited that white racism is rooted in a profound ambivalence on the part of the racist towards the body of the person of color, and examined the ways in which racists create a fantasy that the black body represents the "dirt" they feel envelops their own bodies.

Shelley Fisher Fishkin's exhaustive essay, "Interrogating 'Whiteness,' Complicating 'Blackness': Remapping American Culture" (*American Quarterly*, 47

(September 1995): 428–66) traces the efflorescence in the first half of the 1990s of writing about racial meanings in U.S. literature. Two critics she does not discuss, but who are influential on my work, are Karen Sanchéz-Eppler and Priscilla Wald. Sanchéz-Eppler's *Touching Liberty: Abolition, Feminism, and the Politics of the Body* (Berkeley: University of California Press, 1993) explores the ways in which the abstracted "persons" of American law butted up against abolitionist and feminist rhetorics of fleshed embodiment and physical autonomy. Her recent work on the eroticized body of the child as an avatar for the nation speaks to the developing power of the white "innocent" body in U.S. culture. Wald's *Constituting Americans: Cultural Anxiety and Narrative Form* examines the legal and literary languages of American identity that erased or foregrounded physical or "racial" difference in service of the identity "We the People."

5. For two thorough discussions of spiritualism and related beliefs in the U.S. in the nineteenth century, see Howard Kerr, *Mediums and Spirit Rappers and Roaring Radicals: Spiritualism in American Literature* (Urbana: University of Illinois Press, 1972), and Peter Washington, *Madame Blavatsky's Baboon: A History of the Mystics, Mediums, and Misfits Who Brought Spiritualism to America* (New York: Schocken Books, 1996).

   Both Kerr and Washington discuss the close links between occult beliefs and radical/Bohemian politics in the mid- to late nineteenth century: these connections are relevant to Twain's belief in both palmistry and what he called "mental telegraphy" (people who are emotionally close sharing unspoken thoughts), since he married into the Langdon family, which was well known for its abolitionist and radical politics.

6. These three strands appear throughout the literature on palmistry up to the present day. For example, Andrew Fitzherbert's book *The Palmist's Companion* (1992) describes palmistry as making "three claims":

   (1) That the hands reveal the personality of their owner in very great detail;
   (2) That certain medical conditions can be diagnosed from the hands ...;
   (3) That the lines in almost all hands will reveal some of the past events in the life of the person concerned and will also indicate probable events in the future.

   (p. 11)

   It is worth remarking that Fitzherbert is much more modest than many of his cheirosophic counterparts past or present in enumerating palmistry's powers.

7. For example, John Indagine wrote *Chiromantia: The Book of Palmestry and Physiognomy* and the *Introductiones Apotelesmaticae* in the 1520s, both of which went through many reprintings over the course of 200 years; Richard Saunders published *Palmistry, The Secrets Thereof Revealed* ... in 1663, and *Physiognomie and Cheiromancie* in 1671.

8. Nonetheless, d'Arpentigny did draw upon palm-reading's orientalized past – he attributed his initial interest in palmistry to his encounter with a "gypsy girl" whose expertise "[brought] to d'Arpentigny's mind an echo of some long-lost system of knowledge" (Gettings, 1965: 201).

9. Some of the phrenology and temperament theory texts I consulted were: George
    Sumner Weaver, *Lectures on Mental Science According to the Philosophy of Phrenology*
    (New York: Fowler and Wells, 1852); Furneaux Jordan, *Character as Seen in Body
    and Parentage: With a Chapter on Education, Career, Morals and Progress* (London:
    Kegan, Paul, Trench, Trübner, 1890), Alexander Stewart, *Our Temperaments: Their
    Study and Their Teaching. A Popular Outline* (2nd edn, London: Crosby Lockwood,
    1892); French Ensor Chadwick, *Temperament, Disease and Health* (New York: G.P.
    Putnam's 1892); Daniel H. Jacques, *The Temperaments, or, The Varieties of Physical
    Constitution in Man, Considered in Their Relations to Mental Character* ... (New
    York: S.R. Wells, 1878); Orson S. Fowler and Lorenzo N. Fowler, *New Illustrated
    Self-Instructor in Phrenology and Physiology* (New York: Fowler and Wells, 1859).
10. Spurzheim's work in phrenology was in symbiosis with Samuel George Morton's
    research into the interrelation of race and skull size and shape. The leader of the
    polygenist school of racialism, which believed that different races were actually
    different *species*, Morton had experimented with phrenology until moving into
    craniometry in the 1840s. Morton had an immense collection of skulls from
    around the world – in fact his laboratory was dubbed the "American Golgotha"
    (Gossett, 1997: 58). Gossett's master-work, *Crania Americana* (1839), contained an
    appendix, "Phrenological remarks," written by George Combe, a leading
    phrenologist and student of Spurzheim.
11. For a short but detailed history of temperament theory and Twain's relationship
    to it, see Allen Gribben, "Mark Twain, Phrenology, and the 'Temperaments': A
    Study of Pseudoscientific Influence" (*American Quarterly*, 24 (March 1972): 45–
    68).
12. In *The Gilded Age* (1874), for example, Twain describes the jury selected for the
    murder trial of Laura Hawkins as "a credit to the counsel for the defense. ... Low
    foreheads and heavy faces they all had; some had a look of animal cunning, while
    the most were only stupid" (p. 493).
13. Of course, it is hard to know how seriously phrenology and temperament theory
    were taken, either by scientists or by the general public. The volume of
    phrenology texts suggests its popularity, rather like the explosion in self-help
    publishing today. Although, like the self-help industry, phrenology was open to
    parody and its adherents did not constitute the majority of Americans, its
    terminology and core concepts were absorbed into the popular imagination of the
    late nineteenth-century U.S., as psychoanalysis was in the middle third of this
    century, or as have twelve-step and self-actualization programs in the past twenty
    years. See, for example, David S. Reynolds' *Walt Whitman's America: A Cultural
    Biography* (New York: Knopf, 1995).
14. See Gribben (1972) for a discussion of this visit.
15. Gribben (1972) argues that humorous sketches mocking phrenologists were not
    uncommon in the last decades of the nineteenth century. Twain published one by
    John Phoenix (the pseudonym of George H. Derby) in his *Library of Humor* in
    1888. Twain himself wrote an extended burlesque of phrenology in "The Secret
    History of Eddypus, the World-Empire" in 1901–02 (Gribben, 1974: 63–4).

16. Twain had his skull phrenologically examined at least three times: once by a San Francisco phrenologist, Frederick Coombs, in the 1860s; once by a Professor Beall in Cincinnati in 1885; and once in 1901 by Jessie Fowler of Fowler and Wells, a publishing firm that printed several phrenology and temperament books, including Orson Fowler's *New Illustrated Self-Instructor in Phrenology and Physiology*, and George Sumner Weaver's *Lectures on Mental Science*, both of which Twain owned.

17. For a detailed discussion of attitudes towards personal transparency in the sentimental ethos, see Karen Halttunen, *Confidence Men and Painted Women: A Study of Middle-Class Culture in America 1830–1870* (New Haven: Yale University Press, 1982).

18. Twain was not the only member of his family to be interested in phrenology. In 1869, his wife Olivia copied a quotation into her commonplace book from the *American Phrenological Journal* (known as the *Phrenological Journal and Science of Health* between 1869 and 1911), which was edited by Orson Fowler, co-founder of the Fowler and Wells publishing house and writer of several phrenological books (Gribben, 1980: 545).

19. As Peggy Phelan has argued, it is this complex of knowledge, exposure, visibility, and hiddenness that structures the space of the visual and particularly the space of visual performance. "The dramas of concealment, disguises, secrets, lies are endemic to visual representation, exactly because visual representation is 'not all'" (1993: 32). While "what one can see is in every way related to what one can say" (p. 2), both Phelan and Twain recognize that the visual is often only partial (in both senses of the word), particularly when constructed in the sight-lines of an audience.

20. In his *Book of the Hand* (1965), Fred Gettings reproduces an engraving from Desbarolles that shows another possible locus of palmistry. Sitting on a plush sofa in a well-appointed parlor, a young man reads a young woman's palm as she demurely turns her head away. Both are angled towards the reader, so we see their faces in almost full view. While none of the manuals recommends palmistry as a courting device, this illustration invokes several of the elements that would make it ideal for young couples: the physical proximity and actual touching required for reading, the bourgeois respectability that permitted this closeness, the possibility of access to the interior self, the simultaneous privacy of the act (creating a closed circuit between reader and subject) and the showiness of it, as indicated by the positioning of the couple's bodies towards the reader.

21. Karen Halttunen has a detailed discussion of parlor theatricals, charades, and tableaux vivants in *Confidence Men and Painted Women* (full citation n. 17).

22. While it may be only coincidental, the first test of his abilities that Cheiro underwent during his visit to the United States also concerned identifying the palm of a murderer. A "lady journalist" from the New York *World* challenged him to analyze a series of palm prints. The fourth or fifth print, Cheiro told his audience, was "so abnormal ... that I shall refuse to read it unless you can bring me the consent of the owner to tell what I see" (1912: 111). The journalist had

brought a letter of consent with her, having anticipated Cheiro's hesitation. The palmist identified the hand as belonging to a murderer: "'Whether this man has committed one murder or twenty ... is not the question; at about his forty-fourth year he will be tried and condemned'" (1912: 111–112). At this revelation, the journalist admitted that she had purposely brought Cheiro the print of a convicted murderer.

The striking similarities between this incident and Twain's construction of the conditions around Wilson's palm-reading may not have been deliberate or even conscious on Twain's part. However, they do follow the same paradigm: reading from the body is verified and legitimated by the reading of a text written by the owner of that body.

23. We can recall here Peggy Phelan's insight that "the looker is always also regarded by the image seen and through this regard discovers and continually affirms that s/he is the one who looks" (1993: 15). This raises the complex question: Is the audience Tom or Wilson?

24. According to Anne P. Wigger, Cheiro claimed to have got Twain interested in fingerprints, which certainly adds another layer to the relationship between palmistry and fingerprinting. It is impossible to verify or disprove this claim, however; Twain himself gave credit to Galton alone, but that may also have been because Galton was an accomplished and recognized scientist, whereas Cheiro's reputation was a little less associated with "pure" science.

25. In *Mark Twain's Library*, Allen Gribben argues that Twain's enthusiasm for Galton waned quickly, and that "[a] few years later ... Clemens could not even recall the author's name" (1980: 251). In a letter of June 25, 1895, only three years after reading *Finger Prints*, Twain recollected a "dim impression" of the book, and was not even sure that he could remember the book's title.

26. He must have taken some comfort from the fact that although fingerprints could not be and were not a factor in marriage selection, resulting in "a perfect instance of promiscuity in marriage," the prints themselves were not (metaphorically) miscegenated. "We might consequently [from this promiscuity] have expected them to be hybridized. But that is not the case; they *refuse to blend*" (p. 209).

27. Here we should keep in mind the dual meaning of "show" – certainly the jury's vote is a show (that is, a visible demonstration). But Wilson's use of Chambers' and Tom's prints is pure *show*manship, performance for the benefit of an (appreciative) audience.

28. Here Galton is attempting to find a way out of what Homi K. Bhabha has called "a recognition of the immediacy and articulacy of authority – a disturbing effect that is familiar in the repeated hesitancy afflicting the colonialist discourse when it contemplates its discriminated subjects: the *inscrutability* of the Chinese, the *unspeakable* rites of the Indians, the *indescribable* habits of the Hottentots" (Bhabha, 1986: 173).

29. Percy Driscoll's creditors argue that since "the false heir was not inventoried at that time with the rest of the property, great wrong and loss had thereby been inflicted upon them. They rightly claimed that 'Tom' was lawfully their property

and had been so for eight years" (*PW* 302–3). Needless to say, this is a specious argument if only on the basis of logic. Although the false Tom had not been inventoried, the false Chambers *had*, so the estate suffered no loss at all. However, Twain sacrifices logical accuracy for the sake of rhetorical power here: we can see both how fragile whiteness is, and how central to legal self-ownership.

30. This brings to mind D.A. Miller's analysis in *The Novel and the Police* (Berkeley: University of California Press, 1988) of the role of the detective, both figurative and literal, in the novel: "the detective's final summation offers not a maximal integration of parts into the whole, but a minimal one – what is needed to solve the crime. Everything and everybody else is returned to a ... mute self-evidence" (34). At the end of *Pudd'nhead Wilson* both Tom and Chambers are mute in their identities, although for very different reasons.

31. For example, the early craniometrist and polygenist S.G. Morton sowed the seeds for Galton's obsessive quantification in 1839 in his massive *Crania Americana*. Morton listed thirteen separate measurements for each of the seventy-one crania he surveyed (Stanton, 1960: 31). All these measurements were represented in statistical tables by race (Caucasian, Mongolian, Malay, American, and Ethiopian), and by characteristics such as internal capacity, circumference, and so on. As Thomas Stanton points out, Morton represents the beginning of "the line of demarcation between the old anthropology and the new: mathematical measurement was supplanting aesthetic judgement" (1960: 33).

      However, in many ways Morton's readers were not "ready" for the information he provided. George Combe's appendix "Phrenological remarks" links the mathematical and the personal, equating cranial volume with intellectual ability and speculating about the possibility of estimating skull capacity through *phrenological* (that is, hands-on) examinations. Even as Morton was abstracting racial *identity* from the physical body, Combe was resuturing the body and *character*.

32. In fact he believed that IQ could be used to help children *increase* their intelligence. By identifying students with special needs, teachers could create enhanced learning environments that took their abilities into account. Binet devised a set of what he called "mental orthopedics" for small, student-centered classrooms that would hone disadvantaged children's skills in "will, attention, and discipline" as well as reasoning and retention of information. Binet chronicled the improvements that students in these classes experienced, and "argued that pupils so benefitted had not only increased their knowledge, but their intelligence as well ... [He wrote:] 'We have increased what constitutes the intelligence of a pupil: the capacity to learn and assimilate instruction' "(Gould, 1996: 184).

Notes to Chapter 3

1. I am using Deborah McDowell (ed.), *Quicksand and Passing* (New Brunswick, NJ: Rutgers University Press, 1986), hereafter cited parenthetically as *P* with page number.

2. This is usually the first point at which students realize that *Passing* has a fraught and not altogether trusting relationship with at least some of its readers. Peter Rabinowitz talks about the different audiences *Passing* anticipates, and its deployment of what he calls "rhetorical passing" in " 'Betraying the Sender': The Rhetoric and Ethics of Fragile Texts."

3. This contradicts African American folk understanding that "it takes one to know one," as Ralph Ellison asserts: "although the sociologists tell us that thousands of light-skinned Negroes become White each year undetected, most Negroes can spot a paper thin 'White Negro' every time" ("The World and the Jug," in Ellison, 1995: 124).

4. Larsen often strings adjectival phrases rhythmically like this, creating a series of phrases of equal length. Similarly, during the tea-party scene, Clare pours "the rich amber fluid from the tall glass pitcher into stately slim glasses" (*P* 168); or describing the autumn weather, "cold rain drenching the rotting leaves which had fallen from the poor trees" (*P* 192).

5. See, for example, Robin Wiegman's discussion of the novel in *American Anatomies: Theorizing Race and Gender* (Durham: Duke University Press, 1995); Judith Butler, "Passing, queering: Nella Larsen's psychoanalytic challenge," in *Bodies That Matter: On the Discursive Limits of "Sex"* (New York: Routledge, 1993b); Deborah R. Grayson, "Fooling White Folks, or, How I Stole the Show: The Body Politics of Nella Larsen's *Passing* (*Bucknell Review*, 39(1), 1995); Elaine K. Ginsberg, "The politics of passing," in her edited volume *Passing and the Fictions of Identity* (Durham: Duke University Press, 1996).

6. Quite *how* many has been a matter of debate, as Werner Sollors shows in his chapter on the thematics of passing in *Neither Black Nor White Yet Both: Thematic Explorations of Interracial Literature* (New York: Oxford University Press, 1997). Estimates range from the low millions to the mid-hundred thousands. In "The Vanishing Mulatto," an article he wrote for the October 1925 issue of *Opportunity*, Charles S. Johnson argued that over 300,000 "Negroes" were passing for white. However, figures cannot be accurate, since the more successful the pass, the less easy it is to trace. More importantly, the representation of passing in fiction by both black and white writers is disproportionate to its actual occurrence.

7. Deborah McDowell was the first critic to read *Passing* as a novel that "wanted to tell the story of the black woman with sexual desires," and that Irene and Clare's desires are for each other ("Introduction," p. xxii). In fact, McDowell argues that the novel itself is a text about lesbian sexuality passing as a book about racial passing, and "the erotic subplot is hidden beneath its safe and orderly cover" (p. xxx). For a more explicitly psychoanalytic take on this argument, see Judith Butler's "Passing, queering: Nella Larsen's psychoanalytic challenge," in *Bodies that Matter: On the Discursive Limits of "Sex"* (New York: Routledge, 1993b: 167–85). Butler particularly zeroes in on Irene's ambivalence towards Clare: "To the extent that Irene desires Clare, she desires the trespass that Clare performs, and hates her for the disloyalty that that trespass entails" (*ibid.*: 179).

8. Before I ever heard the expression "C.P. time," I understood this relationship between lateness and subordinated identity from the lesbian and gay community. We talked about "gay time" or "running on the gay clock," with the assumption that we were far too fabulous to be concerned about petty concerns like punctuality. As with "C.P. time," "gay time" had a double meaning: on the one hand it represented our refusal to be controlled by temporal expectations that we had no hand in constructing; on the other, it was a sign of our inability to truly enter the mainstream, to merge into unmarked time.

9. In *Terrible Honesty*, Ann Douglas points out that "fix" had multiple meanings in the 1920s. Jay Gatsby uses the term both clearly to mean illegally manipulating an outcome – Wolfshiem is "the man who fixed the World Series back in 1919" (1995: 78) – and more ambiguously in his vow to "fix everything just the way it was before" Daisy and Tom were married (p. 117).

10. My thanks to a former student, Danielle Pierpaoli, for bringing this passage and its use of class and body size to my attention. Her passionate critique of the class politics of *Passing* and the ways in which fatness and slimness were equated with "trashiness" and "high class" gave me a whole new approach to this novel, some of which I deploy here. Moreover, her courage in confronting my own unthinking sanction of fat-oppression was an inspiration to me as a teacher and as an activist.

11. An instructive contrast to Gertrude is Felise Freeland. Felise is visibly dark-skinned, but shares Irene's class status, perhaps even superseding it. Felise's "dresses are the despair of half the women in Harlem," identified by *haute couture* designers.

12. This scene also complicates what "passing" itself means. One of the debates that has raged around this novel is what is behind or underneath the pass: is there an authentic or originary self that could be revealed as the ground over which the pass is laminated? Thadious M. Davis has shown in her careful biography of Larsen that even Larsen's own everyday identity was a collage of biographical and fictional elements that the novelist wove together to construct a public *and* personal self: "*Nella Larsen* was not only an invented name, a public and private pseudonym, but also a self-created persona, willed and perpetuated from adolescence through old age by a woman who, for a short time at least, attained the meaning of her own daring self-invention" (Davis, 1994: xix).

On the one hand, the concept of passing is itself necessitated by the rigid binaries of black and white that pre-exist and control the lives of the passing characters in this novel – "the limited subversion of the pass always requires that the terms of the system be intact" (Robinson, 1994: 735). At the same time I am wary of defining passing as "any form of pretense or disguise that results in a loss or surrender of, or a failure to satisfy a desire for, identity" (McLendon, 1995: 96). If we accept, as I do, that identity itself is what F. Scott Fitzgerald presciently called "an unbroken series of successful gestures" (1964: 6), then how do we locate the "real" that the language of pretense and disguise presuppose? For, as Samira Kawash convincingly argues, passing is most often understood in opposition to "being yourself" and an assumption of an authentic base. "We ought not to forget," she warns us, "that the exhortation to 'be yourself' is simultaneously a call to liberation and a command of normalization" (1996: 73). Or, put more bluntly, if Clare is "really" black, how can we define what black actually means? How do we not resort to racist measurements of blood or nationalist rhetoric about essentialized culture while still respecting the historical and current integrity of a diverse and multifaceted community of African descent?

13. A 1971 Macmillan edition of *Passing* does not end with this line, but appends another paragraph. See Deborah E. McDowell's editorial notes to the Rutgers University Press edition for more details.

14. A few examples: "Color Question Starts Divorce" (*Chicago Defender*, July 12, 1919), reporting on an annulment procedure initiated by "Francis Dwyer (white) [against] ... Mrs Clara McCreary Dwyer, whom [*sic*] he declares is not a white woman"; "Colored Bride Hides From Klan," a story in the New York *Daily News* from April 1926, in which "Hazel Williams, colored bride of Sidney Barrett, white" was terrorized by the Klan in Peekskill, NY; "Girl's Arrest Opens Mixed Marriage War," by Frank Dolan (*Daily News*, February 25, 1926) following a 16-year-old "bride of a colored youth," arrested for violating New York's anti-miscegenation laws; "Helen Worthing Sues: Her Husband Is Colored" (*New York Telegram*, December 19, 1929), discussing the high-profile separation between "former Ziegfeld beauty" Helen Lee Worthing and her light-skinned "colored" husband (they later reconciled).

15. Throughout my discussion of this case, I refer to both Leonard Rhinelander and Alice Jones Rhinelander by their family names, "Rhinelander" and "Jones," mainly to avoid confusion.

16. For a short but thorough analysis of press coverage of the case, see Mark J. Madigan, "Miscegenation and the Dicta of Race and Class: The Rhinelander Case and Nella Larsen's *Passing*," *Modern Fiction Studies*, 36(4) (Winter 1990): 523–8.

17. High society elopements were not uncommon in the mid-1920s. During the same years that the Rhinelander case covered, the *Times* reported on several elopements within the white New York aristocracy. On the same day that Alice Jones Rhinelander denied deceiving her husband as to her race, the *Times* devoted several column inches to the elopement of Avery Rockefeller (aged 20), great-nephew of John D., and Anna Griffith Mark (aged 19) a year earlier, he from Yale and she from Rosemary Hall, an exclusive boarding-school. Not only did the *Times* assure its readers that "[n]o bar was offered to the match," it also breathlessly described the former Miss Mark's "long and luxuriant curls" of childhood, and her brother's adventures hiking in Yellowstone ("Avery Rockefeller Secretly Wedded"). A year later, the *Times* announced the secret marriage of James Lawrence Lenahan, also a Yale student, and Adele Gardiner, a débutante at Spence, another society girls' school ("Adele Gardiner Secretly Married"). Right next to a front-page article about the jury's finding for Jones, the New York *World* ran a story about the elopement of Arthur Smith, the "second son of the [New York] Governor to elope and be married secretly" ("Another Eloper").

18. According to the New York *World*'s review, Ossip Dymow's comedy *God's Judgment Is Best* was a kind of Yiddish *Inferno* — a story of "the judging of the souls that ascend from Earth" full of topical references, including a riff on the Rhinelander case ("Contrast Striking in Yiddish Dramas").

19. The hyper-saturation of the news market with details of the Rhinelander case spawned a backlash. At a speech to the Women's Press Club, playwright Channing Pollock saw both the density and quality of coverage of the case as an example of "the rising tide of vulgarity which has engulfed every department of our life" ("Criticizes the Press"). Pollock related a telling anecdote about the case: "'An official of the Western Union told me that more than half a million words had been telegraphed out of New York in two weeks to papers throughout the country on the Rhinelander case.'"

20. My main sources for mainstream news about the Rhinelander case are the *New York Times*, the New York *World*, the New York *Amsterdam News*, and the New York *Evening Post*. Each publication had a different reporting focus: the *Times*, in particular, discussed at length Rhinelander's social and racial pedigree, describing him as "a member of one of New York's oldest families," or some variation, with every mention; the *Evening Post* tended towards sensationalism, and the *World* attempted to carve out a discursive space between the aristocratic leanings of one newspaper and the populism of the other, focusing on questions of family and the emotional effects of the trial on both protagonists, while ironically downplaying both the racial and class dimensions of the trial. The *Amsterdam News* reported sparingly on the trial, offering coverage only at the very beginning and at the time of the verdict.

21. Of course, this narrative of historical exclusivity erases those Africans who accompanied, and in some cases even preceded, the original white settlers of the east coast of the United States.

22. See his *Our America: Nativism, Modernism and Pluralism* (Durham: Duke University Press, 1995).

23. Given the odd scriptedness of the Rhinelander case, it is no surprise that the cast of characters contains comic relief in the form of Grace Jones. In the same article, Jones attributes the fuss over her sister's marriage to "jealousy. It was the same way when I got married. ... There are a lot of girls around here who are sore because they didn't cop off a millionaire like my sister."

24. The separation of geography and genealogy was only partial, though. A brief article in *The Tattler* outlining the chronology of the case from the couple's marriage to the jury's verdict explained that "the bride's father was said to be a West Indian and the bride therefore was reported to have colored blood in her veins" ("Famous Rhinelander Case In History"), conflating Caribbean provenance and African descent.

25. See, for example, "Girl's Arrest Opens Mixed Marriage War," in which the marriage of the white Sarah Ziegler and the black Mr Smith (no first name is given) set off "a wave of protest against inter-racial marriages" and led the New York legislature to consider legislation to outlaw miscegenation.

26. The class ramifications of Jones' passing were played out on a variety of levels. One marginal result was that Jones was included in the Social Register for 1925. As the *New York Times* society commentator cattily commented, "[b]y her marriage the former laundress and nursemaid, who is alleged in the papers in the annulment action to be of negro descent, thus passes over hundreds of persons on the fringes of society and makes her debut therein" ("Mrs. L. Kip Rhinelander in Social Register"). In under a week, however, outraged letters from no less illustrious a figure than Emily Post led the Register to drop Jones, claiming that she was "in [high society] but not of it" ("To Drop Mrs. Rhinelander").

    The social implications of the case were subtly clear throughout. As the case was being covered on the front pages of the mainstream case, the society pages maintained a steady ancillary, gossip-oriented commentary about the issues.

27. See, for example, "Bride's Color Starts Suit."

28. In much of the writing of the 1920s, perhaps because of the influence of Rudolph Valentino, darker skinned white people are often described as looking "Spanish." Early reports of Alice Jones characterize her as having "a complexion of Spanish tint" ("Rhinelander's Father-in-Law") or having "coloring ... of a dark Spanish or Indian type" ("Calls Rhinelander Bride's Love Slave").

29. It is interesting, too, that Rhinelander's attorneys deployed a series of arguments to convince the jury that Alice Jones had committed fraud. While her racial background and affiliation with African Americans constituted a large part of their case, Rhinelander's lawyers also argued that Jones had seduced Rhinelander, who was intellectually and psychologically weak (in fact, Rhinelander was in New Rochelle, where he first met Jones, because he was taking a break from the residential psychiatric facility at which he was briefly staying). They represented him as sexually inexperienced and "brain-tied" by the older, more sophisticated Jones (see, for example, "Kip Rhinelander Is 'Brain Tied,' Counsel Pleads," *New York Herald Tribune*, November 10, 1925 (Gumby)). Of course, this dovetails neatly with the racist presumption that black women are sexually voracious gold-diggers, so one might argue that these ancillary arguments only served to bolster the larger accusation of racial fraud – how could a woman who behaved in this way pretend to be anything but black?

30. See, for example, "Rhinelander's Wife Cries Under Ordeal"; "Rhinelander's Bride Said to Be Grieving"; "Mrs. Rhinelander Fails to Testify."

31. Moreover, an issue that peers through the jury's decision but is never explicitly articulated is that of class antagonism. How might the mostly lower-middle-class, white ethnic jurors have identified with the working-class immigrant Jones family over the aristocratic Rhinelander clan, particularly given the repeated references to them in newspaper reports as a "leading New York family," and the estimates of Leonard Rhinelander's inheritance as totalling over $400,000 in 1920s currency?

32. Ironically, three of the jurors' wives who were interviewed by the New York *World* disagreed strenuously with their husbands' decision. The wife of Juror No. 4 declared that "Leonard Rhinelander should have been granted an annulment. It

isn't right for a man of his standing to be tied to a girl of colored blood." At the
same time, the wives could not understand Rhinelander's "blindness": "He should
have been able to see she was colored" ("Jurors Say Facts Beat Kip").

33. This brings to mind a moment in Richard Wright's *Native Son*: the body of Bessie
Mears, the black woman whom Bigger Thomas murdered while he was on the run
for killing Mary Dalton, is wheeled into the courtroom as part of the
prosecution's case against Bigger. Although "he had killed a black girl and a
white girl, he knew that it would be for the death of the white girl that he would
be punished. The black girl was merely 'evidence'" (1940: 306–7).

34. For an excellent exploration of the ambivalence towards primitivism in Langston
Hughes' work see David Chinitz, "Rejuvenation through Joy: Langston Hughes,
Primitivism, and Jazz," *ALH*, 9(1) (1997): 60–78. As Chinitz points out,
"Primitivism ... fetched African Americans credit at far too high a price. While
it proffered a kind of respect, this respect made real acceptance and integration
finally less rather than more achievable. Hughes found himself in the middle
position, trying to affirm, in effect, that African Americans were different, but not
that different" (p. 68).

35. The edition I am using of *The Blacker the Berry* is the Scribner Paperback version
(New York, 1996). I will be citing it within this chapter parenthetically as *BTB*
with page number.

36. For an exhaustive and detailed discussion of the "mark of Ham" thematic in
writings about people of African descent, see Werner Sollors, *Neither Black Nor
White Yet Both: Thematic Explorations of Interracial Literature* (New York: Oxford
University Press, 1997).

37. Kathy Peiss' research on urban African American beauty culture in the 1920s
reveals that "the ideal of brown-skinned beauty [rather than high yellow or near
white] was vigorously promoted by the African-American beauty trade. ... In a
rare study of black consumers' response to advertising, economist Paul Edwards
found that African Americans detested antiquated images like Aunt Jemima ...
but approved of the well-groomed, brown-skinned woman depicted in cosmetics
advertisements" (1998: 235). To that extent, Thurman represents both Emma
Lou's family and the sorority sisters at USC as somewhat provincial in their focus
on very light skin.

38. In fact, as Kathy Ogren points out, Harlem nightlife existed on several planes:
cabarets, restaurants with entertainment, dance-halls, and nightclubs. Moreover,
each venue appealed to a different constituency, which was often echoed by the
color of the performers. The all-white audience of the Cotton Club watched light-
skinned chorines; the black patrons of Small's Paradise applauded dark-skinned
singers and dancers (Ogren, 1989: 74–6).

39. See, for example, David Roediger, *The Wages of Whiteness: Race and the Making of
the American Working Class* (London: Verso, 1991); Toni Morrison, *Playing in the
Dark: Whiteness and the Literary Imagination* (New York: Vintage, 1993); Angela Y.
Davis, *Women, Race and Class* (New York: Vintage, 1983).

40. This process is very close to Julia Kristeva's theory of "abjection" as "a kind of

narcissistic crisis": rather than being the part of the self that is "self-contemplative, conservative, self-sufficient," the abject "takes the ego back to its source on the abominable limits from which, in order to be, the ego has broken away" (1982: 14–15). The encounter with the abject is a violent, nauseating rejection of the "pollution" which the ego constructs in order to distance itself from: "I expel *myself*, I spit *myself* out, I abject *myself* within the same motion with which 'I' claim to establish *myself*'" (p. 3).

   The little black girl is the abjected dark self, the sign of pollution that the Lafayette audience must vomit out and be disgusted by, must ridicule and refuse "in order to be" in a racist world.

41. For a discussion of the popularity of minstrelsy among Irish Americans, see Lott, 1993; of the sentimental ballad tradition in Irish American saloon culture, see Sante, 1991.

42. I disagree with Gubar's contention in *Racechanges* that black appropriation of the minstrel vernacular was and is inevitably degrading. Gubar asks: "How did [Zora Neale] Hurston feel when she could get seated at a restaurant with her traveling companion, Fannie Hurst, only when the white novelist introduced the aspiring black writer as 'Princess Zora'? Or when the folklorist signed letters written to her patron 'Your Pickaninny, Zora'?" as though these events are equivalent (1997: 121). While the incident with Hurst reinforces the powerlessness of African Americans and the exoticization of African primitivism, Hurston's self-styling as "Your Pickaninny" is, I believe, quite a different matter. In taking on the identity of a Topsy, Hurston is sardonically pointing to the unequal power relationship between herself and her white patron. She is, in effect, forcing a white woman to acknowledge the infantilizing nature of their relationship, forcing her to admit that for all her pretense of "color-blindness" she sees Hurston as her "Pickaninny" and acts accordingly.

43. Make-up was a highly politicized issue for African American women from the beginnings of the cosmetics industry. Two of America's first black female millionaires, Annie Turnbo Malone, and Sarah Breedlove, better known as Madam C. J. Walker, made their fortunes from hair care and cosmetics empires. Walker and Malone refused to sell skin lighteners, but other companies had fewer scruples.

   Kathy Peiss chronicles the debates in black communities over skin lightening and hair straightening in *Hope in a Jar: The Making of America's Beauty Culture* (New York: Henry Holt, 1998). In the 1920s, with the rise of Garveyism, "a new aesthetic for dark-skinned people" emerged, championing African features (p. 208). Nonetheless, bleaching creams and hair preparations were an enormous business, and even radical publications like the *Crusader* and *Negro World* depended upon their advertising even as they condemned such products in their editorial pages. Peiss estimates that cosmetics accounted for between 30 and 50 percent of advertising in the black press (pp. 209–10).

44. Thurman's novel captures female Harlemites' familiarity with the cosmetics industry; however, he misrepresents the uses to which the wide array of powders,

rouges, lipsticks, bleaching ointments, and vanishing creams were put. These products were part of a nationwide cosmetics industry and a cultural shift in urban areas towards the use of make-up (as opposed to just skin and hair preparations) in the 1920s. Moreover, black consumers often made choices about how and how much to use the products available to them. As Kathy Peiss points out, while sales for bleaching products like Tan-Off rose dramatically during the late 1920s,

> women applied bleach in various ways. Some dotted it on spots or blemishes to even the skin tone; others sought to fade or dissolve unwanted hair; still others spread bleach across the entire face to peel off the darker epidermis and reveal the lighter layer below. Consumers might have rendered different verdicts on these practices, approving of fade creams, for instance, but looking critically upon those who peeled their skin.
>
> (Peiss, 1998: 226)

Emma Lou's problem with powder was a product of the industry itself, since beauty companies aimed at black women "produced powder in shades ranging from white and rose-flesh to golden brown, but not colors to match very dark complexions" (Peiss, 1998: 235).

Notes to Chapter 4

1. The Public Affairs Committee's purpose was, in its own words, "to make available in summary and inexpensive form the results of research on economic and social problems to aid in the understanding and development of American policy" (Blakeslee, 1948: i). Founded in 1936, the Committee was initially headquartered in the National Press Building in Washington, DC, and was made up of a mixture of academics, policy-makers, and journalists. Pamphlets were printed monthly and were inexpensive: in the 1930s they cost ten cents, and by 1947 had risen to only twenty cents. The dozens of publications embraced diverse topics from "How To Buy Life Insurance" to "How Can We Teach About Sex?" to "This Problem Of Food" (with tips for growing vegetables to support the war-effort) to "The Negro In America." Pamphlets also worked to destigmatize mental illness and epilepsy, help veterans readjust to civilian life, and suggest improvements in schools and other public services. The Committee's focus was on civil liberties and economic prosperity for all classes: pamphlets encouraged readers to save their money but not to look down on recipients of public assistance; to support racial equality and help immigrants fit into the United States; to see marriage as a partnership and children as needing both nurturing and discipline. For a fuller account of the Public Affairs Committee, see the PAC's in-house history by Maxwell S. Stewart, *20th Century Pamphleteering: The History of the Public Affairs Committee* (New York: Public Affairs Committee, 1976).

2. Blakeslee was a long-time science editor for the Associated Press.
3. For a detailed discussion of both the water cure and calomel as major health fads of the nineteenth century, see Joan D. Hedrick's biography of Harriet Beecher Stowe, *Harriet Beecher Stowe: A Life* (New York: Oxford University Press, 1994).
4. The science of agglutination is fairly simple. Agglutination, or clumping, is a life-threatening phenomenon in which blood cells of corresponding types collect in clumps in the veins, transforming the blood from a fluid to a mixture the consistency of curds and whey, and halting circulation. There are two types of agglutinogens (the bodies that clump), which exist in the red blood cells, and two types of agglutinins (the bodies that activate clumping), which exist in plasma. The agglutinogens are called A and B, the corresponding agglutinins a and b. If serum containing A (the agglutinogen) is transfused into a person who has the a agglutinin in her blood cells, a will agglutinate A, that is, cause clumping in the veins. Blood is typed according to what agglutinogens it contains: type A, which has A; type B, which has B; type AB, which has A and B; and type O, which has no agglutinogens in it.
5. In one of the early medical texts that synthesized the discoveries about and ramifications of blood typing, Geoffrey Keynes reported that certain blood types *were* found more commonly in specific national or ethnic groups – for example, what we now call type O was found "in not less than 45% among most European peoples [but is] present in Arabs 37%, in Russians 37% ... in Negroes 27%," and so on (1922: 82) – but was forced to admit that these differences had little meaning. Even if one could trace a connection between race and blood, "the mingling of the hypothetical stocks of which mankind is made no doubt began in a remote antiquity, and it is possible that a serologically pure race does not exist" (1922: 82–3).
6. Twain parodies this notion of the undissolved drops in Roxy's claim to genealogical greatness, in which she lines up the blood of an African chief and of Pocahontas – her putative ancestors –with that of Cecil Burleigh Essex, the father of her son Chambers. The effect, rather than being grand, is absurd: these vestiges of blood are invoked almost as homunculi floating in the serum, in continual friction with each other.
7. The ARC had a hierarchy and bureacracy second only to the Armed Forces themselves. The national organization oversaw local chapters, each of which had its own chain of command, from directors to technical supervisors to publicity managers to the "Gray Ladies" – uniformed Red Cross volunteers who were the foot soldiers of the organization. Manuals and guidelines for all aspects of Red Cross work were issued from headquarters in Washington, DC to local chapters, and everything was expected to go "through channels." Charles Coggin kept a close eye on Red Cross-related media events, and sent out press releases to chapters that they could then personalize by region, or by including local celebrities. Sample news releases were fairly generic: one entitled "Local Red Cross Chapter Launches Appeal for Blood Donors for National Defense" was a basic fill-in-the-blanks affair:

"This appeal," Mr _____ (chair of the center) declared "gives every able bodied citizen of _____ a chance to help our boys in the camps and on the sea."

(Publicity Kit for Chapters)

8. Hence the Red Cross's focus on people with disabilities as ideal blood donors — since they could not sign up for active or auxiliary duties, giving blood was represented as their way of fighting the war. The blind were a population whom the Red Cross often cited as paradigmatic of the "unable to fight but healthy in every other way" disabled, and ARC occasionally featured blind people in its publicity. A November episode of the radio show "We The People" included an interview with a "blind pianist, 16-time donor" (Coggin, Letter, November 6, 1943); "Blood for Defense," a sample radio play in the *Publicity Kit for Chapters* focused on a blind woman who wants to give blood after hearing the Red Cross's publicity campaign on the radio: "A blind woman's blood is as good as anybody's!" (p. 3).

9. Taking collections and signing up people for blood donation appointments in cinemas was a fairly common practice of the Red Cross, starting in 1943. The BDS sent out a pamphlet, *A Tested Theater Recruiting Plan*, to local chapters, outlining successful strategies and reporting on the work of other chapters who had already begun this kind of recruitment drive. According to the booklet, Red Cross workers had signed up 28,000 New York moviegoers for donation appointments between February 1 and July 31, 1943.

    The Bogart trailer was clearly designed with this campaign in mind. Movie studios also arranged for tie-ins with newly released films. For example, the release of a Universal Studios picture *Next of Kin* was accompanied by Red Cross posters in cinemas that declared "Your Blood Could Save *Your* Next of Kin."

10. This ordinariness was played to the hilt in Red Cross publicity about servicemen who had received blood. In a large four-sided "news sheet," *Lives Saved by Plasma*, produced in August 1943 as a promotional tool for newspapers, the ARC outlined in words and photographs "over 60 new case histories" of successful transfusions. The pictures followed the usual iconographic patterns: felled soldiers on stretchers being administered plasma in makeshift hospitals; perky servicemen smiling for the camera; medics reconstituting plasma on the field. The quotations from soldiers emphasize their aw-shucks "normality" to an almost absurd extent: they are cited as saying things like "Boy, I sure think plasma is swell," and "I have seen plasma save an awful lot of lives. It sure saved mine." The headline above these testimonials reads "Your Blood Is Now Theirs," creating an embodied link between these "all-American boys" and blood donors themselves.

11. Similarly, a Paramount News newsreel from late December 1941 posed the question, just weeks after Pearl Harbor, "For 1942 What Can I Do For My Country?" Again, home-front activities are explicitly divided by gender: young men are shown signing up for active duty; fathers buying war bonds and paying bills on time; mothers and daughters knitting, folding blankets and bandages, and participating in volunteer Red Cross work; Boy Scouts collecting scrap metal and

spare tires. The final activity announces the title, is "For Everybody": giving blood. "It is only a pint of your blood and a little of your time, but it may mean life for one of our boys."

12. "I Am An American" day was taken up enthusiastically by Fiorella LaGuardia, then mayor of New York. Press coverage for the first "I Am An American" day in 1941 was spotty: the *New York Times* covered LaGuardia's lavish preparations for the event, but not the celebration itself. In 1942, by contrast, the *Times* devoted several articles to the observance, including a front-page story that was continued on a full-page spread inside the paper, with a quarter-page photograph of a massive rally in Central Park, as well as a patriotic editorial entitled "I Am An American" on the day itself.

13. Theorizing citizenship has mostly been the bailiwick of political scientists. For a brief but fairly thorough historical treatment of Western notions of citizenship from the Athenians to the Rawlsians of the mid-1980s, see Douglas B. Klusmeyer, *Between Consent and Descent: Conceptions of Democratic Citizenship* (Washington. DC: Carnegie Endowment for International Peace, 1996). Another useful source is *Theorizing Citizenship*, edited by Ronald Beiner (Albany: SUNY Press, 1995), which contains essays by such leading political theorists as J.G.A. Pocock and Michael Ignatieff. The classic text of post-WWII theories of citizenship is T.H. Marshall and Tom Bottomore's *Citizenship and Social Class* (London: Pluto Press, 1992), which was originally conceived by Marshall as a series of lectures in 1949 and first published in 1950.

     In recent years, however, interest in the meaning of citizenship has expanded among U.S. literary and cultural critics. See, for example, Lauren Berlant, *The Queen of America Goes to Washington City: Essays on Sex and Citizenship* (Durham: Duke University Press, 1997); Wai-Chee Dimock, *Residues of Justice: Literature, Law, Philosophy* (Berkeley: University of California Press, 1996); Michael Moon and Cathy N. Davidson (eds), *Subjects and Citizens: Nation, Race, and Gender from Oroonoko to Anita Hill* (Durham: Duke University Press, 1995).

14. I do not wish to belabor the distinction between nation and citizenry: certainly they also have a great deal of overlap. Ideas of citizenship in the U.S. were disseminated through many of the same channels as those which Benedict Anderson identifies as the "origins of national consciousness": the assumption of a common language (essential to the project of "Americanizing" immigrants), the rise of print culture, the belief in such a thing as "national character." However, as I want to show here, citizenship should be conceptually distinguished from nationality, and that distinction was drawn by theorists of citizenship in the 1940s. Citizenship's voluntary quality, its connection to a system of rights, and its focus on modernity and democracy separate it from nationalism's deliberate embrace of a mythic genealogical heritage.

15. Citizenship in the United States has an uneven history, to say the least. On the one hand, citizenship was conceived of as a birthright by the nation's founders – to be born in the U.S. was to be a citizen. That seemingly universal statement had a staggering number of exceptions, however. From its inception, the U.S.

contained an entire population of American-born inhabitants forbidden to claim citizenship rights: slaves. African Americans gained citizenship rights through the 15th Amendment in 1870, but these rights were fast eroded with the collapse of Reconstruction. Voting rights were extended to only a minority of citizens until the nineteenth century due to property requirements, and were withheld from women (who could not be both married and hold their own property – a basic right of citizenship – until Married Women's Property laws were passed from state to state from the late 1840s to the early 1890s) until the 1920s. Moreover, as Ian F. Haney López observes, "[i]n its first words on the subject of citizenship, Congress in 1790 restricted naturalization to 'white persons'" (1996: 2).

16. The novel *Wasteland* by Jo Sinclair (1946) is hereafter cited parenthetically as *W* with page number.

17. Of course, Jake's chosen name also resonates with the historical John Brown, an ironic inversion of Jake Braunowitz's unwillingness to stand out. It is hard to tell whether Sinclair had the abolitionist John Brown in mind when she picked out Jake's "American" name. Nonetheless, she came of age in the radical 1930s, and her choice highlights Jake's heroic potential. Thanks to Alan Rice for pointing out this parallel.

18. At the same time that Jake opposes Jewish and American identities in his day-to-day life, he combines the two in his photography. A professional newspaper photographer, Jake takes his "own pictures" in his spare time (*W* 101). He fantasizes taking a series of his parents at home:

> "In the kitchen there, the way they always sit at the table. They're reading the *Jewish World*, see, and I get their faces and part of the paper, the Jewish print showing. . . . I've even got captions for pictures like that. In my head," he said. "That kitchen people I could call, AMERICANS, EVENING. . . . They're Americans after all. . . . Jews, sure, but here they are in their kitchen in America. . . . There's one picture I really want to get. Friday night. It isn't dark yet, but the room is full of that shadow stuff. My mother stands in front of the candles she's just lit. Her hands are over her eyes, her lips are moving. That's the one I'll call IN AMERICA THEY PRAY."
>
> (*W* 102)

The scenarios Jake describes are, in fact, familiar images of Jewish immigrants, images imbued with iconic value by second generation Jews like Jake (or his nonfictional contemporary, Irving Howe, whose *World of Our Fathers* is full of such pictures). They are deeply American images, as American as the ambivalence that brings them into being.

19. In fact, compared with other Southern states, Maryland's segregation regulations were less restrictive: African Americans were not prevented from voting, although they could not marry whites, attend school with them, or frequent public spaces such as parks and swimming pools with them. Buses and streetcars were not officially segregated, although steam trains were, so that black Baltimoreans, for example, could travel freely within the city but were Jim Crowed when traveling to another town.

20. In fact lynching, although not as epidemic as it had been in the first two decades of the twentieth century, continued in civilian life throughout the South. From 1941 to 1946, the *New York Times* reported lynchings or attempted lynchings in Tennessee, Florida, Texas, Missouri, Arizona, Mississippi, and Georgia, and estimated 106 lynchings throughout the South between 1931 and 1941.

21. Perhaps the two most dramatic incidents of racial polarization occurred in Prescott, Arizona, and Alexandria, Louisiana. After weeks of harassment and physical attacks from white military police (MPs), forty-three black soldiers from the 97th Engineer Battalion left Prescott as a group and hitch-hiked back to their former training station in Michigan.

    In Alexandria, in early January 1942, black soldiers protested at the lack of recreational facilities and the army's refusal to appoint black MPs. The demonstration led to the arrest of one of their colleagues, and their subsequent protest of this arrest culminated in a riot by white military police. Twenty-eight of the soldiers were shot or clubbed by MPs, and over 3,000 were arrested by military, city, and state police.

22. The few times the ARC did feature African American soldiers, the content ranged from patronizing to insulting. A *March of Time* reel, produced in co-operation with the War Activities Committee entitled "At His Side," represented the multiple roles that the ARC played in the war. The Red Cross is shown as America's proxy, allowing people stateside to connect with soldiers, and so troops have a link with home. The narrator calls the plasma used in field hospitals "the gift of the American people," as a way to fuse citizens and soldiers.

    Much of the film is taken up with scenes of other Red Cross services, particularly in terms of recreation in ARC clubhouses. Although the film does not comment upon it, the clubhouses are clearly segregated by race. In the white clubhouse, soldiers play checkers, read, write letters, and chat sociably with the female ARC volunteers. The scene in the black clubhouse is rather different: the servicemen are crowded around a piano, listening to a soldier play a boogie-woogie as they clap their hands, roll their eyes and grin.

23. The American Red Cross archives at the National Archives and Records Administration (NARA) in College Park, Maryland, are enormous, numbering almost two thousand boxes of material. The records of the Blood Donor Service take up approximately eight boxes, including office correspondence, promotional material of the kind I have described, and miscellaneous records. Moreover, the NARA has considerable holdings in BDS and Red Cross-related motion pictures, movie trailers, and so on. In all my examination of this material, I did not come across *one* image or written description of a black person either giving blood or receiving plasma. I cannot say for certain that no such image exists, but I never saw any sign of it.

24. In *Yours in Struggle*, Elly Bulkin gives an elegant and arresting example of how effortless it can be to be white in the United States. After participating in a workshop on racism at the 1981 National Women's Studies Association Conference, Bulkin goes to an ice-cream parlor with some other women. One

of her companions, an African American woman, whispers to herself as she walks into the restaurant, "Here I come, white folks!" Up until that moment, Bulkin had not imagined the trip for ice-cream as a "venture into white America," since her whiteness was unremarkable. She is shocked at her own easy return to the assumption of white neutrality: "A few hours after I had been on a panel on racism in the lesbian community, I could imagine going out for ice cream as a simple and uncomplicated act," which it clearly was not for her black companion (Bulkin, 1984: 143).

25. These are only a couple of examples of the numbing insensitivity of this pamphlet. The section entitled "We've Come A Long Way" also juxtaposes an engraving of slavery with a photograph of two black people admiring the Lincoln Memorial. As Audre Lorde reminds us in her "biomythography" *Zami: A New Spelling of My Name*, those tourists would have had a difficult time finding something to eat or a place to stay in most of the area surrounding the memorial, since Washington, DC, was strictly segregated (not to mention the fact that many rural Southern farm-workers were barely a step above the slavery of their predecessors).

26. This remark comes from Freud's discussion of the "narcissism of minor differences" in *Civilization and Its Discontents* (p. 61), an analysis that I have found instructive in my thoughts about the Blood Donor Service. For a detailed discussion of this concept see Ann Pellegrini, *Performance Anxieties* (New York: Routledge, 1998).

27. *What the Negro Wants* has a fascinating publishing history. A white "liberal" Southern historian, W.T. Couch, approached Logan about editing a collection on black political aspirations. Couch, a gradualist who believed in eventual civil rights for blacks but harbored a terror of social equality and the possibility of miscegenation, assumed that his contributors would share his views (considering that they numbered among them Mary McLeod Bethune, the NAACP's Roy Wilkins, A. Philip Randolph, and Logan himself, it is dizzying to imagine how Couch could ever believe this). When he saw the final proofs, including Logan's uncompromising opening essay, and Randolph's radical manifesto for the March on Washington Movement (which I discuss below), Couch was horrified. He insisted that Logan include his lengthy "publisher's introduction" in which he laid out his political program for "Negro improvement." He averred that "the Negro's condition is produced by inferiority but ... this inferiority can be overcome, and prejudice resulting from it can be cured ....The barrier [between the races] may be a tremendous handicap on the Negro, but removing it would result in something worse," such as black social equality (n.p.). Couch dismissed as "obviously untrue" the belief that "the Negro is not inferior to the white man, that he only appears to be so, that his condition is wholly and completely a product of race prejudice, and the consequent disabilities inflicted on the Negro by the white man," and aligned it with social liberals like Gunnar Myrdal, author of the extremely influential *American Dilemma*, a harsh indictment of Northern racism and Southern Jim Crow (n.p.).

Couch's shock at the radicalism of the book's contributors is largely relegated to his footnotes, but they are juicy and near-hysterical. In a lengthy note that begins as a critique of the cultural relativism of contemporary anthropology, Couch veers off in a different direction altogether: all this acceptance is dangerous since "one concession will lead to another, and ultimately to intermarriage. ... *Have we no duty to the remote future as well as to the present?* Does the white man have no right to attempt to separate biological from cultural integration ... ? What problem would be solved if the white South dropped all barriers and accepted amalgamation?" (n.p.; emphasis in original).

What is so striking about Couch's analysis (apart from the fact that the white supremacy is so thinly veiled by a gossamer layer of "progressivism") is the way in which it attempts to deploy both a discourse of citizenship and a discourse of blood. Couch's gradualism will allow for black citizens, as long as they do not insist on displacing the power of genealogy with a politics of fraternity. Rather than "casting social practices as biological essences" as Eva Saks argues miscegenation law does, Couch wants to keep social practices completely separate from biology: those things called "rights" are *only* social (i.e. civic, political). Couch answers his own question: "biological integration" can never "be regarded as a right" because the polity is completely segregated from the family.

28. A 1942 MOWM rally in Madison Square Garden that demanded an end to segregation and discrimination in the armed forces and defense industries attracted a crowd of 18,000, and "black-out" campaigns in Harlem shut down businesses and switched off lights for hours at a time (see Pfeffer, 1990: 58–70).

29. While a resolute anti-communist, Randolph felt comfortable with Marxist economic formulations, and his position was one of democratic socialism. He also believed in mass action organized by a strong vanguardist leadership (particularly him), an ironically Leninist position. For a discussion of Randolph's leadership style, see Pfeffer's analysis of the problems with and ultimate dissolution of the March on Washington Movement.

30. Despite Randolph's credentials as an organizer, and the fact that Macdonald was white, the pamphlet was considered too radical by the black political establishment; the NAACP "declined to distribute it," fearing that they would be associated by its unvarnished attacks on racism in the armed forces (Pfeffer, 1990: 135).

31. This statement also elegantly invokes the U.S. Constitution in its use of the phrase "these United States" which have been brutally riven by racial discrimination.

32. The pamphlet repeats an anecdote first told by Walter White, a "dialogue recently reported between a Negro teacher and student":

> Student: I hope Hitler wins this war.
> Teacher: How can you make such a statement?
> Student: Because I am convinced that is the only thing that will teach these white people some sense – their knowing what it means to be oppressed.

Teacher: But don't you realize that conditions would be even worse under
Hitler?

Student: They can't possibly be any worse than they are for Negroes in the
South right now. The Army jimcrows us. The Navy lets us serve
only as messmen. The Red Cross segregates our blood. Employers
and labor unions shut us out. We are disenfranchised, jimcrowed,
spat up. What more could Hitler do than that?

(Macdonald, 1943: 14)

Macdonald comments on this exchange, "When this dialogue was reported to a
Negro audience recently, it was greeted with cheers" (p. 15).

33. A long-time (and only recently retired) editorial cartoonist and art director at the
Amsterdam News, Tapley was already well known in the black press as the creator
of the "Breezy" comic strip. His work in the *News* was so prolific that he wrote
under pseudonyms such as "Tap Melvin" to obscure quite how much he was
publishing in the paper.

34. This argument was also made in an article in *The People's Voice* (April 28, 1945)
entitled "Army Stands Pat on Jimcro Blood." Brigadier General F.W. Rankin,
advisor to the Surgeon General to the Army, is asked why, since "there is not
biological incompatibility in Negro and white blood" the military insisted on
segregating plasma. The General blamed the "many whites [who] 'out of prejudice
or ignorance' object to having Negro blood inserted into their veins." Rankin uses
the rhetoric of democracy – "He declared that in a democracy the majority rules" –
but the anonymous reporter picks up on the arguments Tapley presents in *An
American Tragedy*. First, the reporter asks, how does the General know "that the
majority of whites objected to having blood from Negroes injected into their
veins"? Second, as though lifting a scenario directly from Tapley's cartoon, the
reporter asks "whether he meant that a dying soldier would stop a transfusion if
the blood was taken from a Negro. The General replied that a dying soldier would
not object, but that a great many people out of the Army would object." Again,
responsibility for blood segregation is placed at the feet of the leadership, not the
common soldier, for whom plasma is a matter of life and death.

35. A superb source of these articles, poems, etc. is the Alexander L. Gumby
Collection of the American Negro, held by the Rare Books and Manuscripts
Division of the Columbia University Library. Arranged in both scrapbooks and
loose boxes, the collection is a treasure trove of Afro-Americana. Articles on the
blood segregation controversy can be found in scrapbooks 74–6.

36. The total number of internees ended up at about 120,000: 110,00 from the west
coast, just over 1,100 from Hawaii, 1,275 who were transferred from other
institutions (hospitals, orphanages, and so on), and almost 6,000 who were born
in the camps. Of the west coast Japanese Americans, almost 80 percent (93,000)
were from California (Weglyn, 1996: 21).

37. For a fuller account of the roots of the Japanese American Citizens League, see Bill
Hosogawa, *JACL: In Quest of Justice* (New York: William Morrow, 1982).

38. The prohibition against non-naturalizable aliens who owned land hit particularly

hard, since a large number of Issei were small farmers. The most common way to dodge this obstacle was to buy land in the names of their minor children and be designated as administrators of the land until the child reached adulthood.

39. This quotation is taken from the *Investigation of Congested Areas: Hearings Before a Subcommittee of the Committee of Naval Affairs, House of Representatives* 78th Congress, 1st session, pursuant to HR 30 (Washington, DC: US Government Printing Office, 1943): 740; hereafter *Hearings*.

40. This quotation is taken from DeWitt's *Final Report: Japanese Evacuation from the West Coast, 1942* (Washington, DC: U.S. Government Printing Office, 1943): 145. Hereafter *Final Report*.

41. Hence the almost obsessive focus on "Emperor-worshipping cults" among Issei, or the practice of sending Nisei children back to Japan for their education: according to this logic, it was not that the U.S. did not wish to extend the rights of citizenship to Japanese Americans, but that they did not want it themselves. They *preferred* the atavistic belief in blood as ancestry, as their allegiance to a dynastic emperor proved.

42. In fact this was patently untrue, as were rumors that Japanese Americans were signaling to Japanese submarines and aircraft off the Pacific coast. DeWitt had released a report citing "hundreds of reports nightly of signal lights visible from the coast, and of intercepts of unidentified radio transmissions" off the coast (Irons, 1986: 39). In terms of the former claim, the FBI had engaged in a series of investigations before Pearl Harbor, as tensions between the U.S. and Japan were worsening. Their subsequent report maintained that "there is no Japanese problem," and loyalty was "not an issue" (quoted in Weglyn, 1996: 34).

   The second charge, which was the basis for the U.S. case in *Korematsu v. United States* (in which a Nisei, Fred Korematsu, challenged the constitutionality of the evacuation), had also been thoroughly investigated by both the FBI and the Department of Justice, who "tore [DeWitt's report] to shreds" (Irons, 1986: 41). The Justice Department affirmed that the accusations of "the use of illegal radio transmitters and ... ship to shore signalling by persons of Japanese ancestry [were] in conflict with information in the possession of the Department of Justice," and requested that the Supreme Court ignore DeWitt's "evidence" (quoted in Irons, 1986: 40). However, the FBI and Justice Department reports were downplayed to the point of suppression by Solicitor General Charles Fahey, who was arguing the government's case from "military necessity." Peter Irons argues that had the FBI and Justice Department reports been available to the Supreme Court, they would not have decided against Korematsu. However, they had considerably less evidence in *Hirabayashi*, and that case was decided unanimously for the government.

43. Ironically, as Eugene Rostow reports, "those subsequently [to Pearl Harbor] arrested as Japanese agents were all white men" (1945: 523).

44. For example, in his dissent to the majority opinion in *Korematsu*, Justice Roberts pointed out that Fred Korematsu was "a native of the United States of Japanese ancestry who, according to uncontradicted evidence, is a loyal citizen of the

nation" (226). However, according to Justice Black, who wrote the majority opinion, loyalty of a given individual is not the issue. There had been "evidence of disloyalty on the part of some," which was enough to cause the relocation of all (223).

45. By the estimation of James Omura, 16,080 Nisei either responded "no," qualified their answers, or refused to answer questions 27 and 28. They were sent to Tule Lake, a camp set aside for "disloyals." Omura suggests that including the residents of Tule Lake, the Nisei imprisoned for draft resistance, and soldiers who resisted in some way after being drafted, the number of resisters could be as high as 16,436, or 21 percent of the eligible Nisei men (Omura, 1989: 75).

46. For an analysis of the role of the Momotaro myth in *No-No Boy*, see Gayle K. Fugita Santo, "Momotaro's Exile: John Okada's *No-No Boy*," in Shirley Geok-lin Lim and Amy Ling (eds), *Reading the Literatures of Asian America* (Philadelphia: Temple University Press, 1992).

Notes to Chapter 5

1. For a discussion of the development of microbiology in the years after World War II, see Gunther S. Stent, "The DNA double helix and the rise of molecular biology," in James D. Watson, *The Double Helix*, ed. Gunther S. Stent (New York: W.W. Norton, 1980, pp. xi–xxi).

2. That is not to say that there is a complete consensus that genetics can answer life's most profound questions. A recent example is the Kansas State School Board's 1999 decision to exclude evolutionary theory from standardized biology tests on the state-wide level, leaving it up to individual districts and teachers to decide whether to teach evolution next to theories such as creationism and intelligent design. While supporters of the decision describe evolution as "one theory among many," its critics point to DNA evidence linking fossils and prehistoric human remains to current organisms, as well as the genetic similarities between all sentient life, as proof positive of Darwinian evolution.

3. For a detailed description of DNA extraction, see A. J. Jeffreys *et al.*, "Individual-specific 'Fingerprints' of Human DNA," *Nature*, 316 (July 1985): 76–9.

4. Ironically, genetics tends to flatten the differences between human beings and other kinds of organisms: tables illustrating the complexity of the human genome in comparison with those of other species reveal that in terms of numbers of genes, human beings have by no means the most involved chromosomal structure, and lie somewhere between fruit flies and pufferfish (Primrose, 1998: 10).

5. PCR was discovered (and a method to induce it invented) by Kary B. Mullis, then a biochemist with the Cetus Corporation, in 1983. For an accessible discussion of the principles behind PCR as well as the process Mullis underwent to understand and replicate it, see "The Unusual Origin of the Polymerase Chain Reaction," *Scientific American*, 262(4) (April 1990): 56–65.

6. A similar blind spot appears in Levy's discussion of those times that DNA evidence has not convinced juries of a defendant's guilt. Talking of a Bronx murder case in which the genetic evidence deployed against the accused was disregarded by the jury, Levy comments that "Bronx juries are notoriously friendly to defendants in criminal cases," without speculating why that might be: why a significant number of Bronx residents might identify against the criminal justice system, or distrust the police, or imagine that evidence was biased (Levy, 1996: 34).

7. More naive is his assumption that exoneration is a necessary sequel to proven innocence. Recently, the U.S. Supreme Court has so tightened the purview of the rights of *habeas corpus* and legal appeal that proof of innocence can come "too late" even in death penalty cases.

8. Another of the manifold analogies between DNA and fingerprinting is that both technologies gained currency during a period of intense fear of violent crime from a perceived underclass. This is not to say that violent crime did not increase during the 1890s and 1980s within poor urban areas (for a terrific discussion of the crime culture of New York's Lower East Side during the turn of the century, see Luc Sante's *Low Life: Lures and Snares of Old New* York (New York: Vintage 1991), for example. However, both periods witnessed a widening of the gap between rich and poor, the intensification of urban poverty (although for vastly different reasons), and extreme economic volatility. Out of these phenomena grew a popular sense, abetted by media reports of lawlessness on the part of immigrants/people of color, that cities were morasses of violence and danger for all legitimate citizens. In fact, the majority of the violence within densely populated poor urban areas was directed inwards, not at the larger population.

9. Between 1993 and 1996, the number of states that required convicted sex offenders to provide blood for DNA data banks almost doubled, from twenty-one to forty-one (Levy, 1996: 135).

10. This is the kind of "blind enthusiasm" for DNA testing that William C. Thompson has criticized in his analyses of judicial uses of genetic evidence (1994: 194). Thompson draws particular attention to the risks of laboratory contamination, intensified by PCR techniques. "The risk of contamination of DNA samples in labs is high enough to be of concern," he argues; "in proficiency tests we found labs produced two false matches out of 100 samples due to accidental cross-contamination" by DNA from other sources (*ibid.*: 187).

11. This issue of *Science* was full of articles about this topic: Lewontin and Hartl's piece, Ranajit Chakrabory and Kenneth L. Kidd's rebuttal (which, oddly, came before Lewontin and Hartl's article in the magazine), and a lengthy article with sidebars charting the controversy over the issue itself, the publication history of Lewontin and Hartl's piece, and an apologia by *Science*'s editor about the controversy. For a detailed description of the events leading up to the publication of all these articles, see Leslie Roberts, "Fight Erupts Over DNA Fingerprinting," *Science* 254 (December 20, 1991): 1721–3.

12. Conversely, Haizlip experiences not being able to connect facial features to

genetic inheritance as profound loss. In her research into her mother's family, Haizlip participates in the now iconic activity of searching slave records for her great-great-grandmother. Cataloged in the 1860 Census for Henrico Country, Virginia, this woman is recorded only by her age, race, and sex: 45 years old, "F" for female and "M" for mulatto. Seeking some sort of affinity with this unknown predecessor, Haizlip touches the words with her fingers in an attempt to "conjure up visions of the woman. ... My fingers just felt sorrow. I look in the mirror and have no idea where I would find that 45-year-old F/M in any of my features" (1994: 42–3).

13. This is also the hypothesis that powers Barbara Chase-Riboud's novel *Sally Hemings* (1979), and the recent film *Jefferson in Paris*, which was in part based on Chase-Riboud's book. For Brodie's account, see *Thomas Jefferson: An Intimate History* (1974).

14. In her thoroughly researched book *Thomas Jefferson and Sally Hemings: An American Controversy* (Charlottesville: University Press of Virginia, 1997), Annette Gordon-Reed lays out the various reasons which biographers and historians gave for the "impossibility" of such a relationship, ranging from Jefferson's asexuality to his love for his children to his purity of mind to his racism and anti-miscegenation sentiments. However, as Gordon-Reed acutely points out, to imagine it "impossible" for Jefferson and Hemings to have been sexually involved, "one has to make Thomas Jefferson so high as to have been something more than human and one has to make Sally Hemings so low as to have been something less than human" (1997: xiv).

15. Alternatively, the coercive nature of slavery is overlaid with and even obscured by contemporary fantasies about sexual attraction and romance. This is clear in the film *Jefferson in Paris* as well as in putatively "objective" accounts of the Hemings–Jefferson relationship: in an article reporting on Foster and his team's conclusions, *New York Times* journalists Dinitia Smith and Nicholas Wade call Jefferson "Hemings' lover."

16. More pointedly, the article quotes LA radio commentator Earl Ofari Hutchinson questioning the refusal of historians to grant credence to the stories of a Hemings–Jefferson liaison, and their claim that Jefferson was too morally upright. After all, as Hutchinson asks, "was having sex with a slave any less moral than owning one, or 200 as Jefferson did?" (Terry, 1998).

Notes to the Epilogue

1. This familiarity can create a feeling of surreality when one is actually in a medical environment. Recently I had to undergo surgery, and in the round of pre-admission testing a medical technician requested an EKG (an electrical reading of the heart), and CBC, Chem 7 and typing blood tests. I had heard these terms dozens of times on *ER* but hearing them applied to the blood that had just been taken from my body, or the picture of my heartbeat that was printed out in front

of me, was very disorienting, as though I had just become a character in a television series. While medical programs on TV give the impression that we are learning about *the* body, and hence our own bodies, my experience was of feeling more distanced – those were tests that occurred to other people in emergency rooms or in Chicago or only between 10 and 11 on a Thursday night, not to me.

2. Or perhaps Sally Hemings is the emancipating Queen of America of whom Harriet Jacobs speaks, a character imagined by an illiterate slave woman who "thought that America was governed by a Queen, to whom the President was subordinate" (1987: 45).

Bibliography

Documents from the records of the American Red Cross, National Archives and Record Administration

Adamson, Hans. Letter to Mrs. Trubee Davison, *Red Cross Courier*, March 1943.

"American Red Cross Reports Many Jewish Donors to Its Blood Plasma Collections." Press release, 17 February 1943.

A Tested Theater Recruiting Plan. October 1943.

"Blood Donors Park Tots at Nursery Center." *Red Cross News*, 1942.

Blood Donor Testimonials — and How to Use Them. 1 August 1945.

"Blood Plasma Brings Fighting Marine Back to Life." Press release, December 1944.

Coggin, Charles. Letter to local blood donor centers and publicity directors, 6 November 1943.

Give Your Blood to Save a Life. Pamphlet, January 1942.

"Hero Sailor Repays Blood for Plasma." *Red Cross News*, 1943.

How to Set up and Operate the New Red Cross Blood Donor Dedication Label Plan. 1944.

Lives Saved by Plasma. News sheet, August 1943.

McIntire, Ross T. Letter to the National Association for the Advancement of Colored People, 16 January 1942.

Publicity Kit for Chapters Participating in National Defense Blood Plasma Resevoir. June 1941.

"Rochester, NY: National Blood Program Launched." *Red Cross News*, 1944.

"Smith Week: May 22–27, 1944." 8 May 1944.

"Statement of Policy Regarding Negro Blood." Press release, 21 January 1942.

"Suggested Newspaper Publicity." 1944.

Teamwork from Publicity to Plasma. Revised edn. Washington, DC: American Red Cross, 1943.

"The Nation's Presswomen Speak." Transcript of radio broadcast, 18 February 1943.

Newspaper and film reports

"Adele Gardiner Secretly Married." *New York Times*, 20 November 1925, late edn, p. 12.

"Al Jolson on Stand in Rhinelander Trial." *New York Evening Post*, 17 November 1925, pp. 1, 8.

"Another Eloper." *New York World*, 6 December 1925, p. 1.

"Army Stands Pat on Jimcro Blood." *The People's Voice*, 28 April 1945, p. 3.

"At His Side." *March of Time*, 24 February 1944.

"Avery Rockefeller Secretly Wedded." *New York Times*, 9 December 1924, late edn, p. 1.

"Betting Is 5 to 1." *New York World*, 28 November 1925, p. 1.

"Bride's Color Starts Suit." *New York American*, 27 September 1924, p. 13.

"Calls Rhinelander Bride's Love Slave." *New York World*, 10 November 1925, p. 1+.

"Calls Rhinelander Dupe of Girl He Wed." *New York Times*, 10 November 1925, late edn, p. 1+.

"Contrast Striking in Yiddish Dramas." *New York World*, 5 December 1925, p. 13.

"Criticizes the Press on Rhinelander Case." *New York Times*, 26 November 1925, late edn, p. 24.

"Denies Ancestry Hunt." *New York Times*, 16 June 1925, late edn, p. 11.

"Family Disinherits L. K. Rhinelander." *New York Times*, 28 October 1925, late edn, p. 27.

"Famous Rhinelander Case in History," in Alexander L. Gumby Collection, Columbia University Rare Books and Manuscript Collection.

"For 1942, What Can I Do for My Country?" *Paramount News*, 26 December 1941.

"Girl's Arrest Opens Mixed Marriage War." *New York Daily News*, 25 February 1926, p. 23.

"Greek Tragedy – Not Bedroom Farce" (Editorial). *The Daily News*, 21 November 1925, p. 18.

"'I Am An American Day' Parade" (1995) *Paramount News*, 1(76) (19 May 1942).

"James Stewart, the Hesitant Hero, Dies at 89." *New York Times*, 3 July 1997, late edn, p. A1+.

"Japanese Americans: Lesson in Loyalty." *Paramount News*, 2(53) (26 February 1943).

John, Gareth. "No Hyphens, Please." Letter to the Editor, *New York Times*, 15 July 1997, late edn, p. A18.

"Jones Interrupts Rhinelander Trial." *New York Times*, 4 December 1925, late edn, p. 3.

"Jurors Say Facts Beat Kip; Race Issue Never Involved." *New York World*, 6 December 1925, p. 1+.

"Lays Son's Plight to Rhinelander Sr." *New York Times*, 3 December 1925, late edn, p. 3.

"Mills in Calm Plea to Free Rhinelander." *New York Evening Post*, 2 December 1925, p. 2.

"Mills Completes Rhinelander Plea." *New York Times*, 11 November 1926, late edn, p. 11.

"Move to Free Rhinelander on Lesser Ground." *New York World*, 25 November 1925, p. 1+.

"Mr. and Mrs. America." *March of Time*, 9(3) (November 1942).

"Mrs. L. Kip Rhinelander in Social Register Despite Race Assertions in Husband's Suit." *New York Times*, 11 March 1924, late edn, p. 1.

"Mrs. Rhinelander Admits Her Color." *New York World*, 11 November 1925, p. 1+.

"Mrs. Rhinelander Fails to Testify." *New York Times*, 1 December 1925, late edn, p. 12.

"New Rhinelander Rumor." *New York Times*, 23 November 1924, late edn, p. 3.

"Rest from Ordeal for Rhinelanders." *New York World*, 15 November 1925, p. 1+.

"Rhinelander an Alert Witness, Brisk in Replies." *New York World*, 12 November 1925, p. 1+.

"Rhinelander Annulment Suit Jury Selected." *New York Amsterdam News*, 11 November 1925, p. 3.

"Rhinelander Bride Fights for Alimony." *New York Times*, 27 December 1924, late edn, p. 4.

"Rhinelander Bride Swears to a Denial." *New York Times*, 9 December 1924, late edn, p. 15.

"Rhinelander Bride's Family Speaks." *New York Times*, 15 November 1924, late edn, p. 12.

"The Rhinelander Case." Editorial, *New York World*, 26 November 1925, p. 16.

"Rhinelander Completes Case; Court Denies Dismissal Plea." *New York Evening Post*, 24 November 1924, pp. 1, 2.

"Rhinelander Jury Warned by Defense." *New York Times*, 2 December 1925, late edn, p. 3.

"Rhinelander Loses; No Fraud Is Found; Wife Will Sue Now." *New York Times*, 6 December 1925, late edn, p. 1+.

"Rhinelander Near Collapse and Trial Halts." *New York Sun*, 18 November 1925, p. 1.

"Rhinelander On Stand Insists Wife Lied to Him About Race." *New York Evening Post*, 12 November 1925, pp. 1, 8.

"Rhinelander Plea Put on Race Issue." *New York World*, 3 December 1925, p. 1+.

"Rhinelander Says He Pursued Girl." *New York Times*, 18 November 1925, late edn, p. 4.

"Rhinelander Shifted Grace's Ring to Alice." *New York Evening Post*, 19 November 1925, p. 1+.

"Rhinelander Sues to Annul Marriage; Alleges Race Deceit." *New York Times*, 27 November 1924, late edn, p. 16.

"Rhinelander Tells of Baring Letters." *New York Times*, 15 November 1925, late edn, p. 1+.

"Rhinelander Trial Suddenly Halted." *New York Times*, 20 November 1925, late edn, p. 9.

"Rhinelander's Bride Replies to His Suit with Complete Denial of Deceit Charge." *New York Times*, 6 December 1924, late edn, p. 15.

"Rhinelander's Bride Said to Be Grieving." *New York Times*, 28 November 1924, late edn, p. 13.

"Rhinelander's Father-in-Law Denies He's of Negro Stock." *The World*, 15 November 1924, p. 1.

"Rhinelander's Wife Admits Negro Blood." *New York Times*, 11 November 1925, late edn, p. 1+.

"Rhinelander's Wife Cries Under Ordeal." *New York Times*, 24 November 1925, late edn, p. 3.

"Rhinelander's Wife Denies She Is Negro." *New York Times*, 29 November 1924, late edn, p. 15.

"Rhinelanders Drop from Public Sight." *New York Times*, 16 November 1924, late edn, p. 13.

"'Save Me from the Gutter,' Rhinelander Told Girl; Plaintiff Near Collapse." *New York World*, 19 November 1925, pp. 1, 6.

"Says Rhinelander Knew of Girl's Race." *New York Times*, 26 November 1925, late edn, p. 3.

"Show-Business at War." *March of Time* (newsreel series), 9(10) (May 1943).

"Society Youth Weds Cabman's Daughter." *New York Times*, 14 November 1924, late edn, p. 1.

"Taking New Measurements for Jefferson's Pedestal." Editorial, *New York Times*, 7 March 1999, late edn, p. 132.

"'Threat' Defied by Rhinelander; Letters Heard." *New York World*, 24 November 1925, p. 1+.

"To Drop Mrs. Rhinelander." *New York Times*, 16 March 1925, p. 19.

"Trial to Go on Avers Counsel to Rhinelander." *New York World*, 20 November 1925, p. 1+.

Books and articles

Abu-Lughod, Janet (1989) "On the remaking of history: how to reinvent the past," in Barbara Kruger and Phil Mariani (eds), *Remaking History*. Seattle: Bay Press, pp. 111–30.

Alexander, Daryl Royster (1998) "The Content of Jefferson's Character Is Revealed at Last, Or Is It?" *New York Times*, 8 November, late edn, p. IV 7.

Althusser, Louis (1990) *Lenin and Philosophy and Other Essays*. London: Verso.

Anderson, Benedict (1983) *Imagined Communities: Reflections on the Origin and Spread of Nationalism*. London: Verso.

Anderson, Frederick, Michael B. Frank, and Kenneth M. Sanderson (eds) (1975) *Mark Twain's Notebooks and Journals*. Berkeley: University of California Press.

Anzaldúa, Gloria (1987) *Borderlands/La Frontera*. San Francisco: Aunt Lute.

Bakhtin, M. M. (1981) *The Dialogic Imagination*, ed. Michael Holquist, trans. Michael Holquist and Caryl Emerson. Austin: University of Texas Press.

Barnes, Barry and David Bloor (1982) "Relativism, rationalism and the sociology of knowledge," in Martin Hollis and Steven Lukes (eds), *Rationality and Relativism*. Cambridge, MA: Harvard University Press.

Barnum, P. T. (1983) *Selected Letters of P. T. Barnum*, ed. A. H. Sexton. New York: Columbia University Press.

Beiner, Ronald (ed.) (1995) *Theorizing Citizenship*. Albany: State University of New York Press.

Benedict, Ruth and Gene Weltfish (1943) *The Races of Man*. New York: Public Affairs Committee.

Benjamin Robert S. (ed.) (1941) *I Am An American: By Famous Naturalized Americans*. Reprinted, Freeport, NY: Books for Libraries Press, 1970.

Bennett, Juda (1996) *The Passing Figure: Racial Confusion in Modern American Literature*. New York: Peter Lang.

Berlant, Lauren (1991) "National brands/national body: *Imitation of Life*," in Hortense J. Spillers (ed.), *Comparative American Identities: Race, Sex, and Nationality in the Modern Text*. New York: Routledge, pp. 110–40.

Berlant, Lauren (1997) *The Queen of America Goes to Washington City: Essays on Sex and Citizenship*. Durham, NC: Duke University Press.

Bhabha, Homi K. (1986) "Signs taken for wonders: questions of ambivalence and authority under a tree outside Delhi, May 1817," in Henry Louis Gates, Jr. (ed.), *"Race," Writing and Difference*. Chicago: University of Chicago Press.

Bhabha, Homi K. (ed.) (1990) *Nation and Narration*. New York: Routledge.

Binder, David F. (1991) *The Hearsay Handbook*, 3rd edn. New York: McGraw-Hill Book Company.

Blackmer, Corinne E. (1998) "The veils of the law: race and sexuality in Nella Larsen's *Passing*," in Kostas Myrsiades and Linda Myrsiades (eds), *Race-ing Representation: Voice, History, and Sexuality*. Lanham, MD: Rowman and Littlefield, pp. 98–118.

Blakeslee, Alton L. (1948) *Blood's Magic for All*. New York: Public Affairs Committee.

Bloor, David (1991) *Knowledge and Social Imagery*, 2nd edn. Chicago: University of Chicago Press.

Bordo, Susan (1987) *The Flight to Objectivity: Essays on Cartesianism and Culture*. Albany: State University of New York Press.

Bornstein, Kate (1995) *Gender Outlaw: On Men, Women, and the Rest of Us*. New York: Vintage.

Brandt, Nat (1996) *Harlem at War: The Black Experience in WWII*. Syracuse: Syracuse University Press.

Brock, Dan W. (1994) "The Human Genome Project and human identity," in Robert F. Weir, Susan C. Lawrence, and Evan Fales (eds), *Genes and Human Self-Knowledge: Historical and Philosophical Reflections on Modern Genetics*. Iowa City: University of Iowa Press, pp.18–33.

Brodie, Fawn (1974) *Thomas Jefferson: An Intimate History*. New York: W. W. Norton & Company.

Brody, Jennifer DeVere (1992) "Clare Kendry's 'true' colors: race and class in Nella Larsen's *Passing*," *Callaloo*, 15: 1053–65.

Bryson, Norman (1988) "The gaze in the expanded field," in Hal Foster, 87–113.

Bucholtz, Mary (1995) "Language in evidence: the pragmatics of translation and the judicial process," in Marshall Morris (ed.), *Translation and the Law*. Philadelphia: John Benjamins, pp. 115–31.

Bulkin, Elly, Minnie Bruce Pratt, and Barbara Smith (1984) *Yours in Struggle: Three Feminist Perspectives on Anti-Semitism and Racism*. New York: Long Haul Press.

Burdette, Franklin L. (ed.) (1942) *Education for Citizen Responsibilities*. Princeton: Princeton University Press.

Butler, Judith (1993a) *Bodies That Matter: On the Discursive Limits of "Sex."* New York: Routledge.

Butler, Judith (1993b) "Passing, queering: Nella Larsen's psychoanalytic challenge," in *Bodies That Matter*, 167–85.

Butler, Judith (1993c) "Critically queer," *GLQ*, 1: 17–32.

Carby, Hazel (1987) *Reconstructing Womanhood: The Emergence of the Afro-American Woman Novelist*. New York: Oxford University Press.

Chadwick, French Ensor (1892) *Temperament, Disease and Health*. New York: George Putnam's.

Chakraborty, Ranajit and Kenneth K. Kidd (1991) "The utility of DNA typing in forensic work," *Science*, 254 (20 December): 1735–9.

Chambers, Ross (1997) "The Unexamined," in Mike Hill (ed.), *Whiteness: A Critical Reader*. New York University Press.

Chandler, James, Arnold I. Davidson, and Harry Harootunian (eds) (1994) *Questions of Evidence: Proof, Practices, and Persuasion Across the Disciplines*. Chicago: University of Chicago Press.

Cheiro (Louis Hamon) (1894) *Cheiro's language of the hand; a complete practical work on the science of cheirognomy and cheiromancy, containing the system, rules, and experience of Cheiro [pseud.] the palmist. Thirty-three full-page illustrations, and two hundred engravings of lines, mounts, and marks; drawings of the seven types*. New York: Self-published.

Cheiro (1912) *Cheiro's memoirs; the reminiscences of a society palmist, including interviews with King Edward the Seventh, W. E. Gladstone, C. S. Parnell ... and others*. Philadelphia: J.B. Lippincott.

Chesnutt, Charles W. (1968) *The Wife of His Youth: And Other Stories of the Color Line* (1899). Ann Arbor: University of Michigan Press.

Chinitz, David (1997) "Rejuvenation through joy: Langston Hughes, primitivism, and jazz," *ALH*, 9(1): 60–78.

Chuman, Frank F. (1976) *The Bamboo People: The Law and Japanese Americans*. Del Mar: Publishers, Inc.

Cintron, Ralph (1997) *Angel's Town: Chero Ways, Gang Life and the Rhetorics of the Everyday*. Boston: Beacon Press.

"Color lines among the colored people." *Literary Digest*, 13 March 1922, pp. 43–4.

Cotton, Louise (1890) *Palmistry and Its Practical Uses, to Which Are Added Chapters on Astral Influences and the Use of the Divining Rod*. London: George Redway.

Cox, James M. (1990) "*Pudd'nhead Wilson*, revisited," in Gillman and Robinson, 1–21.

Cranor, Carl F. (ed.) (1994a) *Are Genes Us? The Social Consequences of the New Genetics*. New Brunswick, NJ: Rutgers University Press.

Cranor, Carl F. (1994b) "Introduction," in *Are Genes Us?*, 1–11.

Crary, Jonathan (1988) "Modernizing vision," in H. Foster, 29–49.

Crary, Jonathan (1990) *Techniques of the Observer: On Vision and Modernity in the Nineteenth Century*. Cambridge, MA: MIT Press.

Crawford, T. Hugh (1996) "Imaging the human body: quasi objects, quasi texts, and the theater of proof," *PMLA*, 111: 66–79.

Crenshaw, Kimberlé, Neil Gotanda, Garry Peller, and Kendall Thomas (eds) (1996) *Critical Race Theory: The Key Writings That Formed the Movement*. New York: The New Press.

Cummings, Sherwood (1988) *Mark Twain and Science: Adventures of a Mind*. Baton Rouge: Louisiana State University Press.

Cutter, Martha J. (1996) "Sliding signifiers: passing as a narrative and textual strategy in Nella Larsen's fiction," in Ginsberg, 75–100.

Daston, Lorraine (1994) "Historical epistemology," in Chandler *et al.*, 282–9.

Daston, Lorraine (1994) "Marvelous facts and miraculous evidence in Early Modern Europe," in Chandler *et al.*, 243–74.

Davis, Angela Y. (1983) *Women, Race and Class*. New York: Vintage Books.

Davis, F. James (1991) *Who Is Black? One Nation's Definition*. University Park: Pennsylvania State University Press.

Davis, Thadious M. (1994) *Nella Larsen: Novelist of the Harlem Renaissance, A Woman's Life Unveiled*. Baton Rouge: Louisiana State University Press.

Deaven, Larry L. (1994) "Mapping and sequencing the human genome," in Cranor, 12–30.

Dedman, Bill (1999) "A Rape Defendant With No Identity, But a DNA Profile." *New York Times*, 7 October, late edition, p. 18.

Degler, Carl N. (1971) *Neither Black Nor White: Slavery and Race Relations in Brazil and the United States*. New York: Macmillan.

Deleuze, Gilles and Félix Guattari (1987) *A Thousand Plateaus*, trans. Brian Massumi. Minneapolis: University of Minnesota Press.

Delgado, Richard (ed.) (1999) *Critical Race Theory: The Cutting Edge*. Philadelphia: Temple University Press.

Dembitz, Nadine (1945) "Racial discrimination and the military judgment: the Supreme Court's *Korematsu* and *Endo* decisions," *Columbia Law Review*, 45: 175–239. Reprinted in McClain, 1994: 9–73.

DeWitt, John L. (1943) *Final Report: Japanese Evacuation from the West Coast, 1942*. Washington, DC: U.S. Government Printing Office.

Dimock, Wai-Chee (1996) *Residues of Justice: Literature, Law, Philosophy*. Berkeley: University of California Press.

Douglas, Ann (1995) *Terrible Honesty: Mongrel Manhattan in the 1920s*. New York: Farrar, Straus and Giroux.

Douglass, Frederick (1987) *Narrative of the Life of Frederick Douglass, an American Slave*, in Henry Louis Gates, Jr. (ed.), *The Classic Slave Narratives*. New York: Oxford University Press.

Doyle, Laura (1994) *Bordering on the Body: The Racial Matrix of Modern Fiction and Culture*. New York: Oxford University Press.

Doyle, Richard (1994) "Vital language," in Cranor, 52–68.

Dubrow, Heather (1996) "The status of evidence," *PMLA*, 111 (January): 7–20.

Dunbar, Paul Laurence (1965) *The Complete Poems of Paul Laurence Dunbar*. New York: Dodd, Mead and Company.

Dyer, Richard (1988) "White," *Screen*, 29(4) (Autumn): 44–64.

Ellison, Ralph (1952) *Invisible Man*. New York: Random House.

Ellison, Ralph (1995) *Shadow and Act*. New York: Vintage Books.

Emi, Frank Seishi (1989) "Draft Resistance at the Heart Mountain Concentration Camp and the Fair Play Committee," in Nomura *et al.*, 41–69.

Erdman, Harley (1997) *Staging the Jew: The Performance of an American Ethnicity, 1860–1920*. New Brunswick, NJ: Rutgers University Press.

Fanon, Frantz (1967) *Black Skin, White Masks* [1952], trans. Charles Lam Markmann. New York: Grove Weidenfeld.

Faust, Drew G. (1998) "Unhappy Echo," letter to Editor, *New York Times*, 9 November, late edn, p. A24.

Federal Rules of Evidence for United States Courts and Magistrates (1990) St. Paul: West Publishing.

Fine, Michelle (1997) "Witnessing whiteness," in Lois Weis Fine, Linda C. Powell, and L. Mun Wong (eds), *Off-White: Readings on Race, Power and Society*. New York: Routledge, pp. 57–65.

Fine, Sidney (1964) "Mr. Justice Murphy and the Hirabayashi case," *Pacific Historical Review*, 33: 195–209. Reprinted in McClain, 75–89.

Fishkin, Shelley Fisher (1995) "Interrogating 'whiteness,' complicating 'blackness': remapping American culture," *American Quarterly*, 47 (September): 428–66.

Fitzgerald, Scott F. (1964) *The Great Gatsby* [1925]. New York: Scribner's Sons.

Fitzherbert, Andrew (1992) *The Palmist's Companion: A History and Bibliography of Palmistry*. Metuchen, NJ: Scarecrow Press.

Foster, Eugene A., M. A. Jobling, P. G. Taylor, P. Donnelly, P. de Knijff, Rene Mieremet, T. Zergal, and C. Tyler-Smith (1998) "Jefferson fathered slave's last child," *Nature*, 396 (5 November): 27–8.

Foster, Hal (ed.) (1988) *Vision and Visuality*. Seattle: Bay Press.

Foucault, Michel (1978) *The Birth of the Clinic*, trans. A. M. Sheridan Smith. New York: Vintage Books.

Foucault, Michel (1979) *Discipline and Punish: The Birth of the Prison*, trans. Alan Sheridan. New York: Vintage Books.

Foucault, Michel (1980) *The History of Sexuality: An Introduction*, trans. Robert Hurley. New York: Vintage Books.

Foucault, Michel (1994a) "The order of things," interview with Raymond Bellour, trans. John Johnston, in *Foucault Live*. New York: Semiotext(e), 1–10.

Foucault, Michel (1994b) "The question of power," in *Foucault Live*. New York: Semiotext(e), 179–92.

Fowler, Orson and Lorenzo N. Fowler (1859) *New Illustrated Self-Instructor in Phrenology and Physiology*. New York: Fowler and Wells.

Freud, Sigmund (1961) *Civilization and Its Discontents*, trans. James Strachey. New York: W. W. Norton & Company.

Frankenberg, Ruth (1993) *White Women, Race Matters: The Social Construction of Whiteness*. Minneapolis: University of Minnesota Press.

Galton, Francis (1892) *Finger Prints*. New York: Macmillan.

Galton, Francis (1909) *Memoirs of My Life*. London: Methuen.

Game, Ann (1991) *Undoing the Social: Towards a Deconstructive Sociology*. Milton Keynes: Open University Press.

Gettings, Fred (1965) *The Book of the Hand: An Illustrated History of Palmistry*. London: Hamlyn.

Gillman, Susan (1989) *Dark Twins: Imposture and Identity in Mark Twain's America*. Chicago: University of Chicago Press.

Gillman, Susan (1990) "'Sure Identifiers': race, science, and the law in *Pudd'nhead Wilson*," in Gillman and Robinson, 86–104.

Gillman, Susan and Forrest G. Robinson (eds) (1990) *Mark Twain's* Pudd'nhead Wilson: *Race, Conflict, and Culture*. Durham, NC: Duke University Press.

Gilman, Sander (1985) *Difference and Pathology: Stereotypes of Sexuality, Race, and Madness*. Ithaca, NY: Cornell University Press.

Gilman, Sander (1991) *The Jew's Body*. New York: Routledge.

Ginsberg, Elaine K. (ed.) (1996) *Passing and the Fictions of Identity*. Durham, NC: Duke University Press.

Ginzburg, Carlo (1989) *Clues, Myths, and the Historical Method*. Baltimore: Johns Hopkins University Press.

Goldsby, Jacqueline (1996) "The high and the low tech of it: the meaning of lynching and the death of Emmett Till," *Yale Journal of Criticism*, 9: 245–82.

Gordon-Reed, Annette (1997) *Thomas Jefferson and Sally Hemings: An American Controversy*. Charlottesville: University of Virginia Press.

Gossett, Thomas F. (1997) *Race: The History of an Idea in America*, 2nd edn. New York: Oxford University Press.

Gould, Stephen Jay (1996) *The Mismeasure of Man*, 2nd edn. New York: Norton.

Gramsci, Antonio (1971) *Selections from the Prison Notebooks*, ed. and trans. Quentin Hoare and Geoffrey Nowell Smith. New York: International Publishers.

Grayson, Deborah R. (1995) "Fooling white folks, or, how I stole the show: the body politics of Nella Larsen's *Passing*," *Bucknell Review*, 39(1): 27–38.

Greenleaf, Simon (1866) *A Treatise on the Law of Evidence* (3 vols), 12th edn revised by Isaac F. Redfield. Boston: Little, Brown.

Gribben, Alan (1972) "Mark Twain, phrenology, and the 'temperaments': a study of pseudoscientific influence," *American Quarterly*, 24 (March): 45–68.

Gribben, Alan (1980) *Mark Twain's Library: A Reconstruction* (2 vols). Boston: G. K. Hall.

Griesemer, James R. (1994) "Tools for talking: human nature, Weismannism, and the interpretation of genetic information," in Cranor, 69–88.

Grosz, Elizabeth and Elspeth Probyn (eds) (1995) *Sexy Bodies: The Strange Carnalities of Feminism*. New York: Routledge.

Gubar, Susan (1997) *Racechanges: White Skin, Black Face in American Culture*. New York: Oxford University Press.

Haizlip, Shirlee Taylor (1994) *The Sweeter the Juice: A Family Memoir in Black and White*. New York: Touchstone Books.

Hall, Stuart (1986) "On postmodernism and articulation," ed. Lawrence Grossberg, *Journal of Communication Inquiry*, 10: 45–60.

Halttunen, Karen (1982) *Confidence Men and Painted Women: A Study of Middle-Class Culture in America 1830–1870*. New Haven: Yale University Press.

Haraway, Donna (1989a) "A manifesto for cyborgs: science, technology, and socialist feminism in the 1980s," in Elizabeth Weed (ed.), *Coming to Terms: Feminism, Theory, Politics*. New York: Routledge.

Haraway, Donna (1989b) *Primate Visions: Gender, Race, and Nature in the World of Modern Science*. New York: Routledge.

Haraway, Donna (1991) *Simians, Cyborgs, and Women: The Reinvention of Nature*. New York: Routledge.

Harper, Philip Brian (1998) "Passing for what? Racial masquerade and the demands of upward mobility," *Callaloo*, 21(12): 381–97.

Harris, Cheryl I. (1993) "Whiteness as property," *Harvard Law Review*, 106: 1707–91.

Haskell, Thomas L. (1977) *The Emergence of Professional Social Science: The American Social Science Association and the Nineteenth-Century Crisis of Authority*. Urbana: University of Illinois Press.

Hearings Before a Subcommittee of the Committee of Naval Affairs, House of Representatives – Investigation of Congested Areas (1943) 78th Congress, 1st session pursuant to HR30. Washington, DC: US Government Printing Office.

Hedrick, Joan D. (1994) *Harriet Beecher Stowe: A Life*. New York: Oxford University Press.

Heron-Allen, Edward (1892) *Practical Cheirosophy: A Synoptical Study of the Science of the Hand* [1887]. New York: G.P. Putnam's Sons.

Hockenberry, John (1995) *Moving Violations: War Zones, Wheelchairs and Declarations of Independence*. New York: Hyperion.

Hofstadter, Richard (1945) *Social Darwinism in American Thought 1860–1915*. Philadelphia: University of Pennsylvania Press.

Hollinger, David A. (1984) "Inquiry and uplift: late nineteenth-century American academics and the moral efficacy of scientific practice," in Thomas

L. Haskell (ed.), *The Authority of Experts: Studies in History and Theory*. Bloomington: Indiana University Press, pp. 142–61.

Holmes, Steven A. "Panel Balks at Multiracial Census Category." *New York Times*, 9 July 1997, late edn, p. A12.

Holmes, Steven A. "Poll Finds Few Support Label of Multiracial." *New York Times*, 16 May 1997, late edn, p. A20.

Hosokawa, Bill (1982) *JACL: In Search of Justice*. New York: William Morrow.

Howells, William Dean (1910) *My Mark Twain: Reminiscences and Criticisms*. New York: Harper and Brothers.

Hurston, Zora Neale (1979) "How It Feels to Be Colored Me", in *I Love Myself When I Am Laughing ... And Then Again When I Am Looking Mean and Impressive: A Zora Neale Hurston Reader* [1928], ed. Alice Walker. Old Westbury, NY: The Feminist Press, pp. 152–5.

Ignatieff, Michael (1995) "The myth of citizenship," in Beiner, 53–77.

Irons, Peter (1986) "Fancy dancing in the marble palace," *Constitutional Commentary*, 3: 35–45. Reprinted in McClain, 143–53.

Jacobs, Harriet (1987) *Incidents in the Life of a Slave Girl, Written by Herself*, ed. Jean Fagan Yellin. Cambridge, MA: Harvard University Press.

Jacques, Daniel H. (1878) *The Temperaments, or, The Varieties of Physical Constitution in Man, Considered in Their Relations to Mental Character and the Practical Affairs of Life, etc. etc.* New York: S.R. Wells.

Jay, Martin (1988) "Scopic regimes of modernity," in H. Foster, 3–27.

Jeffreys, A. J., V. Wilson, and S. L. Thein (1985) "Individual-specific 'fingerprints' of human DNA," *Nature*, 316(4) (July): 76–9.

Jordan, Furneaux (1890) *Character as Seen in Body and Parentage: With a Chapter on Education, Career, Morals and Progress*, 2nd edn. London: Kegan, Paul, Trench, Trübner.

Kaplan, Carla (1997) "Undesirable desire: citizenship and romance in modern American fiction," *Modern Fiction Studies*, 43(1): 144–69.

Kawash, Samira (1996) "*The Autobiography of an Ex-Colored Man*: (passing for) black passing for white," in Ginsberg, 59–74.

Kazin, Alfred (1942) *On Native Grounds: An Interpretation of Modern American Prose Literature*. New York: Harcourt, Brace.

Keller, Evelyn Fox (1994) "Master molecules," in Cranor, 89–95.

Kerr, Howard (1972) *Mediums and Spirit Rappers and Roaring Radicals: Spiritualism in American Literature*. Urbana: University of Illinois Press.

Kevles, Daniel J. (1985) *In the Name of Eugenics: Genetics and the Uses of Human Heredity*. New York: Knopf.

Keynes, Geoffrey (1922) *Blood Transfusion*. London: Hodder and Stoughton.

Kildulffe, Robert A. and Michael De Bakey (1942) *The Blood Bank and the Technique and Therapeutics of Transfusions*. St. Louis: C. V. Mosby.

Klusmeyer, Douglas B. (1996) *Between Consent and Descent: Conceptions of Democratic Citizenship*. Washington, DC: Carnegie Endowment for International Peace.

Korematsu v. United States (1944) 323 U.S. 214.

Kovel, Joel (1970) *White Racism: A Psychohistory*. New York: Pantheon Books.

Kristeva, Julia (1982) *Powers of Horror: An Essay in Abjection*, trans. Leon S. Roudiez. New York: Columbia University Press.

Kunhardt, Philip B., Jr., Philip B. Kunhardt III, and Peter W. Kunhardt (1995) *P. T. Barnum: America's Greatest Showman*. New York: Borzoi Books.

Lander, Eric S. and Joseph J. Ellis (1998) "Founding Father," *Nature*, 396 (5 November): 13–14.

Larsen, Nella (1986) *Passing* (1929). *Quicksand and Passing*, ed. Deborah E. McDowell. New Brunswick, NJ: Rutgers University Press.

Latour, Bruno (1987) *Science in Action*. Cambridge, MA: Harvard University Press.

Latour, Bruno (1988) *The Pasteurization of France*. New York: Oxford University Press.

Latour, Bruno (1993) *We Have Never Been Modern*, trans. Catherine Porter. Cambridge MA: Harvard University Press.

Levy, Harlan (1996) *And the Blood Cried Out: A Prosecutor's Spellbinding Account of the Power of DNA*. New York: Basic Books.

Lewontin, R.C. and Daniel L. Hartl (1991) "Population genetics," *Science*, 254 (20 December): 1745–50.

Lloyd, Elisabeth (1994) "Normality and variation: the human genome projects and the ideal human type," in Cranor, 99–117.

Logan, Rayford W. (ed.) (1944a) *What the Negro Wants*. Chapel Hill: University of North Carolina Press.

Logan, Rayford W. (1944b) "The Negro wants first-class citizenship," in *What the Negro Wants*, 1–13.

López, Ian F. Haney (1996) *White by Law: The Legal Construction of Race*. New York: New York University Press.

Lorde, Audre (1984) *Sister/Outsider*. Freedom, CA: The Crossing Press, pp. 53–9.

Lott, Eric (1993) *Love and Theft: Blackface Minstrelsy and the American Working Class*. New York: Oxford University Press.

Love, Spencie (1996) *One Blood: The Death and Resurrection of Charles R. Drew*. Chapel Hill: University of North Carolina Press.

Lubar, Steven (1996) "Learning from technological things," in W. David Kingery (ed.), *Learning from Things: Method and Theory of Material Culture Studies*. Washington, DC: Smithsonian Institution Press, pp. 31–4.

McClain, Charles (ed.) (1994) *The Mass Internment of Japanese Americans and the Quest for Legal Redress*. New York: Garland.

Macdonald, Dwight (1943) *The War's Greatest Scandal! The Story of Jim Crow in Uniform*. New York: March on Washington Movement.

McKay, Claude (1970) *A Long Way from Home* [1937]. New York: Harcourt, Brace and World.

McLendon, Jacquelyn Y. (1995) *The Politics of Color in the Fiction of Jessie Fauset and Nella Larsen*. Charlottesville: University Press of Virginia.

McNalty, Bernard C. and Morris J. McGregor (1981) *Blacks in the Military: Essential Documents*. Wilmington, DE: Scholarly Resources.

McNamara, Brooks (1976) *Step Right Up*. Garden City, NY: Doubleday.

Madigan, Mark J. (1990) "Miscegenation and the Dicta of Race and Class: The Rhinelander Case and Nella Larsen's *Passing*," *Modern Fiction Studies*, 4 (Winter): 523–8.

Marshall, T.H. and Tom Bottomore (1992) *Citizenship and Social Class* [1950]. London: Pluto Press.

Mead, Margaret (1942) *And Keep Your Powder Dry: An Anthropologist Looks at America*. New York: William Morrow.

Michaels, Walter Benn (1995) *Our America: Nativism, Modernism and Pluralism*. Durham: Duke University Press.

Miller, D.A. (1988) *The Novel and the Police*. Berkeley: University of California Press.

Monmonier, Mark (1991) *How to Lie with Maps*. Chicago: University of Chicago Press.

Moon, Michael and Cathy N. Davidson (eds) (1995) *Subjects and Citizens: Nation, Race, and Gender from* Oroonoko *to* Anita Hill. Durham, NC: Duke University Press.

Moore, David Chioni (1994) "Routes: Alex Haley's *Roots* and the rhetoric of genealogy," *Transition: An International Review*, 64: 4–21.

Morrison, Toni (1988) *Beloved*. New York: Plume.

Morrison, Toni (1993) *Playing in the Dark: Whiteness and the Literary Imagination*. New York: Vintage Books.

Mullen, Haryette (1994) "Optic white: blackness and the production of whiteness," *Diacritics*, 24(2–3) (Summer/Fall): 71–89.

Mullis, Kary B. (1990) "The unusual origin of the polymerase chain reaction," *Scientific American*, 262(4) (April): 56–65.

Munt, Sally R. (1998) *Heroic Desire: Lesbian Identity and Cultural Space*. New York: New York University Press.

Myrdal, Gunnar (1944) *An American Dilemma: The Negro Problem and Modern Democracy*. New York: Harper and Brothers.

Nomura, Gail M., Russell Endo, Stephen H. Sumida, and Russell C. Long (eds) (1989) *Frontiers of Asian American Studies: Writing, Research, and Commentary*. Pullman: Washington State University Press.

Ogren, Kathy J. (1989) *The Jazz Revolution: Twenties America and the Meaning of Jazz.* New York: Oxford University Press.

Omura, James (1989) "Japanese American journalism during World War II," in Nomura *et al.*, 71–7.

Ott, C. Ellis (1939) *The American Citizen in Government.* New Orleans: Pelican.

Owen, Chandler (1943) *Negroes and the War.* Washington, DC: Office of War Information.

Paine, Albert B. (ed.) (1935) *Mark Twain's Notebooks.* New York: Harper and Brothers.

Paine, Albert B. (1912) *Mark Twain: A Biography; The Personal and Literary Life of Samuel Langhorne Clemens.* New York: Harper and Brothers.

Parker, Hershel (1984) *Flawed Texts and Verbal Icons: Literary Authority in American Fiction.* Evanston, IL: Northwestern University Press.

Peiss, Kathy (1998) *Hope in a Jar: The Making of America's Beauty Culture.* New York: Henry Holt.

Penley, Constance and Andrew Ross (1991) "Cyborgs at large: interview with Donna Haraway," in *Technoculture.* Minneapolis: University of Minnesota Press, pp. 1–20.

Petchesky, Rosalind Pollack (1987) "Fetal Images: The Power of Visual Culture in the Politics of Representation," *Feminist Studies*, 13 (Summer): 263–91.

Pfeffer, Paula F. (1990) *A. Philip Randolph, Pioneer of the Civil Rights Movement.* Baton Rouge: Louisiana State University Press.

Phelan, Peggy (1993) *Unmarked: The Politics of Performance.* New York: Routledge.

Phelan, Peggy and Jill Lane (eds) (1998) *The Ends of Performance.* New York: New York University Press.

Pocock, J. G. A. (1995) "The ideal of citizenship since classical times," in Beiner, 29–52.

Pollock, Della (1998) "Performing writing," in Phelan and Lane, 73–103.

Poovey, Mary (1994) "Figures of arithmetic, figures of speech: the discourse of statistics," in Chandler *et al.*, 401–21.

Prial, Frank J. (1998) "Kate Smith, All American Singer, Dies at 79," *New York Times Magazine Online*, 2 July, < http://www.nytimes.com/specials/magazine4/articles/smith1.html >

Primrose, S. B. (1998) *Principles of Genome Analysis: A Guide to Mapping and Sequencing DNA from Different Organisms*, 2nd edn. London: Blackwell.

Rabinowitz, Peter J. (1994) "Betraying the sender: the rhetoric and ethics of fragile texts," *Narrative*, 2(3) (October): 201–13.

Rankin, John E. (1942) "Slandering the Red Cross," *Congressional Record*, 5 June, p. A2308.

Reppy, Alison (ed.) (1949) *David Dudley Field: Centenary Essays, Celebrating One*

Hundred Years of Legal Reform. New York: New York University School of Law.

Reynolds, David S. (1995) *Walt Whitman's America: A Cultural Biography*. New York: Knopf.

Rex, Margery. "Color Line Stressed in Rhinelander Case." *New York Evening Journal*, 10 November 1925, p. 1.

Rich, Adrienne (1986) "Notes towards a politics of location," in *Blood, Bread, and Poetry: Selected Prose 1979–1985*. New York: W. W. Norton, pp. 221–32.

Roberson, Y. Andrew (1922) "Color Lines Among Colored People" *The Literary Digest*, 18 March: 43–44.

Roberts, Leslie (1991) "Fight erupts over DNA fingerprinting," *Science*, 254 (20 December): 1721–3.

Robinson, Amy (1994) "It takes one to know one: passing and communities of common interest," *Critical Inquiry*, 20 (Summer): 715–36.

Robinson, Amy (1996) "Forms of appearance of value: Homer Plessy and the politics of proximity," in Elin Diamond (ed.), *Performance and Cultural Politics*. New York: Routledge, pp. 237–61.

Robinson, Forrest G. (1986) *In Bad Faith: The Dynamics of Deception in Mark Twain's America*. Cambridge, MA: Harvard University Press.

Robinson, G. and M.D. Canby (1946) *American Red Cross Blood Donor Service During World War II: Its Organization and Operation*. Washington, DC: American Red Cross.

Roediger, David (1991) *The Wages of Whiteness: Race and the Making of the American Working Class*. London: Verso.

Rogin, Michael (1990) "Frances Galton and Mark Twain: the natal autograph in *Pudd'nhead Wilson*," in Gillman and Robinson, 73–85.

Rorty, Richard (1989) *Contingency, Irony, and Solidarity*. Cambridge: Cambridge University Press.

Rostow, Eugene V. (1945) "The Japanese American cases – a disaster," *Yale Law Journal*, 54 (June): 489–533. Reprinted in McClain, 1994: 189–233.

Rothfield, Lawrence (1994) "Massaging the evidence," in Chandler *et al.*, 92–7.

Saks, Eva (1988) "Representing miscegenation law," *Raritan*, 8(2) (Fall): 39–69.

Sanchéz-Eppler, Karen (1993) *Touching Liberty: Abolition, Feminism, and the Politics of the Body*. Berkeley: University of California Press.

Sante, Luc (1991) *Low Life: Lures and Snares of Old New York*. New York: Vintage Books.

Santo, Gayle K. Fugita (1992) "Momotaro's exile: John Okada's *No-No Boy*," in Shirley Geok-lin Lim and Amy Ling (eds), *Reading the Literatures of Asian America*. Philadelphia: Temple University Press, pp. 239–58.

Schaffer, Simon (1994) "Self evidence," in Chandler *et al.*, 56–91.

Schmitt, Eric (1997) "Experts Clash Over Multiracial Category." *New York Times*, 24 April late edn, p. A27.

Sedgwick, Eve Kosofsky (1990) *Epistemology of the Closet*. Berkeley: University of California Press.

Sedgwick, Eve Kosofsky (1993) *Tendencies*. Durham, NC: Duke University Press.

Seltzer, Mark (1992) *Bodies and Machines*. New York: Routledge.

Shannon, A. H. (1925) *The Racial Integrity of the American Negro*. Nashville: Lamar and Barton, Agents.

Shapiro, Barbara J. (1991) *"Beyond Reasonable Doubt" and "Probable Cause": Historical Perspectives on the Anglo-American Law of Evidence*. Berkeley: University of California Press.

Sinclair, Jo (Ruth Seid) (1946) *Wasteland*. New York: Harper and Brothers.

Smith, Barbara Herrnstein (1994) "Belief and resistance: a symmetrical account," in Chandler *et al.*, 139–53.

Smith, Dinitia and Nicholas Wade (1998) "DNA Test Finds Evidence of Jefferson Child by Slave." *New York Times*, 1 November, late edn, p. 1 + .

Sollors, Werner (1997) *Neither Black Nor White Yet Both: Thematic Explorations of Interracial Literature*. New York: Oxford University Press.

Spencer, Herbert (1873) *The Study of Sociology*. New York: Appleton.

Spillers, Hortense J. (1994) "Mama's baby, Papa's maybe: an American grammar book," in Angelyn Mitchell (ed.), *Within the Circle: An Anthology of African American Literary Criticism from the Harlem Renaissance to the Present*. Durham, NC: Duke University Press, pp. 454–81.

Spinner, Jeff (1994) *The Boundaries of Citizenship: Race, Ethnicity, and Nationality in the Liberal State*. Baltimore: Johns Hopkins University Press.

Stanton, William R. (1960) *The Leopard's Spots: Scientific Attitudes Toward Race in America 1815–59*. Chicago: University of Chicago Press.

Starr, Paul (1982) *The Social Transformation of American Medicine*. New York: Basic Books.

"The status of evidence: a roundtable" (1996) *PMLA*, 111 (January): 21–31.

Stein, Gertrude (1972) "Composition as explanation," in Carl Van Vechten (ed.), *Selected Writings of Gertrude Stein* [1945]. New York: Vintage.

Stent, Gunther S. (1980) "The DNA double helix and the rise of molecular biology," in Watson, xi–xxi.

Stepan, Nancy Leys (1982) *The Idea of Race in Science: Great Britain 1800–1960*. Hamden, CT: Archon.

Stepan, Nancy Leys (1991) *"The Hour of Eugenics": Race, Gender, and Nation in Latin America*. Ithaca, NY: Cornell University Press.

Stewart, Alexander (1892) *Our Temperaments: Their Study and Their Teaching: A Popular Outline* [1886], 2nd edn. London: Crosby Lockwood.

Stewart, Maxwell S. (1976) *20th Century Pamphleteering: The History of the Public Affairs Committee*. New York: Public Affairs Committee.

Sumida, Stephen H. (1989) "Japanese moral dilemmas in John Okada's *No-No Boy* and Milton Murayama's *All I Am Asking for Is My Body*," in Nomura *et al.*, 222–33.

Sundquist, Eric J. (1990) "Mark Twain and Homer Plessy", in Gillman and Robinson, 46–72.

Terry, Don (1998) "DNA Results Confirmed Old News About Jefferson, Blacks Say." *New York Times*, 10 November, late edn, p. A18.

Thompson, William C. (1994) "When science enters the courtroom: the DNA typing controversy," in Cranor, 180–202.

Thomson, Rosemarie Garland (1996) *Extraordinary Bodies: Figuring Physical Disability in American Literature and Culture*. New York: Columbia University Press.

Thurman, Wallace (1996) *The Blacker the Berry* [1929]. New York: Simon and Schuster.

Tompkins, Jane (1987) "Me and my shadow," *New Literary History: A Journal of Theory and Interpretation*, 19(1) (Autumn): 169–78.

Truscott, Lucian K. (1998) "Time for Monticello to Open the Gate." *New York Times*, 5 November, late edn, p. F1+.

Twain, Mark (Samuel L. Clemens) (1967) *Mark Twain's Letters to His Publishers, 1867–1894*, ed. Hamlin Hill. Berkeley: University of California Press.

Twain, Mark (1996) *The Tragedy of Pudd'nhead Wilson and the Comedy of Those Extraordinary Twins* [1894]. New York: Oxford University Press.

Twain, Mark (1997a) *The Adventures of Huckleberry Finn* [1885]. New York: Oxford University Press.

Twain, Mark (1997b) *What Is Man? And Other Essays* [1906]. New York: Oxford University Press.

Twain, Mark and Charles D. Warner (1997) *The Gilded Age* [1873]. New York: Oxford University Press.

Wade, Nicholas (1999) "Defenders of Jefferson Renew Attack on DNA Data Linking Him to Slave Child," *New York Times*, 7 January, late edn, p. A20.

Wailoo, Keith (1997) *Drawing Blood: Technology and Disease Identity in Twentieth Century America*. Baltimore: Johns Hopkins University Press.

Wald, Priscilla (1995) *Constituting Americans: Cultural Anxiety and Narrative Form*. Durham, NC: Duke University Press.

Wall, Cheryl A. (1995) *Women of the Harlem Renaissance*. Bloomington: Indiana University Press.

Ward, Steven C. (1996) *Reconfiguring Truth: Postmodernism, Science Studies, and the Search for a New Model of Knowledge*. Lanham, MD: Rowman and Littlefield.

Washington, Peter (1996) *Madame Blavatsky's Baboon: A History of the Mystics, Mediums, and Misfits Who Brought Spiritualism to America*. New York: Schocken Books.

Watson, James D. (1980) *The Double Helix: A Personal Account of the Discovery of the Structures of DNA* [1968], ed. Gunther S. Stent. New York: Norton.

Weaver, George Sumner (1852) *Lectures on Mental Science According to the Philosophy of Phrenology*. New York: Fowler and Wells.

Weglyn, Michi Nishiura (1996) *Years of Infamy: The Untold Story of America's Concentration Camps*, 2nd edn. Seattle: University of Washington Press.

Westerinen, Julia Jefferson (1998) "In Jefferson-Hemings Tie, a Family's Pride," letter to Editor, *New York Times*, 9 November, late edn, p. A24.

Wiegman, Robyn (1995) *American Anatomies: Theorizing Race and Gender*. Durham, NC: Duke University Press.

Wigger, Ann P. (1957) "The source of fingerprint material in Mark Twain's *Pudd'nhead Wilson and Those Extraordinary Twins*," *American Literature*, 28: 517–20.

Wilkinson, James (1996) "A choice of fictions: historians, memory, and evidence," *PMLA*, 111 (January): 80–92.

Williams, Raymond (1958) *Culture and Society, 1780–1950*. New York: Columbia University Press.

Williams, Raymond (1977) *Marxism and Literature*. New York: Oxford University Press.

Williams, Raymond (1982) *The Sociology of Culture*. New York: Schocken.

Wills, William (1872) *An Essay on the Principles of Circumstantial Evidence, Illustrated by Numerous Cases*, 5th edn. Philadelphia: T. & J. Johnson.

Winkler, Alan M. (1978) *The Politics of Propaganda: The Office of War Information, 1942–1945*. New Haven: Yale University Press.

Wright, Richard (1940) *Native Son*. New York: Harper and Row.

Wynes, Charles E. (1988) *Charles Richard Drew: The Man and the Myth*. Urbana: University of Illinois Press.

Yogi, Stan (1996) "'You had to be one or the other': oppositions and reconciliation in John Okada's *No-No Boy*," *MELUS*, 21(2) (Summer): 63–77.

Young, Iris Marion (1995) "Polity and group difference: a critique of the ideal of universal citizenship," in Beiner, 175–91.

Zinn, Howard (1980) *A People's History of the United States, 1492–present*. New York: Harper and Row.

Žižek, Slavoj (1990) *Looking Awry: An Introduction to Jacques Lacan's Thought Through Popular Culture*. Cambridge, MA: MIT Press.

Index

De Bakey, Michael 118
Delbrück, Max 141
Desbarolles, Adrien Adolphe 27, 28
Descartes, René 5, 9
DeWitt, John L. 132, 134–6
difference, pathologizing of 146–7
discourses of measurement 15, 16
DNA 21, 142–55, 157–8, 160–1,
    163–5, 167–8
  as bearer of truth 143, 146,
    148–9, 154, 158, 168
  database 145, 150, 154
  dehumanization and 153–5, 167
  as a discourse 10
  as evidence 11, 143, 147–50,
    154–5, 160, 164–5, 167
  as genealogy 141, 143, 147,
    157–60, 163
  genetic mutation 146–7
  genetic traits 142, 144, 154,
    158–60, 168
  as human identity 142, 147,
    149–50, 153, 155, 157, 160–1,
    168
  metaphors for 142, 145, 148,
    154, 157, 160, 167
  as ontology 142, 144–5, 147–8,
    153
  racial matching 151–3
  as unifying force 143, 147,
    157–8, 160–1, 166–7
  use in criminal
    investigations 143, 147–8,
    151–2, 154
  visible on the body 157,
    159–60
Douglas, Ann 61, 81
Douglas, Mary 16
Douglass, Frederick 23
Doyle, Laura 6, 9
Dr Who 11

Drew, Charles 120
DuBois, W. E. B. 83
Dunbar, Paul Laurence 83

Eads, Jane 106–7
Ellis, Joseph J. 164
Ellison, Ralph 65, 124
eugenics 18, 43–5, 50
evidence
  analysis of 20
  circumstantial 12–13, 38
  details 19, 20
  Frye standard 152
  of identity 19, 46–8
  legal 11, 12, 13, 14, 18, 39, 47
  racialized bodies as 4
  rhetoric of 19, 21
  versus facts 13
  visibility of 8, 10–11, 23, 29
  see also DNA; bodies; blood
Executive Order 9066 133
eyewitness testimony 11–12, 14

Fair Play Committee (FPC) 137–8
fatness 60–1
  as a class indicator 61
Faust, Drew G. 166
fetal images 20
Field, David Dudley 13
Fine, Michelle 124
fingerprint technology 7, 11, 15,
    26, 38–41, 43–50, 52, 147,
    153–4
  expert in 17
  Twain's use of in *Pudd'nhead
    Wilson* 24–6, 38–41, 43–4,
    46, 48–50
forensic science 33, 43
Foster, Eugene A. 163–5
Foucault, Michel 4, 6, 10, 20
Frankenberg, Ruth 48, 124